AFTER SHOCKS

AFTER SHOCKS

REBOOT SERIES, BOOK 2

PHILL FEATHERSTONE

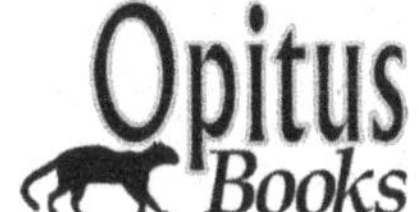

Typeset in Fanwood 11pt by Opitus Books

Cover by Rica of 100 Covers

ISBN 978-1-9993324-2-6

eISBN 978-1-9993324-3-3

Opitus Books, Sheffield, England

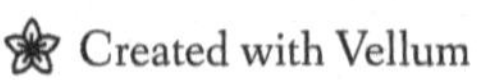 Created with Vellum

Paradise Girl (REBOOT series Book 1)

After Shocks (REBOOT series Book 2)

Jericho Rose (REBOOT series Book 3)

The God Jar

What Dreams We Had

I Know What You're Thinking

The Poisoned Garden (Leopard's Bane series Book 1)

Undiscovered Countries (short stories)

For John and Sarah

Aftershock

[ˈɑːftəʃɒk]

NOUN

The second, third or subsequent event following an initial calamity

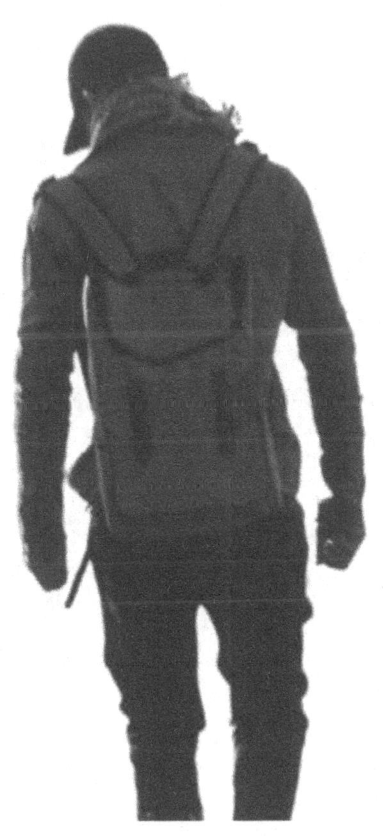

ONE
LEAVING

LANDER REVIEWED THE items he'd spread out on his bed. It was the fourth or fifth time he'd checked them. There were:

- His ID card: essential in case he was picked up by a patrol.
- Chocolate bars: also essential, but for a different reason.
- Maps: he knew where he was going but he intended to avoid main roads, so they would be important.
- A Bowie knife in a sheath: because you never knew.
- His favourite fleece: it was probably cold in Belarus, and in any case summer was ending.
- A pair of binoculars: useful for spotting patrols, with luck before they saw you.

- A torch: electric power was becoming less reliable.
- A compass: he could usually find south during the day, but at night it might be different.
- A water bottle: obvious
- An envelope containing two hundred and seventy-four pounds in notes and coins: also obvious

Money was probably not much use any more, but having it was a comfort. Some of it was his own savings, but most had come from the tin he'd found in the bottom of their Mam's wardrobe. It was where she kept her cash. He felt bad helping himself, even though she wasn't around to ask. He'd been scrupulous in taking no more than half, leaving the rest for his sister, Kerryl. Their Mam would have wanted that.

When he'd stowed all the items in his backpack there was one more thing left on the bed: a USB flash drive.

Lander tossed it in his hand. He was trying to decide what was the best thing to do with it. It had taken him a long time to compose the letter it contained. Writing was not his thing, that was more Kerryl's scene, and putting it together had been hard work. Where should he leave it to be sure his sister wouldn't miss it? Not downstairs; their Gran might clear it away before Kerryl saw it. He might put it under her bedroom door but she might miss it. Besides, he couldn't be sure she was asleep and he didn't want her to know about it until after he'd gone. It had to be somewhere she'd see it and want to investigate, so that she would read it and understand why he had left them all.

He took a reel of tape and stuck the USB drive to the notice board over his desk. He chose purple (her favourite colour) so it would catch her attention, and to make sure he pinned a sheet of A4 next to it and with a black marker wrote a big letter K, filling the paper. Then to be on the safe side he added an arrow pointing to the drive. There. He knew that she'd come into his room to look for him and there was no chance of her missing it when she did. He was assuming she'd be curious enough to put it in her computer right away.

Suddenly there was a sound on the stairs: his grandparents were coming to bed. Quickly he pushed the backpack under his bed, lay down, shut his eyes, and pulled the duvet up to his chin.

The loose board on the landing creaked. Then his bedroom door opened a crack and a shaft of light striped the bed. It was Gran. In the few days since the death of their Mam she'd taken to looking in on him and his sister last thing before she settled down herself. She didn't do anything, didn't come in to straighten their bedclothes or give them a goodnight kiss, she just stood in the doorway. He didn't know why. Mam had stopped doing that when they went to secondary school, but Gran seemed to think it was a good idea. She closed his door gently and moved on to Kerryl's room next door.

He lay still. He couldn't risk leaving the house until he was sure his grandparents were asleep. They had been talking downstairs for so long he wondered if they were ever going to bed. Their voices had been too muffled for him to hear what they were saying but he could guess. It would be about the Infection. That's the only thing anybody ever talked about now. What else was there?

There was the usual coming and going to the bathroom. Teeth were cleaned, the lavatory flushed, Granddad let go his nightly, world-class fart. Normally Lander would have thought that funny, but not tonight. He was about to leave everything he knew, so there was not much that could make him laugh tonight.

The door to his grandparents' bedroom closed and there was silence. He'd been hot, lying fully clothed under the duvet, and he was glad to throw it off. It was nearly midnight. He told himself to wait for another quarter of an hour, just while everything settled down. The minute hand on his watch moved with glacial slowness. After a while he heard the rhythmic rasp of Gran's snoring, but he knew better than to trust that. She was the lightest of sleepers. Granddad always said a mouse belching would wake her. Was Kerryl asleep? He'd heard nothing from her room for ages but he knew she often spent hours reading. Maybe she was doing that now.

At last the minute hand reached quarter past the hour. He got up from his bed and took the spare pillows from the bottom of the wardrobe. He arranged them under the duvet to make a lumpy shape. It wouldn't pass close inspection, but to a casual glance in the dark it might look as though he was sleeping.

He stood in the doorway and took a last look at his room. There were only a few things he'd miss. His laptop, of course. There was no point taking that. There was the match ball from the time he'd played for Yorkshire Colts. That had been a day. He'd taken 5 wickets for 16 against a Derbyshire Youth XI, and they'd given him the ball as a souvenir. They'd also offered him a place at the Yorkshire Cricket Academy. He'd been over the moon for a while, but he needed their Mam's consent and she'd refused to give it. 'You need to pass your GCSEs, get some qualifications behind you,' she'd said. 'Then you can think about playing games.' They'd rowed about it for days but she wouldn't budge. He'd given up on school after that. He'd done it to punish her, and it had only recently dawned on him that really the one who was being punished most was himself. That was particularly true now that Kerryl was all set to go to Cambridge. Not that he'd want to go there anyway. He'd better things to do than rub shoulders with a load of toffs. The ball was small enough to take and he was tempted to slip it into his pocket, but he told himself no. It was part of his old life, a life he was leaving behind; at least for now.

He slung his backpack over his shoulder, took his trainers, and tiptoed on to the landing. The squeaky board was right in the middle and he was careful to avoid it. He bent to look under Kerryl's door. There was no chink of light, but that didn't mean anything. She might be

Snapchatting on her phone, or listening to music on her earbuds, or she might be reading by torchlight. He pressed his ear to the door, straining for any sound. At first he could hear nothing, then he picked out the sound of steady breathing. She was asleep, all was clear.

There was a sudden snort from his grandparents' room. He froze in case it was a prelude to other nocturnal activity, but everything stayed quiet. It was a timely nudge, though; stop messing about and get moving.

He could have gone down the stairs with his eyes shut, but faint moonlight through the landing window made it easier. He knew that the third and seventh treads creaked, and he was careful to avoid those.

Buster looked up as Lander entered the kitchen and gave a welcoming whimper. He rose from his basket and stretched. Lander bent and fondled the dog's ears and tried to still his tail, which was beating a noisy tattoo on the cupboard door. Clearly Buster had high hopes of what this nocturnal visit might mean: a walk? an early breakfast? both? His tail wagged even more vigorously and Lander heaved the animal's swaying rump aside.

'Sh. You'll wake the whole house,' he murmured.

Buster was Lander's dog and a good friend. He would miss him. He'd thought about taking him, but decided that although he could imagine him being useful, the upheaval wouldn't be fair on the old dog. Besides, it would be harder for him to hide from the authorities with a big sloppy Labrador in tow. And he would be another mouth to feed.

Lander squatted. 'No, mate, you've got to stay here,' he said.

Buster looked disappointed. Lander opened a tin of Dog Star beef and jelly, his favourite, and filled his bowl. That would keep him busy while he slipped out of the house.

'See you, boy,' he whispered, giving him a pat. 'Look after everybody. Kerryl will see to you, and I'll come back. I promise.'

He crept out of the kitchen.

For as long as Lander could remember the door to the yard had not been locked at night. Grandad said there was no point. 'Who's going to bother coming all the way up here to thieve from us? Anyway, we've got nowt worth pinching.'

That had changed. The Infection had made everybody cautious, and for the last few weeks Gran had insisted on it being secured. 'You never know. There's all sorts of strange folk about now,' she'd said.

He took the key from its hook, slid it into the lock and turned it gently. He wouldn't be able to lock the door behind him but that didn't matter. By the time the others noticed he'd be well on his way.

The air was chilly and he shuddered. Summer it may be, but over a thousand feet up in the hills the nights could be sharp.

He tiptoed quickly and quietly across the yard and let himself into the barn. He took out his phone and turned on the torch, shielding the beam with his hand to avoid the light spilling outside. Their three cows watched him lazily as he went to the far corner, where there was a heap of sweet-smelling hay. He knelt and rummaged. He'd hidden his two motorbike panniers there. He'd packed them three days ago. In one were clothes – a spare pair of jeans, socks and underwear, three or four t-shirts and a couple of sweatshirts. Was that right? Would it be enough? It was difficult to pack for a trip to another country, one that you'd barely heard of let alone located on a map. Anyway, if he was short of anything he could probably find it somewhere. There was plenty of stuff in abandoned stores. And of course he had money to buy things, if that still worked.

He turned to the other pannier. In that were his waterproof jacket, his sleeping bag, a groundsheet, his washbag, and a spare pair of trainers. The rest was taken up with food. For the past week he'd been sneaking tins and packets from the store in the pantry. He'd felt a bit guilty about this, but their Mam always used to say that Gran kept enough food to feed an army, and he was sure the rest of the family wouldn't need the little he'd taken. He'd probably be able to get plenty of food on the way too, but it was best to have something put by in case there was a problem.

The cows studied him with mild curiosity. How was it that cows managed to look as though they understood everything that was going on, when in fact they were as thick as gateposts?

He was satisfied, and pleased with himself. Had he forgotten anything? He told himself that if he knew that it wouldn't be forgotten, would it? He smiled at his own joke. One of his school reports had said that he needed to pay more attention to planning. Well, take a look at this lot for planning, Mr Teacher.

He took a pannier in each hand and went out to the yard. He was careful to be very quiet as he passed Joey's stable. Horses don't sleep much, and the last thing he wanted was for Joey to whinny. He was Kerryl's horse and she could hear him from a mile away. If he did sound off she'd be sure to wake up.

Beyond the stable was the shed where he kept his motorbike. It was a 125cc Yamaha that he'd got almost a year ago, soon after his seventeenth birthday. He loved that machine. At least once a week, sometimes more, he gave it a good clean and polish and the chrome shone in the torchlight. He took out his knife and cut off the L-plates. He was a superb rider, he just hadn't taken his test yet. Having to show the plates was demeaning in normal times, and these weren't normal. If he ran into the law the lack of plates would be the least of his problems. He was glad to be rid of them.

He clipped the panniers to the bike, rocked it off its stand, and wheeled it out of the shed. The moon was higher now and brighter, and Lander kept in the shadows. He was well aware that his Granddad never got through a night without getting up several times for a pee. If he were to do that at this moment and look out of the landing window there was a good chance he'd see his grandson in the yard, so her needed to move.

At the edge of the farmyard he got astride the bike but he didn't start the engine. Instead he pushed with his legs and scooted towards the top of the track down to the valley, where he stopped and looked back towards the house. There were no lights on and the building was a dark shape against the sky. All clear. Phase one complete. He'd got away without anyone noticing.

He was sad, but he was also excited. He'd lived on Paradise Farm all his life and he couldn't imagine being anywhere else. He felt a choke in his throat and he was tempted to turn back, but he knew he couldn't. It was for their good, Kerryl's and his grandparents', that he was going. He owed it to them to get away as quickly as he could. He'd explained why in the letter on the USB stick. He hoped they'd understand. Would he ever know?

He took a deep breath, pushed forward, lifted his feet off the ground and the bike picked up speed. He'd often free-wheeled down to the town but that had been for fun, not because of a need to leave in silence.

The first part of the track was easy because he could see well. Further down the moonlight didn't penetrate the tree canopy and it was hard to make out the road surface well enough to be sure where he was going. He slowed down for fear of hitting a rut that would send him tumbling down the embankment and into the stream below. Years ago their Dad had gone over the edge on a tractor and not lived to tell of it.

Ahead of him a pale shape fluttered across the path; an owl seeking a kill. That afternoon he'd seen three roe deer grazing in the field. How strange it was that wild things seemed to be carrying on as normal, untouched by the menace that was clearing out their human rivals.

He reached the bottom of the track where it joined the main road into Walbrough and waited, checking to make sure that there was no one around. The last time he'd been into the town was when he'd collected their Mam's ashes. The place had smelt bad then, but now it was worse: a mixture of failed drains, excrement and decay. There was also a whiff of something burning, and over to the south towards Manchester he thought he could see a red glow in the sky. He pulled a scarf over his mouth and nose and pressed the bike's starter.

The racket as the engine exploded into life was deafening in the quiet night. They'd hear it in Leeds! Previously Lander had liked the noise his bike made. He'd even tinkered with the silencer to make it louder, but now in the still of the night when he wanted to sneak away it was a curse. Best to move on quickly, before he woke the whole town.

He pulled onto the road and revved away. The sound of the engine bounced off the blank walls of the buildings, rattled around the streets, cannoned off the steep sides of the valley. With luck that would make it harder to locate his precise position. It was helpful that the brightness of the moon meant he didn't need lights; they would have been a dead give-away.

He roared out of the town, leaving behind the only life he had ever known.

TWO
NIGHT

ONCE OUT OF Walbrough, Lander opened up the bike and did a wheelie. He didn't feel in high spirits, far from it, but he wanted to exit the bottleneck of the valley as quickly as he could and that meant giving the Yamaha its head. He was used to slowing down for the speed cameras but nobody was going to bother about speed limits now and he shot past the first one, giving it a middle finger as he went.

He began to relax. He was confident he'd be well clear before anyone had time to wonder what the din in the middle of the night was. Of course, there was always the possibility that some busybody would report him as a nuisance on the citizens' response line and a patrol would be ordered to look for him. That was a risk he had to take.

The moon had gone behind clouds and he needed his lights, so he switched them on and settled into the saddle, prepared for a long ride. He loved being on his bike and was enjoying the prospect of travelling through the night to Hull, even though it was taking him away from his home. At the coast he would find one of the illegal ferries that his internet contacts said made regular trips to the continent. Then he'd slip out of the country and across the sea. He hoped he had enough money. According to the online chatter the ferry prices had been going up and up, which seemed crazy because money was of less and less use now. What was the point of having cash if there were no shops, no entertainment, no services, nothing to spend it on?

He didn't hear the car over the noise of his bike but suddenly it was there, racing towards him on his side of the road. It wasn't showing any lights. Lander swerved at the same time as the driver saw him and they missed each other by a whisker. It was a big convertible, a white BMW with the top down. He caught a glimpse of three passengers, at least one of them a girl. They turned and shouted at him as the car shot past. They might have been friendly but Lander wasn't inclined to find out; he gunned his bike to get away.

He was on a long straight section of the road and starting to think that the BMW wasn't interested in him, when he saw in his mirrors twin headlights spearing the dark. Was it the BMW? Or was it a patrol? If it was the BMW it meant that whoever was driving it had turned around to come after him. It was hardly likely they'd just want to say hello. The fact that now they didn't seem to care about being lit up like a Christmas tree was troubling.

These were people who weren't afraid to break the rules about being out after curfew.

He twisted the throttle as far as it would go. The little bike screamed, but the headlights behind him were gaining fast. Whatever the vehicle, it was certainly in a hurry. Now he could see the broad spread of the beams sweeping the road at either side and beyond him. It was the BMW, no doubt about it. Perhaps that was all right. He'd only had the briefest glimpse of the driver but he hadn't looked any older than Lander himself. They were only kids. They wouldn't be a problem, would they?

He didn't want to find out. His mind raced. How could he dodge them? He could do a U-turn, but even if he could get past the car would only turn and come after him again. How could he escape?

The Yamaha was at its limit, he could get no more out of it. The highway was level and smooth, and the BMW was way quicker. It would only be a few seconds before it caught him. Then he remembered. On the left at the end of this straight was a lane. Somebody Lander had known at school lived up there. It was a narrow, twisting track and the surface was so rough that only a four-by-four or a tractor could manage it easily. A four-by-four, a tractor, and a dirt bike.

The BMW was now just a few metres behind. It could have overtaken him, driven him off the road, but it seemed to be taunting him. His heart raced. The car's horn blared a fanfare. He swerved across the road and it followed. They were going to run him down! He knocked his mirror to deflect the dazzle and peered ahead, searching for the entry to the lane. It must be close. Had he passed it? No, there it was. He might just do it.

He delayed braking until the very last second and skidded sideways, speedway fashion, as he aimed for the corner. He almost lost control but he hung on and raced up the hill, bouncing over the ruts, spitting stones behind him. Taken by surprise, the BMW shot past the turning. It might come back but even if it did it would take time, and Lander knew that the car would find it hard to get up the track. He eased off the throttle and killed his lights. Suddenly he began to tremble, so much that it was hard to keep the bike straight. He came to an open gate, and with a feeling of immense relief went through it and into a field. He killed the engine, leant the bike against the stone wall and sank down beside it. He was still shaking, but gradually he calmed down. He got to his feet and closed the gate, leaving the bike where it was, hidden from the track by the wall so that anyone looking over would have to peer down to see it. He retreated to a clump of trees further along the field's edge.

It was a few minutes before he saw the headlights down the lane. Now, though, the BMW was moving slowly, its lights leaping like a kangaroo as it bounced over the bumps. It seemed an age before they drew level with the gate. The driver clearly had no idea how to drive on a surface like this, and his answer to wheel spin was to rev harder, so the car wallowed and slid and the tyres threw up rubble and grit that rattled on the underside and fizzed along the track. There was a smell of burning rubber.

The occupants were shrieking and squealing and the stereo blared. They were all young. Lander guessed they must be high on something. What did they want with him? Just a bit of fun? Probably, but you never knew. Things had changed since the Infection, the usual customs out of the window. Once you would have ignored a stranger, or acted with guarded friendliness. Now strangers were fair game, an entertainment, butts and receptors of whatever you wanted to inflict on them.

He waited while the noise of the car receded up the hill. His pursuers had taken no notice at all of the gate, probably not even seen it. He guessed they'd go on to the end of the lane where it met the hilltop road. There'd be an argument about whether the Yamaha had gone right or left. They might choose one, or they might simply lose interest and carry on to wherever they'd been going in the first place. In either case it was unlikely they'd find their way back here. He felt relief for the first time since the beast had come hurtling around the corner at him.

The darkness was easing and he could make out a small copse a little way across the field. The trees were feathery silhouettes against the faintly lightening sky. He checked his watch. It was just before 4 o'clock. Three hours since he'd left the farm. It seemed longer than that, but at the same time shorter. Soon it would be dawn. Dawn! Lander couldn't remember when he'd last been awake early enough to see the sun rise. Mornings were definitely not his thing.

He thought about home. Kerryl was always up first. She'd go across to the cows, Dolly and Molly and Bonny, and milk them before anyone else stirred. She did the mornings, he did the evenings. That was the way they'd arranged it. It was strange that they were twins but so different in something like that, him a night owl and his sister liking to rise with the lark. Although when he thought about it, Kerryl seemed easily able to do what their Gran called 'burning the candle at both ends'. She could manage on just a few hours' sleep a night, whereas Lander needed a solid eight at least, preferably more.

He had a choice: he could continue for another hour or so, or he could call it a day – well, call it a night really – and hole up until it got dark again. It was tempting to go on, to get closer to Hull, but the daylight would increase his chances of being spotted by a patrol. And if not by a patrol by somebody else, perhaps by another load of idiots like the ones in the BMW. No, better play safe. Besides, he hadn't slept for twenty hours. He was knackered. He needed to rest.

The mate he'd known at school who lived nearby was called Simon. His house must be close, probably no more than half a mile away. Should he drop in and see if he could sleep there? Simon had been the wicket keeper in his school's first eleven, and in the year above him. He'd not really been a mate, but Lander had visited his house once. It had not been a success. It turned out that Simon was gay. That had been a surprise. On the whole, the gays at King's Heath Boys' School didn't try to hide their orientation and everybody knew, but Simon had kept his dark. However, it seemed that he had made a miscalculation. Lander had missed all the signs and it had been an embarrassing encounter for both of them.

That wasn't what put him off calling, though. The thing that did was that since the Infection struck nobody wanted a surprise visitor arriving on their doorstep. It was a visitor who had brought the disease to his own home. The man who had turned up with his sick boy asking for help hadn't meant them any harm but by coming to the farm he had killed their Mam. No, Simon and his family wouldn't welcome Lander suddenly appearing without warning; assuming they were still alive themselves. And if they weren't, he didn't want to go into another house of death. Over the past few weeks he had discovered that the chances were that he was not going to die from the virus that was killing everyone else. And probably neither was Kerryl. But he didn't want to put it to the test. The sensible option was to bed down here.

He took his groundsheet and sleeping bag from one of the panniers. From the other he got a tin of beans, his water bottle and a packet of chocolate biscuits. It seemed best to get away from the road so he went over to the copse. He decided not to venture too far into the trees in the dark because you couldn't be sure what you might find in a place like that. Anyway, it was choked with brambles so he sat down on his groundsheet at the field's edge. He opened the beans and tipped the tin into his mouth as if drinking. He alternated mouthfuls of beans with bites of chocolate biscuit as he watched the sky lighten. When he'd finished he filled the empty bean tin with small stones and pushed it into a hollow at the base of the nearest tree. It was a beech. He knew that from the smooth bark and the mast around it. He could recognise beech; he also knew oak, ash, silver birch, holly, but not much else. Kerryl, who knew every plant, flower and tree that ever was, often ridiculed him. 'Call yourself a country boy and you don't know what that is!' she'd jibe when he failed to identify something she thought was obvious.

He took a swig of water and belched. He felt better for the food. He was weary, but he didn't feel sleepy. Nevertheless, he thought it best to prepare for when he did drop off. He didn't want to experience dream walking here.

He spread out his bed. It was hard to find a comfortable spot because of the stones and the roots, and he wished he had a foam roll-up. Eventually he found a space where the ground was not too bad, the vegetation gave him some cover, and he could keep an eye on his bike.

'Dream walking'. That's what the online people called it. It sounded cool. Sexy even. But it wasn't. Dream walking was the way some – just a few – responded to the Infection. Dream walkers were deadly, either to themselves or to others. It was because he was afraid he might be one that Lander had decided to leave home.

There was a reel of elastic in his backpack. It was from their Gran's sewing kit and he'd taken it because, as Gran would say, 'A bit of elastic is always useful.' He cut off a couple of metres, anchored one end to the beech tree and knotted it firmly. He tied the other end around his wrist. He took some time to get the tension right, so that the elastic was secure enough not to slip over his hand and firm enough to wake him up if he tried to move, yet not so tight that it would cut into his skin and block his circulation when he slept. He'd been doing something similar at home for the last few nights. There was not much harm he could do dream walking here, but who knew where he might end up?

When he was satisfied with his arrangements he made sure his knife was tucked underneath him where he could get at it quickly. Then he rested his head on his backpack, and closed his eyes.

THREE
IN DREAMS

SLEEPING IN THE daylight wasn't usually a problem for Lander. His bedroom was on the sunny side of the house but he never had any trouble snoozing till lunchtime, even in the summer, even with the curtains wide open in the way their Mam always left them after she'd been in to wake him. She always used to say that Lander could sleep for England, anytime and anywhere. However, today was an exception. Perhaps it was the effect of walking out on his home and family in the middle of the night. Perhaps it was the adrenaline still pumping around his system after the brush with the BMW. Perhaps it was the hard ground and not being able to find anywhere free from the tree roots and sharp stones which seemed to be competing to bore into his back, his hip, his shoulder. A bed roll would have been great, but they'd used the only one they had for their Mam. She'd lain on it in the barn when she was sick. It had got spattered with her blood and smeared with her vomit, and after she'd died their Granddad had burnt it.

As if the hard ground wasn't enough, there was a surprising amount of noise. Lander had assumed that the Infection would keep everyone indoors. Besides, everything was closed now so there was no reason for anybody to go anywhere. And of course, there were the government warnings against any sort of travel. By rights there should have been a funereal quiet; but no, on the contrary there was no end of activity.

There were vehicles on the valley road – not lots, nowhere near as many as there would have been a few months ago, but more than he expected. There were emergency sirens. There was a train – he'd thought they had all stopped. Somewhere along the hillside a tractor was working. He wondered why. Was someone really tending the land in the expectation that they'd still be alive and farming next year? Nearby a dog barked; then another, further away, answered. Sheep bleated. A donkey brayed. A horse whinnied. It sounded just like Joey. For a second he thought it might be Kerryl, who'd ridden after him to give him an earful for slinking off like a thief in the night, but that was crazy. One horse sounded very like another, and how would she know where he was? Late in the morning a police helicopter passed over, flying low in a series of big sweeps. Was it looking for him? Don't be daft. The police wouldn't send a helicopter to search for one teenager, not with everything else that was going on. Anyway, who would have reported him?

Eventually things quietened down and he managed to arrange himself in a position where he could avoid most of the lumps. However, sleep still eluded him. He got out his phone and brought up Kerryl's number. His thumb hovered over the call icon. Should he call her and explain? Perhaps no one had missed him yet. Perhaps they thought he was having a lie-in and had decided not to disturb him. Possible, but unlikely.

He thought of his home – the comfortable farmhouse with its cosy kitchen smelling of Gran's baking, its tidy yard, Buster, Joey, the cows. What would they all be doing? Gran would be busy with housework. Granddad would be out and about in the barn or the fields. Would they be OK without him? The farm barely scraped by. Granddad was getting on, and over the past year he had been depending more and more on Lander to do the heavy work. How would he manage on his own? Kerryl would be all right. By now she would have done the milking and she would be in her room skyping, QuickChatting, or perhaps writing her diary. She seemed to spend ages doing that. She wouldn't be at school, the schools had all shut. Lander remembered how upset Kerryl had been when St Winifred's closed. She'd told him about the assembly where the head had announced it to them all, and some girl had done a soppy reading and everybody had cried. It had been different at his own school. At

King's Heath Boys' the news of the closure had come in a simple note taken to all the classrooms; no assembly for them. He laughed to himself, imagining the reaction if there had been. There wouldn't have been any tears there. Instead there would have been cheers you could have heard a mile away. Lander had been right that there was no point in school. The Infection had proved as much.

His phone still had plenty of charge and there was a good signal. He opened his browser and clicked on the top tab in his list of favourites. It took him to a home screen, anonymous, just a throbbing light in the centre of the screen, and below that a log-in box. He wondered if the site was still live. One way to find out. He put in his user name and password, and clicked. For a second nothing happened. Then the light shuddered and grew. It swelled, and words began to hurtle towards him, one by one: *the ... truth ... will ... make ... you ... free!*

He knew the site well. As soon as it was obvious that the Infection was serious, Lander had wanted to find out more about what was going on. Kerryl had accused him of being gruesomely fascinated by the whole business, but he'd told her that the more you knew about what was happening the better your chances of staying alive. That was why he got annoyed when their Mam grumbled at him for spending so much time on his computer. He was doing it for them. It was what Dad would have done.

To begin with he had restricted himself to collecting online reports and clips from news broadcasts. Then he'd started to follow breadcrumbs, and they'd led him further afield, into chat rooms and issue groups. That was how he'd found *www.thetruthwillmakeyoufree.by*, or just *thetruth*, as its members called it.

The content was all in English, so at first it didn't register with him that the *.by* suffix stood for Belarus. When he did find out he'd no idea where Belarus is but it sounded pretty exotic. The site seemed to be only lightly curated and made no concessions. There was no welcome, no explanation, no guidance to lead you in. You simply applied for admission, waited a few days, then got a password and went straight to it, making of it what you could. It had taken Lander several long sessions to tap into the key forums and bulletin boards, and to learn what it was all about.

As far as he could see the users were all men. The thing that made them special was that every one of them claimed either to have had the Infection and recovered, or to be immune to it. There was a single rule: members must avoid hearsay or speculation. You could only report and comment on things that had happened to you directly, or that you had witnessed first-hand. Many of the accounts were of casual and accidental contact with the virus, like Lander's own, but a few members actually courted it, deliberately trying to get infected in order to prove that they couldn't. However, what emerged from all these stories was that there was no such thing as immunity; everyone who was exposed to the virus caught it. Everyone. But not everyone reacted in the same way.

Their Mam had died of the virus. It had been awful, as bad as people said. No, worse. He'd fully expected that sooner or later the rest of the family would go the same way, probably Gran and Granddad first, then Kerryl and him. He waited for the symptoms, but time went on and nothing happened. Now *thetruth* was telling him it might never. The realisation that he might survive this thing that was killing everyone else was like having a death sentence removed. He had been ecstatic, but not for long.

Four days ago he'd got an alert. It was a message from someone who said he represented a group of people who called themselves *The Chosen*. They had formed a 'Community of the Immune', and they invited him to join them. In Minsk. Lander didn't even know that Minsk was a place. It sounded to him more like a name you'd give to a soft toy. Or something you got. Where was it. He looked it up. Fucking miles away, that's where. Go to Minsk? No way! Besides, travel was restricted and movement illegal. Train and bus services had all been stopped, and vehicles were regularly intercepted by army patrols. Anyway, moving around was dangerous. He'd seen on TV a report of a Nottingham family who'd left their home to look after a relative in another town. Local people accused them of coming in from an infected area and a crowd attacked them. They set the family's car on fire and chased them away.

Then the next bombshell hit, the one that convinced him that whether he went to Minsk or not, he had to leave the farm as soon as possible.

The Chosen started posting accounts from people who had all had the same experience. It was a kind of sleep-walking, but with a difference. The sleep-walkers looked to other people to be wide awake. While in that state they did extraordinary things, but afterwards they had no recollection of what. Some of them had tried to investigate what was happening. One managed to leave a video camera running and record a whole episode. It showed him in bed. Then without warning he got up. He looked to be wide awake and started to move about his room. He went to a dresser and started to pick up items and drop them on the floor. Some of them smashed. Then he grabbed one of the drawers and upended it. This went on for a few minutes, after which he got back into his bed and resumed normal sleep. The video ended by cutting to him talking to the camera. It panned around the room and showed the damage he'd done. He explained that he had no memory of it, that the same sort of thing had happened to him several times before, and that the incidents only started after he'd been exposed to the virus. It was as if another version of him, a ghost of his normal self, was doing things independently of his will. He called it "dream walking".

A couple of days later Lander noticed that some of the things in his bedroom had been moved. The plastic car models were gone from the shelf where he kept them. They'd been tossed into the waste bin and some of them were broken. He was furious. He'd had some of those models since he was a kid and a few of them were worth a bit. He'd been thinking of selling them but he hadn't got around to it. He certainly wouldn't just chuck them out. He stormed into Kerryl's room and accused her of being responsible. She denied it, and they had a huge row.

He was sure it was Kerryl's fault – who else could have done it? – but she'd looked so surprised when he blamed her, so hurt. He remembered *thetruth* bulletins and decided to do an experiment of his own. Overnight he locked the door to his room. The first few times nothing happened and in the morning the place was just as he'd left it. Then one day he found that things had been moved. There was only one key and no one else could have got in. It had to be he himself who had done it while he'd been sleeping, but he just couldn't remember it. He had become a dream walker.

He logged into *thetruth* and went to the bulletin board to report what had happened to him. There was a new and frightening post. It told him that some people, only a few, responded to the virus in a way different from the majority. For this group, instead of causing the terrible and familiar cramps, vomiting, bleeding, and the failure of the nervous system, the virus settled in their brains where it launched a different type of destruction. They called the condition it created D.I.D., 'dissociative identity disorder'. Episodes occurred when the sufferer was asleep, and resulted in outbreaks of extreme violence. It was lethal; not to the sufferer, but to those around him.

He'd been trying to decide what to do about this when there was a ping, and another post appeared. This one was the most harrowing of them all. It was another video.

It opened with shots of four bloody corpses. It was clear that these people had been brutally murdered, hacked to pieces. All of them had had their throats cut. The arm of one had been almost cut through, fingers were missing from another. A stomach had been opened. The floor was awash with blood. The video showed all this in ghastly detail. The author of the post came on next. He was hysterical, hardly able to speak, but he managed to get out that the dead were members of his own family. The night before they had all gone to bed as usual. He had felt strange and been restless, but at last he had fallen asleep. He had woken up to find himself covered in blood with the bodies all around him. In one hand he held a carving knife.

'I killed them,' he wept. 'All of them. I couldn't help it. I didn't know what I was doing. I was asleep, and I killed them.'

This was what convinced Lander that for the sake of Kerryl, Gran and Granddad he must leave. That's what he had said in the note he had left. Had Kerryl found it yet?

FOUR
HELP ON A TRACTOR

LANDER WOKE AND the sun was low. He sat up, blinking and trying to work out where he was. He looked at the long shadows of the trees stretching across the grass. Then he remembered. He was running away, and he was in the middle of a field. He was stiff and sore. The ground certainly hadn't got any softer while he'd been sleeping and it was now getting cooler. He stretched and looked towards the lane. Something was missing. His bike!

He shook himself out of his sleeping bag and dashed across the field to where he'd left it beside the gate. He spun around, half expecting to find it further along the wall, but of course it wasn't. There was the flattened grass where it had been. And the field gate was open, whereas he could clearly remember shutting it. Somebody must have come along, looked over the wall and seen it. Like a fool he'd left the key in place. He just hadn't thought it would be a problem, that anyone would be around to nick it. But they had.

'FUCK,' he shouted. 'BASTARDS. FUCKING FUCKING BASTARDS,' louder with each iteration. He didn't care if somebody heard him.

Whoever had taken his bike had come in through the gate. Had they also seen him?

He went back to where his sleeping bag lay crumpled under the trees. His backpack was there because he'd been using it as a pillow. But his phone! Where was his phone? He remembered reading the post from *thetruth*, but then he must have dozed off. Had it fallen from his hand? He turned the sleeping bag over, lifted it up, shook it. Nothing; the phone was gone. So were his trainers! An almost new pair of Arco Sport Professionals that had cost him two months allowance. His spare pair was in one of the panniers, and that had been on the bike.

'SHIT. HELL FIRE FUCK!'

The panniers had also contained all his food. His stomach grumbled even as he took this in. He picked up a stone and threw it as hard as he could at a tree. It rebounded off the bark and bounced into the undergrowth.

Lander flopped onto his sleeping bag and buried his face in the crook of his arm. He was the closest he'd been in a long time to tears; but he hadn't cried when their Mam died and he was fucked if he was going to cry now. He wiped his face on his sleeve, sat up and forced himself to take stock. What did he have?

He had his backpack, which held some of his clothes. There was also a forgotten chocolate bar, which he immediately ate. He had the little money that had been in his pocket, and some basic information about *thetruth* people. It didn't help at all in finding the exact location of the group, or the address in Bruges where he could connect with the network. He had the roll of elastic. He had his knife, binoculars, compass and torch. He had his water bottle, now empty. He had a black felt-tip pen. He had a map. It was a large-scale motoring version that covered the whole of the north of England. It wasn't any use for minor roads but it showed the way to the coast. He had his sleeping bag.

What did he not have? He had no food. That was a problem but only a temporary one. There'd be plenty of places vandalised shops, abandoned houses – where he'd be able to het things to eat. Same for water, and in the meantime he'd just have to risk the streams. He had no phone. He had no ID; he'd put that, together with most of his money, in a compartment in the bottom of one of the panniers because he'd thought it would be safer there. Finally – and he was beginning to think this was the worst of all – he had nothing to put on his feet. Until he could do something about that he was more or less stranded.

A little way down the field he'd noticed a large white sack which had blown against the wall and lodged there. It was the sort used for building materials – sand, gravel, rubble, that kind of thing – woven from thick stands of plastic and very tough. They had lots of them back at the farm. They weren't returnable but Granddad wouldn't throw them away. He'd tie them and put them in the barn in case one day they'd "come in". Well this one had "come in" now.

He dragged the sack back to his camp beside the trees, sat down, unsheathed his knife, and spent the next half hour fashioning himself some footwear. He started by cutting one of the side panels from the sack. That gave him a sheet of material about a metre square. He put his foot on the edge and drew loosely around it with the felt-tip. Then he began to cut out the outline with the knife. It was harder than he expected, but with a combination of hacking and sawing he managed. Next he used the shape he'd made as a template, and drew round that until he'd filled the whole of the plastic sheet with feet, more than twenty of them. He cut these out, and gathered them into two equal piles.

He took three pairs of socks from his backpack and put them on. Then, using the roll of elastic, he strapped half a dozen of the plastic shapes to the soles of his feet. He cut a strip from the remainder of the sack and tied it tightly around each one. He stood up and hobbled a few steps. Not too bad. He wouldn't be running a marathon, but he could walk. He was not sure how far, but he hoped it would be far enough to reach somewhere he could find a pair of replacement trainers. He stowed the rest of the plastic in his backpack and put away the other things.

He thought for a moment about going home but immediately rejected the idea. The only thing to do was to stick to Plan A and keep going. There was no chance of getting in touch with Kerryl or his grandparents now that his phone had gone. He'd have to see if he could get hold of another phone somehow, so that he could find out how they were and let them know he was safe. He left the field and walked out to the track.

He decided to carry on up the hill, reasoning that because the main settlements were in the valley the hilltop road wouldn't be as busy and so there would be less chance of being spotted. The down side was that there would be nowhere near as many opportunities for finding transport, footwear and food.

It wasn't too bad. The ground was rough and sometimes sharp stones dug into his feet but he reached the head of the track with his makeshift footwear still more or less intact and turned right. The road was too small to be marked on his map but it was going in the right direction. He knew that if he followed the general line of the M62, away from the setting sun, he would eventually get to the east coast.

Progress was slow. The knots in the plastic strapping kept working loose and needed frequent attention. Then the binding on his left foot slipped right off and the whole assembly came apart. It seemed he was having to stop every few minutes. And it seemed as though all the sharpest stones had lined themselves up just for him. He walked for an hour, and it was obvious that his foot protection wouldn't last much longer. He could understand why this style of footwear hadn't caught on. The four-inch heels Kerryl had bought on her last trip to Manchester would have been more comfortable.

He guessed he'd gone less than two miles when he heard the unmistakable sound of a tractor. At first he thought it must be in a field, but then he saw its lights on the road behind him. They were a long way off. Should he try to hide? Or just carry on as normal, looking as though he knew what he was doing and had every right to do it? It couldn't be anything official. The police or the army patrols wouldn't be going around in a tractor. No, it had to be a farmer. Most of the farmers he knew were like Granddad, not well-disposed towards the authorities. It was unlikely that a farmer would report him as a vagrant. He might even help him.

The noise grew louder. The road was narrow with high stone walls on each side, and there wouldn't be much room for the tractor to pass. He stopped by a niche in the wall and squeezed himself in so that it could get by. Except that it didn't; it stopped right beside him.

It was big and green with yellow wheels, a late model John Deere, and it was pulling a cattle trailer. The driver leaned down from the cab window.

'Out late, lad,' he said.

Lander said nothing. Yes, he was. Who was this guy? A specialist in the fucking obvious?

'Yer looks as though yer needs a lift.'

He was an old man, probably as old as Granddad, red faced, with grey hair poking from under a greasy cap. He looked friendly. He wouldn't be going far, but a lift for even a short distance would be very welcome.

Lander nodded. The farmer opened the door and he climbed in. He pulled his scarf over his mouth and nose.

'What yer doin', lad?' said the old man. Lander looked at him with a puzzled expression. 'Wi' yer face. Why are yer doin' that?

'I'm covering my mouth and nose. To protect you from the Infection.'

'There's no need for that,' the man said. 'If I'm going ter get it I'm going ter get it. At my time o' life it makes no odds.'

Lander let the scarf fall. There was a tired old collie sitting on the jump seat. The farmer pushed it off and it settled resentfully at the back of the cab. There was a clunk and the tractor moved forward.

'Where yer makin' for?'

Lander thought it best to tell the truth, or something close to it. 'I'm heading for the coast. I want to see if I can get a boat over to Belgium. I've got friends there.'

'Makin' for t'coast. Well, I can get yer as far as Knottingley.'

Lander had never heard of it. 'Where's that?'

'T'other side o' Castleford.'

This was good, much better than Lander had expected. It was well on his way. He wondered why the farmer would be going so far.

'I'm teckin' some beasts,' he said, nodding over his shoulder towards the cattle trailer. 'I've got three steers.'

'Oh,' said Lander. He thought that it was a bit late to be delivering cattle, but it seemed rude to say so.

The tractor cab was cosy. Lander looked down at the road, picked out by the lights. The collie decided to see whether he was friendly, stood up and sniffed him. Lander patted it and remembered Buster. Would he know he'd gone? Kerryl would look after him, and he'd be good company for her. Would he miss him? Probably not. As long as Buster got his four square meals a day he'd be happy.

'What's up wi' yer feet?'

'What?'

'Yer feet. Yer've got bandages on 'em.'

Lander laughed. 'They're not bandages.' He lifted up a foot where the farmer could see it. 'Somebody nicked my trainers while I was asleep in a field back there.'

'Never! The buggers.' The old man tutted. 'What's it all comin' to?'

'I had to make these out of an old sack I found, but they don't work too well.'

The farmer thought for a moment. Then he said, 'Look in t' back there. There's an old pair o' boots.'

Lander found them. They were wellingtons, indeed old and quite smelly, but they seemed sound and looked to have plenty of wear left in them.

'Teck 'em if yer want.'

'Really? Are you sure?'

'I've got five pairs o' boots and only two feet. If yer wants 'em, teck 'em.'

Lander slid the bindings off his feet and put on the boots. Without the extra socks they would have been too big, but with them they were fine. He felt a great relief. With no shoes his options had been severely limited. Now, with something on his feet and a lift to take him closer to the east coast harbours, things were looking up. All that was left was to find something to eat.

'Ay up.' The farmer pointed.

Lander saw bright lights in the road a couple of hundred yards ahead.

'Road block. Army I shouldn't wonder.' The farmer rummaged on the cab floor and tossed Lander a blanket.

'Get thissen down, an' cover thissen wi' that. An' say nowt.'

The blanket was old and smelt strongly of dog. It was clearly the collie's, but Lander had no choice. He squeezed into the footwell and covered himself. A minute later the tractor came to a stop and the farmer turned off the engine.

'You do realise it's past curfew,' said a crisp voice.

'Aye, I do that,' said the farmer. 'I've got an Agricultural Movement Permit.'

'Have you now? So where are you going and what's the purpose of your journey?'

'I'm going to Knottingley wi' some beasts.' The farmer reached under his seat, took a plastic wallet and climbed down from the cab. Lander made himself as small as he could, shrunk himself into the confined space, and looked out under the blanket through a small Perspex window. The area was bright with floodlights. He could see the farmer's back and an army Land Rover.

'A bit late to be moving cattle, isn't it?' said a different voice.

'I'm teckin' 'em now 'cos it's safer. Last time I took some beasts in daylight they was nabbed.' The farmer laughed, but without humour. 'I don't know what's got into folk sin' all this plague business started. You can't sell steers for love ner money, nobody wants 'em, but when you try to move 'em some bugger thieves 'em. So it's best to go at night.'

The guards seemed satisfied, and there were a few muttered courtesies. It seemed to be all over when Lander suddenly felt cramp seize his leg. He straightened it, he couldn't help it, and he knocked a spanner which was on the cab floor. It made a scraping rattle.

'What's that?' the voice said. 'Have you got somebody in your cab?'

'Nay,' said the farmer. 'It's on'y me dog.'

Lander heard the door open. He froze. He was in agony but he had to keep still. If the road block found him he'd be in trouble, and so would the farmer. The collie got up and stuck its head out of the cab door.

'See?' said the farmer, reaching up and fondling the animal.

'All right,' said the guard. 'On your way.'

The old man climbed back into the cab and started the engine. Lander stayed down in the footwell until they were some distance along the road. Then he got back into the jump seat. Irritatingly his cramp had vanished as soon as they pulled away from the check point.

'Thank you,' he said.

The farmer shrugged. 'Yer welcome.'

Lander thought it would be polite to introduce himself. 'My name's ...'

'Nay!' The farmer cut him off, holding up his hand. 'It's as well I don't know yer name. I don't know who y'are, where yer goin' or what yer up to, and it's best we keep it that way.' He paused, then added an explanation. 'Suppose yer told me yer name was George, an' then a patrol stopped me and asked me if I'd come across some'dy called George. I'd have to tell 'em yes. But if I don't know yer name, I can't tell 'em owt, can I?'

There was no answer to this logic. Lander watched through the window as the walls and hedgerows passed by. His stomach growled and he wondered where he could get something to eat, and when.

A CHOICE

LANDER RECKONED HE had a good two hours of travel time left. After that it would be too light for him to still be about. The farmer had dropped him at the gateway to a farm just past Knottingley. He'd tried to thank him but his benefactor didn't seem to want that and had driven off with the briefest of goodbyes. They never knew each other's names.

There were few dwellings and the villages were far apart. He walked through one, unlit and deserted, and saw no one. The only sign of life was a nasty looking dog, mangy and drooling. It snarled at him, but its heart wasn't in it. Lander threw a stone at the animal and it ran off.

There should have been signs of dawn, but there was thick cloud and it was still very dark. He decided he'd keep going. The farmer's boots were not the most comfortable footwear he'd ever had but they were all right, certainly a vast improvement on the plastic sack, and he settled into a mindless plod, an almost trance-like progression that allowed his mind to wander. His thoughts were miles away, so the woman's voice startled him.

'Are you my knight in shining armour?'

Lander jumped, looked around and located the speaker. 'What?'

She was sitting in the garden of a small cottage at the roadside. The building was unlit and the hedge in front was high so that he would have walked past without seeing her at all if she hadn't spoken.

'I wished for a strong young man to come along to help me. I think you must be he.'

Lander looked more closely. It was an old woman, and she was definitely crazy.

'I don't think so,' he said, and started to move off.

'Please,' she said. 'Give me a moment of your time. You have so much of it and I have very little. It's not a lot to ask.'

Lander paused. 'What do you want?' he said, guardedly.

'Ah,' said the woman. She rose stiffly from her chair and came closer, and Lander could see that she was even older than Gran. 'I need a favour,' she said. 'I need your help with a task.'

'What?' She probably wanted something shifted or lifted. Lander would help her, because in similar circumstances he'd like someone to help his Gran, but he couldn't afford to stop for long.

'I can see you are eager to continue your journey,' she said. Her voice was not exactly posh but it was educated, a bit like some of his teachers. 'What I'd like you to do won't delay you greatly. It's not dangerous, at least not for you, but I have to admit it is something you might find difficult.'

Lander doubted it. He was used to heavy work on the farm and there wasn't much he was unable to tackle.

'Come into the house,' she said. 'I'll make us a cup of tea and I'll explain.'

Lander hesitated. The prospect of tea was welcome, and there might be something to eat with it.

'Come, do,' she said, walking towards the door. 'There is nothing here that will harm you.'

Still Lander hesitated. The woman seemed to be all right, but the house could be infected. There were lots of warnings about going into unfamiliar buildings. He reached for his scarf again but something told him that the old woman might see covering his face as rude so he didn't pull it up.

'I have cake,' she said. 'Carrot cake. I hope you like carrot cake.'

That swung it. Lander had been checking out the house, looking for tell-tale signs of movement inside, but there were none. An old woman, a very old woman, couldn't be a threat, even if she did seem a bit weird.

He followed her through the door into a small kitchen. The woman indicated for him to sit at the table while she put a kettle on the hob. Neither of them spoke while it boiled.

'How do you like your tea?' she said.

Lander liked tea the way his Granddad drank it. 'Milk and four sugars, please.'

The woman raised an eyebrow and poured the milk with a hand that trembled slightly. She pushed the sugar bowl towards him. 'Help yourself,' she said.

She went to a cupboard and took out a large cake. Lander watched as she cut him a very large slice. She took a smaller piece for herself.

'Carrot cake used to be one of my late husband's favourites,' she said, 'and my son's. I see you like it too. I have a Rayburn and I'm still able to bake while my oil supply lasts. Once it's gone I'm afraid that will be the end of it.'

The woman took a seat opposite Lander and watched him while he ate. When he'd finished she didn't bother to ask but cut him another slice. She hadn't touched her own piece.

'Now, please tell me your name,' she said when he'd finished.

'Lan... I mean Alexander.' He thought this woman deserved his proper name; the carrot cake was excellent. 'Shaw,' he added. 'Alexander Shaw.'

'Alexander. A noble name. A Greek name. My own name is Louise Fisher. I used to be Professor of Classics at the University of Bristol. There is some of my work.'

She pointed to a shelf holding half a dozen impressive looking hardbacks. Lander scanned the spines and read her name and some of the titles. *Feast and Famine in Minoan Crete. Athens, Sparta and the Struggle for Peloponnesian Supremacy. Socrates and the Birth of Modern Thought.* Lander couldn't see himself reading any of them. They seemed more Kerryl's cup of tea than his.

'This is my most recent work,' said Louise, picking up a volume and putting it on the table.

It was called *Luck, Chance and Fate in the World of Homer.* Was she expecting Lander to read it? Was that the favour she wanted? Some hopes! She'd said that what she had in mind wouldn't take him long. This was a thick book. Reading it would take for ever. And it could be dangerous, a serious case of brain strain.

'The Greeks had some interesting ideas about chance and fate,' she said. 'You have read Homer?'

Lander shook his head. At least he knew enough to understand she was talking about the author of the Trojan War, not one of the Simpsons.

'Well, that is a treat you have to come,' said Louise. 'In Homeric Greece one of the words for fortune was moira, meaning a portion or a share. The concept of providence as a share is an interesting one, because it implies there is a whole to be divided. It also implies that if one person has a larger share of it, there is less left for others.'

She pointed her knife at the remains of the carrot cake. 'Consider this cake. You may cut it into equal slices so everyone gets the same size piece. Or you can do what I did and make the slices different sizes, some large, some small. Now imagine the cake represents good fortune. Some people get larger slices. Very nice for them. But that means that there's less of the cake left, so others will get smaller slices. The cake is a finite size. If my portion is larger than the average, someone else's must be smaller to compensate. Very good fortune for me means slightly less good fortune to share between everyone else.'

Lander hadn't expected a lecture on ancient history, but what the woman was saying was interesting. It would have appealed to his grandfather, who was a rampant socialist and raged against inequality and privilege.

'I think everybody's slice must be smaller now,' he said, 'after the Infection.'

'Ah,' said Louise, 'an interesting point. However, what the Infection means is that the whole cake is smaller. It doesn't affect the proportions of the individual slices.' She looked at him steadily for several seconds before going on. 'I think that my own slice of the cake has been generous. Born into a well-to-do family, happy childhood, happy marriage to a wonderful man, good career and two lovely children. Yes, I think a pretty fat slice, don't you?'

Lander agreed.

'So,' she said, 'tell me about you. What has your portion been like, so far? Happy home?'

'Yes.'

'Enough to eat and drink, caring parents?'

'Yes. My dad died a while back, but yes.'

'I'm sorry to hear that.' She looked away. 'Would you say you've had a good education?'

'I suppose so. I don't like school much.'

'Ah, well, I can't say whether that's their loss or yours, but you seem to me to be an intelligent young man, so who knows? At your age it's too early to ask about unrealised dreams, but I assume you have some?'

'Yes.'

'So, despite the sad loss of your father, a pretty good share of the cake for you too, up to now.'

'Yes.'

'Would you like another slice?'

She was looking at the carrot cake, and Lander certainly would have liked another piece of that. However, he had the feeling that he was being tested so he said, 'No thank you.'

'Good,' said Louise. 'I think it's right that we should recognise our good fortune and not take more than is necessary, don't you? No need to panic, I'm not coming on to you with religion, telling you to count your blessings, all that sort of thing. In reality I'm a devout atheist, but I think it's good for us to review the balance of our lives from time to time.' She stood up. 'I want you to meet someone whose slice of the cake is somewhat smaller than yours or mine. Come this way. Please.'

She waited for him at the door, holding it open. Lander hesitated. Should he go? Was this the reason she'd waylaid him? Who was he to meet? He had to follow her, it would have been impossible not to.

He stepped into a small room lit by a single candle. It was stuffy and cramped, and had an antiseptic smell. There was a bed in the centre, and a lifting device like a beige crane. Beside the bed was a hospital table covered in plastic boxes and jars. There was somebody in the bed. Lander leant forward to get a better look at the figure. It was a boy, perhaps his own age, maybe a little older. The head turned slowly and a pair of large, grey eyes gazed at him.

'This is Spencer,' said Louise. 'Spencer, this is Alexander.' The figure in the bed made no response. Louise stroked his head, the lock of hair falling over his brow. 'I always talk to him,' she said, 'even though he can't hear me. And even if he could, it's doubtful he would be able to understand.

'Spencer is my grandson. He's nineteen. Three years ago he'd been to spend an evening with one of his friends. He was cycling home when he was hit by a car. Two young men in a souped-up Golf, out to impress their girls and going too fast. The driver had been drinking and said he didn't see Spencer because he was not showing any lights. That was ridiculous; Spencer always used lights when cycling, during the day as well as after dark. The people in the car got away with minor injuries, but Spencer's skull was shattered and his back broken. He was in intensive care for three months and came out like this. He can see and he can breathe. He can swallow but he can't chew. He can move his head but nothing else. He needs constant care throughout the day and the night, all day, every day. The car driver was disqualified from driving and sent to jail for eighteen months. Spencer's sentence is much longer. He is imprisoned in his own body for the rest of his life.'

Lander was struck by the emptiness in Louise's voice. Spencer's plight was similar to that suffered by other young people he'd heard of, but he'd never met any of them. Now he did he felt the terrible unfairness of what had happened to the boy in the bed, the blind injustice of it. Louise had said the favour she wanted would only take a moment or too, so she couldn't want ongoing help with his nursing. Was it something quick, like toileting? Feeding?

'What do you want from me?' he said. He was dreading the answer, but the one he received jolted him to the core.

'I want you to kill him,' she said.

It was so unexpected, such a hammer blow that Lander couldn't answer. Was she serious?

'I've shocked you,' she said, 'but please hear me out. Spencer's brother and sister, and his parents, my son and daughter-in-law, are dead. All his relatives are dead, victims of the Infection. For reasons I cannot fathom, he and I are not. I've tried to infect us both, even putting the linen from his mother's deathbed on our own beds. To no avail. We, Spencer and I, seem to be immune, and I guess you are too. That's not the blessing it might seem for any of us. In fact it's a burden which reduces the size of our slices of the cake by quite a bit.

'I am the only carer Spencer has. I am eighty-seven. I have rheumatoid arthritis. I've had two heart attacks and I've run out of my medication. I could die any day. What will happen to Spencer if I do? When I do?'

Lander had no answer, although he knew there must be one.

'What will happen to Spencer then is a slow death. He will starve, but it will probably be thirst that kills him. He will die from dehydration, wrapped in a parcel of his own faeces and urine. It will take some time. He may be in a near vegetative state but he can feel pain. He will suffer. If you kill him, he will be spared that. And I can then put an end to my own life too.'

Lander shook his head, trying to bring some sanity, some reality into this crazy room. 'I can't. If you think it's right, why don't you do it yourself?'

Louise smiled ruefully. 'I've tried. I have a shotgun which would do the job swiftly and painlessly, if a little messily. I have carving knives. I have aspirin in the cupboard. I have brought all of them into this room at various times, and not been able to go any further.' She stroked Spencer's head again. 'He's my grandson. I played with him when he was a baby. I changed his nappies. I lifted him on to my knee and read him stories. He would always come to me if he had any worries or problems. I cannot do it. Could your grandmother kill you?'

Lander knew she couldn't, whatever the circumstances.

'You're all right here,' he said. 'Why don't you wait till the Infection's over and the authorities will look after you. You can even ask them to come now. Phones are still working. You could use my mobile, except it was nicked.'

Louise looked sadly at him. 'Do you think that after all that's happened an old woman and her paralysed grandson will be on anyone's list of priorities? The 'authorities', as you call them, will have much more pressing things to attend to, and rightly so.'

She turned to the corner, where a shotgun rested against the wall. She picked it up.

'You've used one of these before?' she said.

Lander nodded.

'And you've killed things with it?'

'Yes, but only magpies and rabbits, and once I had to slaughter a calf.'

'We could have a long debate about the value of a human life, even one as reduced as Spencer's, against the value of all the things you've shot, but there is no time. I promised that what I wanted of you would only take a moment, and it will. A second to pull the trigger, that is all. Then you can go. It will be a mercy, a service to Spencer and to me, a favour we can never repay.'

Lander was torn. He could see the reasoning behind what Louise was saying, but could he bring himself to contemplate what she was asking of him? Surely there was someone else she could go to.

She could see him wavering, and spoke again. 'Solon, the Athenian statesman and poet, said, "Judge not the measure of anyone's good fortune until they are dead". My grandson's slice of the cake was once larger even than your own, but on that night three years ago it was reduced to a mere sliver. By a simple act you could increase the volume of Spencer's good fortune, and mine. And although you might not think it now, your own too.'

Still Lander hesitated. Did Spencer understand what his grandmother was proposing? There was no sign that he did. The grey eyes moved from him to Louise and back again, but sluggishly and not, as far as he could see, in response to anything.

'There is another thing,' said Louise, and Lander thought he detected a new edge to her tone. 'Now that you know what I have told you, I think you are confronted with a moral dilemma, a quandary which leads to an imperative. If you are not prepared to do us this service, to end the life which is a trial to Spencer and a burden to me, then your only ethical course is to remain here and look after my grandson yourself.'

Was that right? It was like being hit in the face by a slamming door. This was blackmail. He couldn't stay. It was impossible. Technically he could do what she wanted. He was a good shot, but he wouldn't need to be. Both barrels in Spencer's mouth, pull the trigger, and it would be done. She was right, it would be over in an instant. The boy would feel nothing. He wouldn't even know what was going on. It wouldn't be murder, it would be mercy killing, like putting down a stricken animal. It would make a terrible mess. Shotguns close up did; he remembered the calf. Should he then help Louise clear up? Help her bury him? She hadn't asked him to do that.

Louise handed him the gun. 'The safety catch is on. You don't mind if I don't watch.'

She went back into the kitchen, pulling the door closed behind her. Lander weighed the gun in his hands. It was a good one, well balanced. There was a cartridge in each barrel. Spencer's hand was limp on the duvet. Lander took it.

'I'm sorry, old pal,' he said.

Was it his imagination, or did he feel the tiniest, gentlest of pressures from the inert hand? He looked into the eyes, grey and steady on his. Killing was the right thing to do in the circumstances, Louise had convinced him of that. And now Spencer had convinced him of something else. If it were to be done, it should be done not by a stranger but by somebody who knew him, who loved him. It must be done by Louise.

He opened the door to the kitchen. Louise was sitting at the table and looked up at him in surprise.

'I can't,' said Lander. 'I'm sorry, I can't do it. It has to be you. There's no one else.'

He walked out of the front door, leaving the gun against the wall.

It was light now but still early, the morning bright and fresh. He set off along the road, his pace brisk but his heart heavy. Always before – at home, at school, hanging out with his mates – he'd known what had been the right thing to do. He'd not always done it, but he had always known what it was. This time there was no right thing, and he bled for the pair he'd left behind.

He'd gone a hundred yards when he heard the percussive thump of a gunshot. He stopped and waited, and then, a moment later, there was another

He didn't go back.

SIX

DESERTED

LANDER SPENT THE day under a hedge. Even though it was only early autumn it was cold and he slept badly. It was not only the cold, the uneven ground and the daytime noises. It was the vivid images of the carnage in the cottage that plagued his imagination. The helpless boy and his wise, troubled grandmother haunted him. He wondered what Louise had thought as she looked at Spencer and pulled the trigger, as she took away the meagre life he had left. Should he have done what she asked of him? That would have spared her having to do it herself, but he couldn't. Shooting birds, small animals, even the bull calf he and Granddad had slaughtered had been one thing. Murdering another human being was different. The Infection had made life even more precious, and he knew now that he was not a killer.

It was a relief when dusk came and he was able to continue his journey. It meant he could get on with things, instead of going over and over in his mind what had happened in the cottage.

The land was flat, nothing like the hills and valleys of the Pennines, the home he'd left what seemed like months ago. He thought that if he walked briskly he could probably cover ten or twelve miles before he needed to hide again. Something to eat was a problem. All he'd had for twenty-four hours was a chocolate bar and two slices of carrot cake. His stomach had stopped growling and all he felt now was a gnawing ache. He drank a pint or more of water from a stream and that helped, but he needed something to give him energy.

He'd not gone far when he came to a fork in the road. One signpost said Goole. He knew that was close to his final destination. He'd not been there, but he thought it was probably quite big and so best avoided for now. The other signpost was to a place called Snaith. What sort of a name was that? It sounded slithery, like a snake. He'd never heard of it, but it was in roughly the right direction and it was much closer than Goole. He might find food there.

He took the Snaith road and half a mile later came to a painted welcome board: Parish of Snaith. Beneath the name was the legend pop 3779. Using spray paint, somebody had crossed out the 3779 and written instead 24. Then, presumably later, the 24 had been sprayed through and replaced by the figure 0. To Lander, always one to spot and point out an illogicality, that was absurd. The population couldn't have been zero. What about the person doing the spraying? Pleased with himself at that thought, he set off down the gentle slope into the town. He passed what a sign told him was The Robert Mellor Secondary School, but the gates were locked and the building showed no signs of life.

The streets were very different from what he was used to in Walbrough. There they were all stone, grey-black and stern. Here everything was warm brick, apart from a few buildings that had been washed with pastel colours. The biggest difference, though, was in the overall appearance of the place. The valley towns he'd left behind were desolate. Windows that weren't boarded up were smashed. Graffiti defaced every surface, there was rubbish, there were stray animals, there was the odour of putrefaction and the smell of death. Snaith was completely the opposite. It was clean, tidy, well cared for and picture perfect. There were no signs of decay or destruction. So where was everyone?

His watch said it was just after nine o'clock, and you might have expected there to be at least somebody about, but doors and windows were closed, curtains drawn. He came to a convenience store, the sort that would normally be open from first light until well into the evening. It was shut up. He looked through the window. On the shelves were magazines, cans and bottles of drinks, dried and tinned food. He could see packets of cereal and biscuits, and his stomach churned. In a corner were beers and wines. There were even neat racks of face masks and plastic bio-suites that some places had started to stock when the Infection first approached. The amazing thing, though was that the place was intact. Nobody had broken in, there had been no looting, everything was as it should be. In Walbrough the shop wouldn't have lasted five minutes.

What to do? He was ravenous, and behind that window was food. To the side was a high gate, which presumably led to a yard behind. He looked around. There was nobody in the street, no tell-tale curtain-twitching in the houses opposite. He gave the gate a push but it was locked. It would be simple to climb over, smash a window and get in. But he hesitated. There was something odd about the place. Suppose it was a trap. Suppose there was an alarm and people came running from all directions to set upon him. Where was everyone? Then he remembered the zero on the roadside sign. Did it really mean that there was no one here? If so, where had everybody gone? They couldn't all be dead. Surely these buildings weren't housing corpses. But they might be. He left the shop. It would be better to explore a bit more before he did anything he might regret.

He continued further into the town. Everywhere was the same; shops, homes, a primary school, offices, all shut up, all lifeless, like on Christmas Day. The curtains on most windows were closed, those with shutters had them drawn. He passed a pub, a fish-and-chip shop, a chemist, a newsagent and post office, all in the same state. Another unusual thing struck him: there were no stray dogs. Every street in Walbrough had its pack, all of them hungry and many savage. Here there wasn't so much as a cat. It was a ghost town.

He glanced down a side street and saw a close of prim-looking homes, four and five bedroom detached houses, goals of an aspiring middle class. One at the far end caught his eye. It was in prime position and the only one with a double garage. Go for the top, he thought, and he walked towards it past the other, silent buildings. He expected that at any second there would be hostile shouts and he would be accosted, but everything stayed quiet.

There was a short, tarmac drive and a concrete path across a lawn to a smart looking front door. He tapped on it and listened. Nothing. He pressed a bell push and heard a chime from inside. Still nothing. He tried the knob. The door was locked, as he'd expected. It looked solid, impregnable. Might the garage offer easier entry? There was no handle on the door, nothing to get hold of. Presumably it was one of those electric up-and-over jobs. To the side of the house was a gate. That was unlocked and he went through to the back.

The garden was neat and tidy, with a patio, a few bushes, a children's swing, and a small shed and vegetable patch at the far end. Then he saw something very interesting; one of the windows was open. It was an upstairs one, and a top pane. He could see from the ground that it was too small for him to get through, but there was a casement below and he thought he might be able to reach in far enough to open that. The best bit was that it was over the garage.

Making it on to the garage roof was easy enough. PE had been Lander's best subject at school, and jumping to grab the edge of the roof and pulling himself up was no problem. Getting into the house was harder. It meant getting on to the narrow window sill and squatting there while he reached inside to undo the fastening for the casement. At first he couldn't reach it, but after a struggle he managed to get his fingers to the handle. This was the sort of house that would have window locks, he thought, and he prayed there wouldn't be one here. There was not. The catch turned, he eased the window open and crawled through.

He was in a bedroom, obviously a girl's. There were posters of boy-bands on the wall, make-up on the dressing table, a floral bedspread, a purple rug with an image of a unicorn, a couple of soft toys on a neatly-made bed. There were books – school texts and fiction – furry slippers, a pink bath robe on the door. It could almost have been Kerryl's room. Thinking of her brought a pang of sorrow. He missed her. He missed his grandparents. Had she found the memory stick yet?

There's something about an empty house that gives off its own vibe. If it had been occupied Lander would have felt it, but he knew from the start there was no one in. He opened the door onto a large landing with more doors. One of them was ajar; a bathroom. He used it, then went downstairs, not bothering yet with the other rooms. He went to the back door. There were bolts top and bottom and a key in the lock. He wondered about opening it.

Might there be an alarm? He told himself that was silly, because if there was an alarm he would have set it off by now. He opened the door and retrieved his backpack from where he'd left it outside. He didn't lock the door again; if somebody came to the front he might need to make a quick exit.

The hallway was spotlessly clean. Nothing had been left out, there were no marks on the carpets, no dust. It was perfect, like a show house or those room mock-ups you see in IKEA. On one side was a huge sitting room, with two sofas in cream leather, a white faux-fur rug, and a massive TV. On the other side was a kitchen/diner. There wasn't much in the kitchen. The fridge was empty apart from a sealed carton of long-life milk and two eggs. He broke the eggs into a glass, sniffed them and decided they were OK. He whisked them up with most of the milk and added some sugar. He drained the concoction in half a dozen gulps and gave a burp of appreciation. The larder cupboard wasn't much better. He found some rather soft cream crackers in a plastic box, and some tins of sardines. He opened one and ate the fish with his fingers, wiping the juice off his chin with his sleeve. There were a few more cans on the shelf – grapefruit segments, passata, beans, new potatoes. Who eats tinned potatoes? Gran would have a fit. He was going to try them but he couldn't find an opener, so he had some more sardines because they opened easily with a key that came with the tin. He ate some cream crackers, drank two glasses of water, then he went back upstairs.

The master bedroom was luxurious: an enormous bed with a comfy looking duvet, a vast en suite, another TV. There were a couple of built-in wardrobes, and one of them was full of men's clothes. There were suits, jackets, business shirts. They had no interest for him, but there were also some plain t-shirts and a pile of pressed pairs of jeans. He recognised Gucci and Armani, but he'd never heard of the other brand names. There were also four pairs of trainers. They would come in very handy, he'd gone about as far as he could in the farmer's boots.

He lay down on the bed. Why was this place deserted? Everything was so ordered; that meant that the people hadn't left in a hurry. Neither were there the sad signs – the stained sheets, the soiled clothing, the human mess – that there would have been if large numbers of them had perished from the Infection. It was as if everyone had simply walked out, and recently too. There were cars on the drives, so what had they left in? Would they all come rushing back, pouring out of buses and marching down the street?

The bed was heaven. His last resting place had been hard and uncomfortable, and he soon fell into a deep sleep. It was late afternoon before he awoke, suddenly sitting bolt upright and wondering where he was. There was a rattling sound downstairs. Had somebody come in? He rolled out of bed, tip-toed onto the landing and crouched behind the bannister. At the foot of the stairs was a large ginger cat, looking primly up at him. He placed the rattle; it had been a cat flap. The cat slowly mounted the stairs and wove itself around his legs. He stroked its head and it purred, rolling on to its side. It was sleek and well fed. Another mystery.

He went to the en suite, turned on the shower and waited for it to run hot. It didn't. Still, better than nothing. He got under the spray, poured soap on his head and scrubbed himself. The water was wickedly cold and he could stand it for no more than half a minute. There were plenty of towels, dense fluffy ones, and he rubbed himself dry. Then he helped himself from the wardrobe to fresh undershorts, a t-shirt and a pair of jeans. They were a bit short in the leg but not a bad fit, and anyway, who was there to see him? He left his own clothes on the floor. They were showing that they'd been well worn and he certainly wasn't going to wash them. He stuffed some more clothes into his backpack, including several pairs of socks to make up for the ones he'd worn out.

Downstairs he opened two more cans of sardines, gave one to the cat and ate the other himself, with the rest of the crackers. There was a phone in the kitchen. He picked it up and heard the familiar purr of the dial tone. It was so reassuring that again he marvelled at how normal things seemed to be here. His fingers hovered over the buttons. Should he call home? It was tempting, but what would they think if he suddenly contacted them now? Besides, if they tried to persuade him to come back, to dissuade him from what he was meaning to do, he would find it hard to refuse. It would be better to wait until he was at the coast, or even across the Channel.

Then he could tell them exactly where he was going and why. Of course, they would already know that from his letter on the memory stick. If they'd read it.

The wall clock told him it was 5.30, time to get ready for the next leg of his journey. With luck he'd be at the coast by morning, especially if he could find some transport. He looked out of the window. He weighed up whether to go outside and see if one of the cars parked out there was unlocked. Not yet. Perhaps after dark, although ideally he'd rather be gone by then.

There was a door in the kitchen that he guessed led to the garage. He was right. Half the double space was empty, but in the other was a car. It was an Audi, low, sleek, and red. He could be at the coast in no time in that. He tried the door. Locked. There was no sign of any key anywhere. He wished he knew how to break into a car and start it. Kevin, a lad at his school, had claimed he knew how to do it. Lander wished he'd had a teach-in.

He might not be able to start the car, but there was something in the garage that he could use. In the corner was a mountain bike, a bright yellow Specialized Stumpjumper. It was in beautiful condition, almost new. It had front and rear suspension, disc brakes and custom gears. Lander reckoned it had probably cost the thick end of three grand. That would certainly get him to the coast. Even better, it would make no noise, and he wouldn't have to risk attracting the attention of anyone who might be watching by opening the garage door. Not that he thought anybody would be. Apart from the cat, he hadn't seen a single living thing all the time he'd been in the town. It was like a film set, just that there were no actors or technicians. If he was into sci-fi he might have thought he'd slipped into another dimension.

He decided to leave it another hour before setting off. It wouldn't be properly dark even then, but it would be good enough. Besides, there were no lights on the Specialized and the twilight would help him to get a good start.

In the pantry he found a carton of custard, and he ate that. He put the last two tins of sardines in his rucksack, and some cartons of beans and soup. It was too heavy, so he put the sardines back. The cat looked relieved.

A little before 8 o'clock he wheeled the Specialized through the kitchen and into the back garden. He put on his rucksack, propped open the side gate, mounted the bike and set off along the close towards the road, all the time glancing from side to side for watchers from the houses. He was so engrossed that he rounded a corner and almost rode into it: a large, white van the size of an ambulance, with blue emergency lights. It was stationary, it's engine off, and standing one on each side of it were two people in white biohazard suits and masks. They looked like Storm Troopers from Star Wars.

Without slowing Lander did a U-turn and pedalled back up the close, fast. He'd seen a narrow path beside the house. He had no idea where it went, but the ambulance – if that's what it was – wouldn't be able to get along it and the Storm Troopers wouldn't be fast enough to catch him.

His heart was thumping. It was not only the surprise, it was the shock of seeing the people. Biohazard suits! Did that mean the area was infected? Was that why there was nobody around?

He came to the end of the path, turned on to the road, and there was another vehicle, exactly like the first one. It couldn't be the same, there wouldn't have been time for it to get there. Inside were two other people, also in masks. As soon as he appeared blinding searchlights flooded the street.

Across the road was another jitty. He dropped the bike and ran for it. It was narrow and in places seriously overgrown. He sprinted for a hundred yards but there was no sign of anyone following and he stopped, leaning on the fence, gasping for breath. Who were these creepy dudes? Were they really after him? Why hadn't they followed him? He soon found out.

The top of the fence was just above his head and he scrambled up it to see what was on the other side. Allotments. Excellent, there'd be huts where he would be able to hide. He hauled himself over and was straightening up when he heard a whispering, whirring sound, like moth wings. He looked up. Above him was a drone, a white one. There was another a little further away. And a third coming across the allotments to join them. He turned to vault back over the fence, and there was a fourth, two metres away and head height. It had two stereoscopic lenses that observed him like the eyes of some giant bug. There was a tube pointing at him. A gun barrel.

In the second that he realised this the drone fired. It shot him full in the face. At point blank range.

SEVEN
CAUGHT

THE SAME FIVE questions, again and again and again.

> *Who are you?*
> *Where are you from?*
> *Where are you going?*
> *Why?*
> *How did you know about Snaith?*

The questioning didn't start immediately. To begin with he spent what he later learnt were three days recuperating. The drone had sprayed him with a nerve agent. He'd felt panic when they'd told him that, but they assured him that the substance used was very mild and he would quickly make a full recovery.

At the start it had been awful; pain all over and great difficulty breathing. This lasted forty-eight hours, by which time he was so weak he could barely move. After that the pain receded, leaving him exhausted and with sore eyes, a weeping nose, and a headache. Then quite suddenly he felt better, and he was able to take in his surroundings.

He was in a white room that had all the trappings of a hospital ward, but he was the only person there. He had tubes running into his arm, another up his nose, and some sort of sensor with a wire to his chest. For most of the time he was left alone but in the afternoon a nurse came in, or maybe it was a doctor, he wasn't sure because in their bio suits and hoods they all looked the same. She stood beside the bed and checked the machinery that seemed to be monitoring him. Then she bent over him and in turn raised each eyelid and examined his eyes, shining a pen-torch into the pupils. When she'd done that she took off her surgical gloves and removed her hood.

'Well,' she said, 'the good news is that you're not infected. All your blood work has come through clear.'

That was no surprise to Lander. He could have told them that. 'I know. I'm immune,' he said.

The nurse raised an eyebrow. She had a friendly face and looked strong and capable. She reminded him of his mother.

'Are you now?' she said. 'That may be. A few people are immune, I know that, but they can still carry the virus. You don't appear to be a carrier either.'

'Good. So what now? Can I go?'

'Not my decision,' she said, 'but I very much doubt it. I'm afraid you're in trouble.'

This was unwelcome news. He'd heard the broadcasts telling people to stay at home, and he'd ignored those when he decided to start his journey. But that wasn't really serious, was it?

'Trouble? What sort of trouble?' he said.

'It's bad. But not as bad as it would have been if you were a carrier. My advice is to get some sleep and eat some food. You'll need all your strength.'

The next day the questions started. To begin with he made no answer but they just repeated them, so to combat the boredom he made things up.

> *'Who are you?'*
> *'The Doctor.'*
> *'Where are you from?'*
> *'Mars.'*
> *'Where are you going?'*
> *'To the Moon.'*
> *'Why?'*
> *'To see the man there.'*
> *'How did you know about Snaith?'*
> *'A little bird told me.'*

The drill was always the same. He was taken into a bare room where three people would be sitting at a table. He was made to stand in front of the table. One of the three would put the questions to him and another would write down his answers, while the third looked on. Sometimes it was the same people, sometimes different ones. No matter what he said, the three interrogators received his answers without comment. Then he would be returned to the cell he'd been put in when he left the hospital ward, and half an hour later they'd bring him back to the interrogation chamber and ask him exactly the same questions again. He tried giving different answers from the ones he'd given before, or the same ones, or a mixture. Whatever he did, they would hear them without responding, he would be taken away, and after another half hour he'd be subjected to the very same ritual again. This went on constantly, throughout the day and into the night.

He asked where he was but they ignored him. He asked if he could make a phone call, because in all the police dramas he'd seen on TV that was a given. They ignored him. He asked if he could have a lawyer. They ignored that too. They ignored him completely except for the questions. Over and over and over again, every half hour. They interrupted his meals to ask them. They woke him up to ask them.

By the end of two days he was dizzy. By the end of the third he was so tired he could barely stand. By the end of the fourth he was delirious. He never saw daylight, and the harsh white light in his cell and the interrogation chamber was always the same. He had no idea whether it was day or night.

Sometime during day five he collapsed. He'd been escorted to the chamber, led to his usual place before the table, then somebody took hold of a corner of the room and turned it upside down.

He came round lying on the bunk in his cell. A woman was sitting beside him, a man was leaning against the wall.

'Ah, you're awake,' said the woman. Lander blinked. His eyes felt as if they were full of sand.

'Who are you?' he said.

His question was ignored.

'We're not going to stop this,' said the woman. 'We can't. We will go on asking these questions until you answer them truthfully.'

Lander felt as if his head was made of kapok. 'Why?' he said. 'What do you want from me?'

'We've told you. We need to know who you are, where you are from, and what you were doing.'

Lander couldn't understand. The whole situation was insane. Who did they think he was? Why was it so vital to them to know? With the Infection raging all around, didn't they have better things to do?

'I'm nobody important,' he said. 'I'm just a boy from a farm. Why won't you leave me alone? I wasn't doing any harm.'

The woman made a clicking noise with her tongue. 'Oh yes you were doing harm,' she said. 'You were doing a great deal of harm in Snaith.'

Snaith. The empty town. 'What's so special about Snaith?'

'We were hoping you might tell us that.'

Lander was lost. He felt bereft and alone. 'But I don't know,' he said, helplessly. 'It was just a place I came to. I'd never even heard of it till I saw the name on a signpost.'

'So why won't you answer our questions? They're very simple, and we shall go on asking them until you do.'

There was something in Lander that hated being told what to do. That had been one of his problems at school. It was the same characteristic that made him good at sport: he refused to give in.

'What if I don't?' he said.

'Then you will die, but first you will lose your mind.'

Lander's blood ran cold but he said nothing.

'You will die if we have to keep this up,' the woman continued. 'You haven't thought of that, have you? Human beings cannot manage for very long without sleep. If we keep you awake like this, in the end your brain will shut down, your bodily functions will cease, your blood pressure will fall to critical levels, you will relapse into a series of comas of increasing severity, and eventually you will die. It may take some time, but it will happen. That is unless you co-operate.'

Lander was scared. He had no doubt that the woman was serious.

'And what if I do co-operate?' he said.

'Then your life will continue.'

The man by the wall spoke for the first time. 'It's a no brainer, literally,' he said, and laughed at his joke.

They both left. Lander forced himself to focus on what the woman had said. He couldn't remember ever having been so tired. He felt as though his brain had already shut down. Everything was woolly. He felt sick, a trembling ache in the pit of his stomach. Would they really kill him? Why? What had he done to deserve that?

Twenty minutes later he was roused and a single guard took him to the interrogation room. There had been two guards to start with. Lander was aware enough to realise that he was now in such a weakened state that he was no longer considered a threat. He was led to stand before the usual table and the guard withdrew to the door.

'What is your name?' said one of the interrogators.

'Alexander Shaw,' said Lander.

Two members of the panel looked at each other. 'Do you have any other names?' said the one who had spoken before.

'James,' said Lander.

'James Alexander Shaw? Or is it Alexander James?'

Lander felt he was in a madhouse. They were talking nonsense. His head was reeling. He was going to faint again. 'Yes,' he said.

'Which? Which is it?'

'Alexander James,' he managed to say.

'Very good. That's a start. Next question: where are you from?'

'Walbrough. It's in West Yorkshire.'

'Where in Walbrough?'

'I live on a farm. Paradise Farm.'

The interrogator nodded. 'And where were you going?'

'The coast,' Lander said. His mouth was so dry he could barely get the words out.

'Why?'

'I'm trying to get across the channel.'

'Why?'

Lander shook his head. He couldn't get into all *thetruth* stuff. His brain was too befuddled to explain it. He just stood there before his torturers, trying to remain conscious, trying to stay on his feet.

'Never mind,' said the interrogator. 'Tell us how you knew about Snaith.'

'I didn't know about it. I'd never heard of it. I just saw it on a signpost.'

'So why did you go there?'

'I needed food, and somewhere to rest.'

The interrogator muttered something to the note taker but Lander didn't catch it.

'How did you get there from Walbrough?' said the interrogator.

This was unfair. They'd told him that if he answered their questions they'd stop. He had, and now they were asking more.

'I had a motorbike. It was stolen, so then I got a lift. Then I walked.'

'Who gave you a lift?'

'I don't know.'

The interrogator looked sceptical. There was a long pause.

'It was a tractor,' said Lander. 'The guy didn't tell me his name.'

'Why don't you have your ID card?' This was the third member of the panel, who hadn't spoken before. The question was fired at him, sharper than any of the others.

'It was stolen. When my bike got nicked.'

There was another pause, even longer than the first one. Lander was on the point of collapse.

'Take him away,' said the interrogator. The guard opened the door and Lander stumbled after him.

His captors kept to their bargain, but only in part. He was allowed to sleep. He slept for a long time, and that was good. When he awoke he was given a bowl of meaty broth and some bread. That, too, was good. Then he was taken out into a small, enclosed courtyard. There was daylight. There was grass, trees, birds singing. Lander sat on a bench and savoured the pale sunshine washing over his face and limbs. He felt better, although he still had a headache. They'd said that if he co-operated he would be able to carry on with his life. What did that mean? Would he be freed? Would he be able to continue his journey?

He soon learnt that a sleep, a meal and a walk in the garden was as far as it went.

For the rest of the day he was left alone. The following morning he woke up, used the lavatory in the corner of his room and crawled back into his bunk, looking forward to another lie in. He was just dropping off again, when without warning his door opened and a different guard came in. He was brisk and abrupt. He dropped some clothes on to the bench, and a second guard placed beside them a plate of what looked like scrambled egg.

'Eat that and get dressed,' said the guard. 'You've got twenty minutes.'

Lander was ready sooner than that. He was in a buoyant mood. They were going to let him go. He would be able to carry on towards the coast. Or go back home. That was tempting, but the original reasons why he'd left hadn't changed.

In fact, neither of these options was available. What did happen was that he was taken out to a car and made to get in the back. Alongside him was yet another guard, a very burly looking one with a ring of tattoos around his neck. Lander asked him where they were going but his question was ignored. It was only then that he realised where he was. There was the Minster, there were the walls, there was Clifford's Tower. He was in York.

The car drew up outside a yellow brick building and Lander was ushered inside. He was led down a long corridor and through a heavy door at the end. He was astonished to find himself in what he could see straight away was a courtroom. There was the bench, on a platform with a large chair like a throne in the middle and smaller chairs on each side. There was the witness stand, just like he'd seen on TV. There were half a dozen other people at the front of the room. They were in suits and gowns, and they had their arms covered in plastic sleeves and their hands in surgical gloves. The combination looked ridiculous. They were sitting with wide spaces between them. All of them turned to look at him as he came in, and their eyes followed him to the dock.

The dock? What was going on?

He had only just sat down when the door behind the bench opened, a woman came in and everyone stood up. She, too, was wearing a black gown over a business suit, and she had the bio gloves that seemed to be a part of the uniform in there. She sat in the large, middle chair. Everyone else sat down too, apart from Lander, who had never got up in the first place.

The woman spoke.

'This court is convened and will operate under the abbreviated procedures set out in Section 4 of the Emergency Powers Act. We have one case before us this morning. Would the defendant please stand.'

Nobody moved. Then the guard who had settled himself in the dock next to Lander jabbed him with his elbow and Lander realised that the woman was talking to him. Defendant? What was that about? Was he on trial? What was he supposed to have done? He wasn't a criminal.

A man at the front of the court stood and faced him, a sheaf of papers in his hand.

'Alexander James Shaw, you are accused on three counts under the Emergency Powers Act. One, that you committed the crime of vagrancy by wilfully and without permission leaving your place of residence, your place of residence being defined as an area within one square kilometre of your home. How do you plead? Guilty or not guilty?'

Lander didn't respond. What was this guy talking about?

'Do you plead guilty or not guilty?' said the man, rather sharply.

Still Lander didn't reply. This was unbelievable. Guilty? Of what?

The woman, he assumed she must be a Magistrate, spoke. 'You must answer the question put to you by the Clerk of the Court. Did you or did you not leave the town of Walbrough without permission?'

He supposed he had. He'd heard you weren't meant to travel, but that was about going to work or school or things like gigs. Surely it didn't apply to what he was doing. Anyway, how did you get permission? Who did you ask?

'Well,' said the Magistrate, 'did you do that?'

'Yes, I suppose so.'

'You suppose so, ma'am.'

'I suppose so, ma'am.'

'Enter a plea of guilty,' the Magistrate said.

The Clerk spoke again. 'On count two, that you were in public areas without a valid Identity Card. Do you plead guilty or not guilty?'

'I don't know. I mean I'm not sure,' said Lander. What did they want him to say? He didn't have his ID when they'd picked him up because it had been stolen, but he'd had it when he left home.

The Magistrate sighed. 'Mr Shaw, you must try to understand what is being said to you and to reply. Otherwise this business is going to take a very long time and the Court will lose patience with you. When you were apprehended by the authorities did you or did you not have an Identity Card?'

'No,' said Lander, 'I didn't. But I did have it when I started out. It was nicked, along with my other stuff.' Why weren't they trying to find who'd robbed him, rather than blaming him for something he couldn't help?

'He pleads guilty,' said the Magistrate.

The Clerk smirked. 'On count three, you are accused of entering and being at large in a classified area. How do you plead? Guilty or not guilty?'

They must mean Snaith, thought Lander. That was where they'd picked him up. What was it about that place?

'Do you mean Snaith?' said Lander.

'Of course,' said the Clerk. 'Were you there or were you not?'

'Yes, you know I was. Shouldn't I have been there? How was I supposed to know that? There wasn't anything to say it was off limits.' Lander was beginning to feel angry. This was ridiculous. It was like Alice in Wonderland.

'Take that as a further plea of guilty,' the Magistrate said to the Clerk.

'Very good, ma'am.'

The Clerk sat down and Lander started to do the same, but the guard poked him so he remained standing.

'You have pleaded guilty on three counts,' said the Magistrate. 'All of them are serious offences. Any one of them would merit a custodial sentence. However, you are a young man, and I shall take your age and inexperience into account. On count one, the count of vagrancy, you are sentenced to eighteen month's detention. On the count of not being in possession of valid ID you are sentenced to six month's detention. On the count of entering a classified area, you are sentenced to five year's detention. All three sentences are to run concurrently. Take him down.'

The Magistrate rose and so did everyone else. Lander exploded. Five years in prison for doing nothing? This was unjust. It was beyond belief, ridiculous, a farce.

'What the fuck?' he shouted at the back of the Magistrate as she turned to go through the door. 'I haven't done anything. I didn't do anybody any harm. I was just trying to get away. You're all bloody mad!'

By the end of the speech he was screaming. The guard grabbed him from behind and got him in an arm lock, forcing his head forward and banging it on the rail. The Magistrate turned to him.

'Be very careful, Mr Shaw,' she said. 'In the circumstances, I have been very lenient with you. One more word and I'll hold you in contempt of court. That will mean an even longer sentence.'

She went through the door and it slammed behind her.

EIGHT
SPRUNG

IT ALL HAPPENED very quickly. Lander was driven to what he assumed must be a prison, although it didn't look like the pictures of prisons he'd seen on the TV. Those had tiers of cells on separate floors, but this one was small, just a single subterranean corridor, and he seemed to be the only inmate. His cell was barely two metres square. He'd been expecting to share because he'd seen that on the TV too, but he was the only occupant. It had a bed bolted to the floor, a table, also bolted down, and a plastic chair. In one corner there was a stainless-steel lavatory with no seat or lid. On the floor beside it was a roll of very coarse toilet paper. There was nothing else, but despite the sparse furnishings there was hardly room to move.

He'd only had time to test the bed and conclude that it was probably the most uncomfortable one he'd ever encountered, when the cell door opened and two people came in. Both were wearing biohazard suits and masks.

'We're going to run some tests,' one of them, a woman, said. 'We need to find out if you're infectious.'

Lander sighed. 'I'm not,' he said. 'I've already been tested. I don't have the Infection and I'm not a carrier.'

Her companion, a man, leant forward until his face was only a few inches from Lander's.

'Shut your fucking gob, arse wipe,' he said.

They put a needle in his arm and took some blood, they swabbed his mouth, they poked a thermometer into his ear, they felt his pulse. Then they went.

The rest of the day he was left alone. There was nothing to do, no TV, not even anything to read. For some of the time Lander slept. Then he did some stretches, some squats and some press-ups, all he could manage in the tiny space. For the rest, he lay on the bunk and stared at the ceiling. Five years of this? Did they really mean to keep him in this room for five years? He would go crazy. Nobody knew he was there, and that frightened him even more. They could do what they liked to him and no one would have any idea.

Half way through the day a guard brought in a plate of fish and chips. Lander asked for ketchup but the guard gave a humourless laugh. The meal wasn't bad. At least he was being fed.

The next morning the man and woman came back, this time with a third person. As before they were in full biohazard gear, complete with face masks, and one of them was wheeling a metal trolley with various items of equipment on it. He was told to lie down and the trolley was pushed close. He had a moment's panic as the word 'torture' flashed through his mind, but it wasn't like that.

They fitted sensors to his chest and connected them to one of the machines. They shaved the hair from his temples, fixed more sensors there and connected them too. One of the trio studied a screen on the trolley, and a printer beside it whirred. They took his temperature again. They took more swabs from his mouth and several more blood samples. Finally they uncoupled him from the machines and gave him a flask.

'Fill this,' the woman said.

Lander looked at it with puzzlement. Fill it with what?

'Pee in it, dimbo,' said one of the men. 'Over there, in the corner.'

'Don't worry, we won't look,' said the woman.

The three turned around and Lander went over to the lavatory in the corner. He found peeing to order difficult, but he managed a splash in the bottom of the flask. Sheepishly he handed it over and the three left.

The rest of the day he was again on his own, and he lay on his bunk, wondering what all this was about. Why all the medical stuff? They must know he was immune from the Infection, so what were they looking for?

He soon discovered that by far the worst thing about being in prison was the boredom. Three times a day two guards came in with his meals and to check on him. One of the guards would be carrying a plastic tray of food, and the other would be holding what looked to Lander like a cattle prod. The tray would be placed on the table, where it would remain until the next one was brought in and that in turn taken away. The fare wasn't bad. Cereal and buttered toast in the mornings; cold meat with salad for lunch; chicken or fish, with chips or mashed potatoes and greens for supper. The cutlery he had to use was plastic. At the start the guards would both be in full biohazard gear, but after a few days they swapped this for white coats and sterile gloves, so he concluded that all the tests they'd done confirmed what he'd told them: he was clean.

For two hours each day he was allowed out of his cell to exercise in an enclosed yard. He found an old tennis ball in the corner and spent most of the time hurling it against a wall and catching the rebound. Then he'd do some sit-ups, star jumps and burpees. Back in his cell he'd lie on his bunk, wondering how things were back on the farm. He tried to talk to the guards but they must have been under orders not to have anything to do with him. He asked how many other people were in the prison. No response. He asked if he could have a TV. Cold shoulder. He thought he had the right to make a phone call and asked the guard he judged to be the friendlier of the two if he could. He was told that it was out of the question. The other one added that the Infection was getting worse, and all telephone lines and cell phone circuits were reserved for the emergency services. He was lucky to be in here, they told him.

He didn't feel lucky. He thought he would go mad. All the days were running into each other. How long had he been there? He understood now why prisoners made marks on their walls to record the days. He simply had to keep some sort of record of the passing days. At the next meal he kept back the plastic fork and hid it under his pillow. The guards didn't seem to notice, and after they'd gone he used it to scratch the wall low down by his bed. He didn't know how many marks to make but he put seven. That was a starter. Seven days. One week. How could he manage five years of this? Why had he left the farm? Why had he abandoned his family? What good was he doing here?

He'd scored another seven tally marks on the wall when one morning his cell door opened – nobody ever knocked – and an elderly woman came in. She was pulling a battered wooden trolley behind her.

'I'm Marjorie,' she said. 'You are?'

'Lander,' he answered. There was no way you could not answer this lady.

'What?'

'Alexander.'

'Right. I shall call you Alex. I am the prison librarian. I shall come to your cell at this time each week for you to choose some books from my trolley. You may select up to three.'

Three books, thought Lander. What would he do with three books? That was more than he'd read in the last three years! Kerryl was the reader, not him. But at least it would be something to do.

Marjorie mistook the reason for his hesitation. 'Don't worry,' she said. 'All the books are sterilised between uses. You won't catch the Infection from them.'

Lander looked at the selection. He hoped there might be something on computing there. Or a copy of Wisden. Or a lads' mag or two. But they were all rather battered looking hardbacks, and there was nothing that seemed less than a hundred years old.

'Spoilt for choice, are we?' said Marjorie. 'Well take your time. I'm in no hurry.' She walked over to the lavatory, looked in it, sniffed and pressed the flusher.

There was a book called *Middlemarch*. He could remember Kerryl talking about reading that, but bloody hell, it was the size of a brick! There was *Moby Dick*. He remembered Kerryl mentioning that one too, and Granddad saying that moby dick wasn't something you read but something you caught if you weren't careful. Lander had laughed, but Gran hadn't thought it funny and she'd said he ought to wash his mouth out.

'I'm not really one for reading,' said Lander. 'I'd rather see a movie.' He felt he should apologise for this rejection. 'I'm sorry.'

'No need to be,' said Marjorie. 'It's your loss. No time like the present to start a good habit, though.' She took the copy of *Middlemarch* from his hands and gave him another book in its stead. Lander read the spine: *A Tale of Two Cities*. 'Try that,' she said. 'You don't have to finish it, and if you don't like it you can change it for something else when I come back next week.'

She left, and Lander sat on the edge of his bunk holding the book. This one was enormous too. He flicked to the back. Almost 500 pages. Published in 1859. What was it about people in those days? Where did they get all the time for this stuff? Didn't they have anything else to do? He opened the book, read the first sentence... and carried on. The language was old-fashioned and some of the sentences were very long, but somehow it drew you in. When the lights of his cell went out at 10 he was still reading.

Lander was not going to turn into an avid reader overnight, but he did read some more of the book the next day, and again he became absorbed. The ornate and convoluted language grew easier to follow, and although he didn't fully understand some of the vocabulary he got enough of it to be able to keep moving forward with the story and to get involved with the characters. How about that Dr Manette? Put in prison not for five years, but for eighteen!

How could he stand it? Lander felt he had another point of contact with this character: his name was Alexandre. He had a fit daughter too, and that was a definite plus.

He found that with care he could skip pages without losing track of the story. It did need care because you could miss something crucial, but with a bit of thought he managed to get into the rhythm of the book and spot when Dickens was going to say something important and when he was coasting. If Kerryl had learnt to do this – and he bet she had – why hadn't she let him in on the secret? He felt resentful. There she'd been, setting herself up as Princess Bookworm and she'd probably only read half of all the stuff she claimed she had. Was that what Advanced English was all about, picking up the gist of a book and then talking as if you'd read every word of it?

He looked at how much he'd got through. Close to half an inch. He set himself the target of finishing the book before Marjorie came next. That would surprise her. He liked Marjorie, she seemed a decent old bird. He wondered why she didn't wear a biohazard suit, like the guards. Too tough, he thought. The virus would never get through that hide.

In fact he never got the chance to finish *A Tale of Two Cities*, at least not then. Neither did he see Marjorie again. All at once his stay in prison was over.

He was finishing his breakfast – porridge, so it must have been Sunday – when there was noise in the corridor and his usual pair of guards came in, this time wearing their full anti-germ apparel. They were followed by two soldiers, also in protective clothing. Oh my god, he thought, something's gone wrong.

'Time to go,' said one of his guards. Then, when Lander didn't move, 'On your feet, pretty boy. Chop chop.'

'What's going on?' said Lander.

'You're getting out of here, that's what,' said the other guard.

'Right enough,' said the first one, when Lander still didn't move. 'You're to accompany these fine gentlemen to Oxford.'

'Why?'

'They must have decided to do something about your education,' said the second guard, and they all laughed.

'You're being sprung,' said the first one. 'You're out of here.'

'Friends in high places,' said the guard. 'You're clearly too important for the likes of us.'

'Time to pack up.'

Lander had nothing to pack. Everything had been taken from him. He had no clothes other than the prison fatigues and the underwear he was wearing. The toothbrushes and grooming gear they allowed him were in a locker in the washroom, and anyway they were disposable. He picked up *A Tale of Two Cities*.

'Leave that,' said the guard, sharply.

'Prison Service property,' said the other. 'Besides, you don't want Queen Marjorie to come after you, do you?'

Lander was fairly sure that Marjorie wouldn't object if he took the book with him, but he put it on his bunk, took a final look at his cell and followed the two soldiers along the corridor.

NINE
GWEN AND ADAM

'CALL ME GWEN.'

That was not what Lander had expected. The plaque on the door said *Dr Gwendolyn Matthews, Director of Special Programmes*, and he thought as he knocked that the person behind it would be old, serious, and formal. Instead he found a striking looking black woman who was probably not that much older than he was, and who greeted him with a massive smile. She motioned to the chair in front of her desk.

'Please sit,' she said.

'Call me Gwen' was wearing the white coat which seemed to be a uniform for everybody in the Oxford hospital. She also had a sterile face mask which was tied loosely around her neck, and she had the latex gloves they all wore. Lander hadn't been given any of this kit and he was feeling left out, as if everybody else merited protection but not him.

'I expect you're wondering why you've been brought here.' Gwen had such a broad, open smile that it would have been hard not to smile back, and Lander did.

'Well yes, you could say that,' he said.

'I just did,' said Gwen. Lander immediately liked her. She had his own sense of humour. 'I suppose you can guess that it's about the Infection. What isn't? So let's start from the beginning. How much do you know about the virus?'

'Enough,' said Lander. 'I watched my mother die from it.'

'Yes, of course you did. I'm sorry, that was insensitive of me. The tragic thing is that everybody one meets has lost someone, often their whole family. It's easy to become blasé about what are terrible personal losses.'

'That's all right,' said Lander.

His remark about his mother had come out differently from the way he'd meant it. He hadn't been digging for sympathy. What he'd been trying to convey was that after seeing somebody consumed by the virus he didn't think there was much more to learn about it.

'All I know really is that sooner or later just about everybody gets it, and hardly anybody gets over it,' he said.

Gwen nodded. 'Let me give you some background. The Infection caught everybody by surprise. We knew about Ebola of course. We, that is medical and health professionals, have been fighting that for years, but although this one has similarities it's in a different league.'

'But it came from Africa, didn't it? Like Ebola.'

'Yes, it did, but only incidentally. We think, and this is only theory mind, that this virus was actually created in a laboratory.'

'You mean somebody made it?'

'We believe so. We think it was developed as a weapon of biological warfare. Something so devastating that it would be comparable with the H bomb. The ultimate deterrent.'

Lander couldn't believe it. 'Who would do that?'

'It's hard to say. There are only a few countries with the capability to do it. It wasn't us, or so our government says, and there are only three or four others it could have been.'

'So what is it?'

'This virus, its official label is I/452, we think is derived from Ebola, but its effects are even worse and it's harder to stop. The reason why so many people catch colds and influenza, and why those who have 'flu jabs need them renewed each year, is because those viruses change all the time. They evolve, and that gives the body's immune system little opportunity to develop the antibodies to combat them. As fast as the immune system learns how to counteract one mutation, another appears. We think that whoever designed I/452 took a virus of this type – it may even have been a cold or 'flu virus – and somehow spliced it with a particularly powerful strain of Ebola. As an added extra they managed to make this virus mutate much more quickly than any of the influenza or cold viruses we've met so far.'

Lander was flabbergasted. The idea that human beings could make something like this was incomprehensible. 'But why Africa?' he said. 'Surely it wasn't an African country that did this.'

'Heavens no. We think the originators are certainly from the northern, 'civilised' hemisphere. It appeared in Africa because whoever designed it wanted to test it. They couldn't do that in their own back yard. An outbreak of something that looked like Ebola in Moscow or Beijing or New York would arouse too much attention. Where better to test something that looked like Ebola than in a place where Ebola is endemic? And where lives are cheaper.'

Lander caught the bitterness in Gwen's last remark. Maybe her own origins were in one of those places. 'You mean they released it amongst real people on purpose? Just to see if it worked? That's unbelievable.'

'To the likes of you and me, yes,' said Gwen. 'To any decent person it's completely unbelievable. But to the twisted minds that go in for this sort of thing there's a perverse logic to it. Where it all came unstuck was that the "cure" they thought they had for it didn't work. They probably meant to try it in a single village, and when they'd observed it and were satisfied they'd learnt all they could, to snuff it out. However, the thing got out of the test area and developed a momentum all of its own. It slipped from the grasp of its controllers...'

'...and look what happened!'

'Yes, look what happened.'

Lander sat for a moment in silence, digesting the awful account Gwen had given him. Would people really do something like that deliberately? Well, they'd dropped the Atom Bomb on a living city, hadn't they? Twice. And fired gas into World War I trenches. And blanket bombed Dresden. And executed six million Jewish civilians. And blown up children, women and men going about their ordinary lives in arenas, mosques and marketplaces. So yes, some people really would do it deliberately. But what did it have to do with him?

'Why tell me all this?' said Lander. 'There's nothing I can do about it.'

'The reason I've told you is the same reason we've had you released from prison and brought you here. And that's because we think there is something you can do about it. Or, rather, something you can help us to do about it. I'd like you to meet my colleague.' She leant across the desk and pressed an intercom button. 'Andrea, would you ask Adam to come in.'

A minute passed while Lander waited. He felt awkward. It was not only the awful account Gwen had given. It was also that she was a very attractive woman, and she seemed to be staring at him. He didn't want to simply stare back, so he looked at the floor, the wall, the picture behind her desk, her stapler. At last the door opened and a young man came in. He was dressed in a white shirt and black chinos. His face was tanned and his head covered in blond curls. Lander noticed he wasn't wearing either surgical gloves or a face mask.

'This is Przemysław Adamski,' said Gwen. 'We call him Adam for short. He's one of our research team.'

Adam held out his ungloved hand and Lander took it. That was unusual. Shaking hands had vanished as a means of greeting since the virus arrived. He pulled up a chair beside Lander and sat down.

'I've been telling Alexander here what we know of the origins and nature of the virus,' said Gwen.

Adam grinned. 'Alexander, eh? Using your Sunday best name now, are you? I think I'll call you Lander.'

Lander nearly fell off his chair. 'How do you know my name?'

'I know quite a lot about you,' said Adam. There was a hint of middle Europe in his accent. Polish? Czech? 'Don't look worried,' he continued. 'You've not been spied on or anything like that, but I had to find out about you to be sure you were who we thought you were, and that you were in a position to help us.'

'And I am?'

'Yes, I – we – think you are.'

Lander wasn't sure he wanted to co-operate with people who'd arrested him, tried him and jailed him, and now apparently investigated him, but he'd give them a hearing.

'How?' he said.

Adam looked at Gwen, who nodded.

'My team has been studying responses to the virus,' he said. 'As I expect you've realised, the vast majority of people have no defence against it. This is particularly true of the very young and the very old, who contract it most easily. Mature adults succumb more slowly, but well over ninety-five percent of those who are exposed to the virus develop the Infection and die. That means that most of the UK population is now dead, or soon will be. The same is true in Europe, the USA and, as far as we know, the Russian Federation, Africa, the Indian sub-continent, and south and east Asia. Actually, the whole world, although since communications have become dodgy it's hard to know exactly what's happening where. The virus doesn't discriminate and it has no mercy. It cuts across all ages and all ethnic groups. It penetrates all income groups, even getting into the bolt holes of billionaires, although the better off do have more places where they can hide.'

'You said over ninety-five percent,' said Lander. 'That's not everybody, then. What happens to the rest?'

'The rest fall into two groups. Some of them initially show only a mild reaction to the virus – headaches, joint pains, sore throat and sniffles, bleeding gums. Then they get better, or they appear to.'

'But they don't,' said Lander. 'The virus attacks their brains.'

Adam looked surprised. 'You know this?'

'Yes. Before I left home I was in contact with an online group. They told me all about it.'

Adam looked at Gwen. 'Did they? What else did they tell you?'

'Well, people who posted said that the effect was like a split personality, kind of two people in one. The two don't know about each other, and they behave separately. One of them can do something without the other being aware of it. They said that usually it's harmless, but it can be violent. Sometimes one of the personalities will attack other people, sometimes it will think it's attacking somebody else but it will really be turning on itself.'

Adam shook his head. '*Dr Jeckyll and Mr Hyde.*'

'What?'

'It's a book,' said Gwen. 'By Robert Louis Stevenson. Dr Jeckyll, a good man, invents a serum that turns him into Edward Hyde, an evil murderer, and back again, so he can live two lives.'

'Oh,' said Lander. He had heard of it. He wondered if Kerryl had read it.

'I wish I'd known about this online forum of yours,' said Adam. 'Their information might have saved me a lot of work.'

Lander was going to point out that he'd been on his way to join the group when he'd been arrested, but he thought better of it.

'Anyway,' said Adam, 'people who respond in this way are, as far as we know, all males. We haven't yet come across any women showing a similar reaction, although of course there may be some that we just haven't found.'

'What's the other group?' said Lander.

'That group consists of people like Gwen and me. Young adults, under thirty, fit and healthy. We have a certain immunity in that our bodies seem able to dodge some of the strains of the virus. However, only some. We can go on with our lives but it's Russian roulette. Sooner or later the chamber will be loaded, we'll encounter a mutation that we're unable to cope with and then we'll join the rest. Unless a means of stopping it can be found first.'

'Which group do you think I belong to?' said Lander.

'Neither,' said Adam. 'You and Kerryl are a group on your own.'

For the second time Lander was thunderstruck. What did he mean a group on their own? And how did he know about Kerryl?

'What are you talking about? Have you been spying on my sister too?'

'Calm down,' said Adam. He took out a mobile phone and swiped through some pictures until he found one and handed it to Lander.

Lander was astonished. 'That's our house,' he said. 'Where did you get this?'

'I took it.'

'When?'

'A couple of days ago. Scroll on to the next one.'

He did. It was the house again, but from a different angle. There was somebody crossing the yard.

'That's Kerryl,' he said.

'Yes. Keep swiping.'

There were eight more pictures, and Kerryl was in several of them. They must have been done on different days because she wasn't wearing the same clothes in all of them. In one of the best ones she was on her horse, Joey. It was taken from quite close, she had no riding hat, her hair was loose. She looked happy. Lander felt an actual physical tug. They had often had rows lately, but despite that he missed her. Oh how he missed her.

'Why did you take these? Do you know Kerryl? Are you some sort of Peeping Tom pervert or something?'

Adam smiled. 'Hardly. I'll tell you what I've been doing and why, but first I want you to know that your sister is safe and well. Sadly, I don't have the same news about your grandparents. I'm sorry to have to tell you that they are both gone.'

It was painful to hear, but Lander was not surprised. He'd expected that Gran and Granddad would catch the Infection at the same time as their Mam had. They hadn't, and when he'd left he'd been hoping that they'd managed to escape, and that if no one else came to the farm spreading the virus they'd be able to hang on. But in his heart of hearts he'd known that it was unlikely he'd see them again.

'I'm sorry,' said Gwen.

Lander sniffed. He wasn't one for tears, but the mention of his grandparents and their fate, together with the pictures of Kerryl apparently normal and healthy, had brought on an almost intolerable homesickness.

He nodded to Gwen. 'Thanks.' Then to Adam, 'So if you're not a Peeping Tom, why have you been watching her and taking pictures of her?'

'For a very good reason,' said Adam. 'When you were first spotted the army thought you were just some vagrant seeing what he could steal. You didn't appear dangerous so they let you be. Then you went into a restricted area...'

'Snaith.'

'Yes, Snaith. They thought then that you must be up to no good, so they arrested you and put you in jail. From our point of view, and I think yours and Kerryl's too, that was an excellent thing. The authorities need to know whether a prisoner is infectious, so everybody who's committed to prison is screened for the virus. They did some tests on you, the basic stuff – DNA swabs, blood samples, pulse, temperature and urine checks.'

'I remember them,' said Lander. 'Then the next day they came back and did some more.'

'Yes. That was because when they analysed your samples they found that there was something odd about them, and so they did another batch, more extensive and elaborate this time. They confirmed what they at first thought. That was when they called us in, and we had you brought here.'

Lander began to tremble. Confirmed what? What had he got? This was going to be something terrible. 'What's wrong with me?' he whispered.

'Oh, nothing's wrong with you,' said Gwen. 'In fact everything is right with you. You see, you're immune.'

'I'm what?'

'Immune. The most thorough tests were done and it's clear. There is no trace of the virus being active anywhere in your system, although there are signs that you've been in contact with it.'

Lander pondered this. He'd been exposed to the virus, he knew he had. His mother and grandparents had caught it, so it must have been around in the house.

'Are you sure?'

'Yes. Completely and absolutely sure.'

'You see,' said Gwen, 'it seems that your system is able to produce antibodies unusually quickly. Unlike the rest of us, you can respond to each new strain of the virus almost immediately.'

'What does that mean?'

'For one thing,' said Adam, 'it means you won't die of the Infection. Not this one, anyway. You can go anywhere, do anything in safety.'

'How did you find out about Kerryl?'

'We ran your DNA through our database. You may have lost your ID, but you can't lose that. It told us about you, and your sister.'

'Is Kerryl the same as me?'

'Yes. She's your twin.'

'But we're not identical, our Mam said so.'

'What she probably meant is that strictly speaking you're not. You have a Y chromosome and Kerryl doesn't. But your DNA is so close that there's barely any difference.'

Lander's mind was racing. What was the significance of all this? What did it mean for him and his sister? He was sure he'd been infected and he knew he'd started to show the split personality symptoms. He'd checked with *thetruth* and the behaviour he'd seen discussed there fitted with what he'd been experiencing. He'd had hallucinations. Bad dreams. Periods when he was sure he'd done things without realising it.

'But I've had the split personality thing, I know I have. They call it "shadow walking", when you behave like a zombie.'

Adam looked surprised. It was a term that was new to him.

'Interesting. However, you were observed while you were in prison, and your case looks to be mild. Several nights you got up in your sleep, but all you did was stand for a few minutes before getting back into bed. You seem able to control your condition, and while you can it won't result in any danger to you or anyone else.'

Lander wasn't aware of any such control. As far as he knew the business was random. 'How do I manage that? How do I control it?'

'At present it seems to be involuntary, a sort of safety device that you've developed unconsciously. We wonder if you might be able to learn to control it voluntarily.'

'You mean switch it on and off, like taking Dr Whatsit's potion?'

'Yes.'

'Are there any others like us?'

'We've not found any in this country yet, although these online people you talked about might know more. When it became clear that the Infection couldn't be stopped the government set up a number of isolated areas where people could go to be safe from exposure to the virus. They call them 'arks'. Four thousand people have been selected to fill them. The idea is that they'll stay there until the Infection dies out...'

'...or a cure is found,' Gwen interrupted.

'Of course. Then they'll come out and it will be their job to rebuild the country, and to repopulate it.'

Lander had heard rumours of the arks but had never been able to discover anything concrete about them.

'All the arkies, as we call them, are in Adam's and my age group,' said Gwen. 'Every one of them was tested and they were all found to be like us, semi immune but not completely so. Just FYI, Snaith had been set up as a reserve ark. The whole place had been isolated, sterilised, and prepared for extended occupation. That's why people were so upset when you wandered in there.'

Half an hour ago Lander had thought his future was plotted. He would find a way to carry on to Belarus, and once there he would wait with others for the time when his disordered personality would kill him, or when he would be removed because he'd become too dangerous to live with. Now everything had changed.

'If I'm immune,' he said, 'and Kerryl is too, I can go home now. We can live on the farm.'

Gwen and Adam glanced at each other.

'You could do that, in theory,' said Gwen. 'But don't you think it would be rather selfish?'

'How do you mean?'

'You and your sister are the only two people we've found who have this particular characteristic. That means there must be something in your genes that the rest of us don't have. If we can isolate what it is, we might be able find some way of replicating it and protecting people.'

'There's also the possibility,' Adam added, 'that we may be able to use what we can learn from you to engineer the DNA of the babies that the arkies will have, so that they produce children who are immune to the virus from birth.'

There was a long pause.

'So,' said Gwen, 'will you and Kerryl help us? What do you say?'

TEN

EXPERIMENT

THE IDEA THAT the virus had been released as some ghastly experiment was almost beyond belief, but even worse was the thought that struck Lander in the small hours.

He remembered that in the months leading up to the Infection a hot topic had been the pressures on the earth's resources placed by an increasing global population. In fact it had replaced climate change as the top environmental issue. There had been a conference of world leaders in Tokyo, which had concluded that if the human race continued to grow at its present rate, within less than fifty years the planet would be unable to sustain it. It wasn't just food. Resources of all sorts simply wouldn't go round. The outcome of the conference was that there was a strong possibility that human society would simply implode.

Of course, there were the usual sceptics – the *Daily Mail* ran a piece with the headline "Tokyo Joke-yo" ridiculing the whole thing – but on the whole people seemed to take the issue seriously. Lander remembered a General Studies session at school where the teacher had asked the class to come up with solutions to the problem of too many people. The boys made a range of suggestions, most of them fascistic: compulsory sterilisation, limiting life by requiring euthanasia after fifty years, aborting foetuses that showed signs of malformation or other problems. Finally somebody said, 'Why don't we just reintroduce The Black Death?' Everybody had laughed, but suppose that's what had happened. Suppose the Infection was not a test that had gone terribly wrong, but a deliberate stratagem to remove a huge number of people. Granddad had often said that the world was run by a secret bunch of anonymous, faceless zillionaires, and that politicians were simply their puppets. Lander had thought it was just another of his rants, but it made a sort of insane sense. It kept him awake most of the night.

In the harsh light of morning he returned to what Gwen and Adam were proposing, and when he saw them again he gave the only answer he could. Yes, he would do what they wanted. He would have preferred to consult Kerryl, but communication systems were down and there was no way of getting in touch with her. He wanted to bring her to Oxford, where he thought they'd want them both for the tests, but Adam and Gwen had other ideas. Gwen put it to him that the two of them being in different environments offered a unique opportunity to study their behaviour.

'Both of you are in sterile surroundings,' she said. 'Provided Kerryl stays at home she won't be exposed to the virus. Neither will you, as long as you remain in this hospital. What we can do is give a new strain of the virus to both of you...'

She held up her hand as Lander began to protest.

'...You know you're immune. We can introduce the virus to you both, and while your bodies are coping with it we can in Kerryl's case observe how that affects her ability to function in day-to-day practical situations, while in yours we can see what's happening inside your head.'

'Observe how?'

'Well, we have equipment that can look into your brain and nervous system and see exactly what's going on. As far as Kerryl's concerned, we'll watch her.'

'Who's "we"?'

'I'll do it,' said Adam. 'I'll monitor her from a distance and keep a record of what she does and how she is. Don't worry, she won't know I'm there.'

'And how will you infect us?'

'It's best if you're not aware of when or how you're in contact with the virus,' said Gwen. 'If we're to make a fair comparison between you and Kerryl we'll have to expose you both at the same time and in the same way. We need to think about how to do that, but be assured you'll know nothing about it.'

'If you co-operate with us in this,' said Adam, 'there's a good chance that we can learn enough about the virus to enable us to defeat it.'

'And thereby ensure the survival of the human race,' said Gwen.

'It really is as big as that,' Adam added.

Lander knew he had no choice. 'How long will this go on?' he asked. 'How long will you need for these tests?'

Adam said six months; Gwen said three; Lander settled on two.

'At the end of two months I want this all to be over,' he said. 'I want Kerryl and me to be together.'

'All right.'

'Also I want to be able to talk to her.'

'Not possible,' said Adam. 'For one thing, all the phone systems have collapsed – landlines, mobiles, the internet, the lot. More important for the programme, though, is that you don't communicate. The best thing would be for neither of you to know that the other exists. That can't happen in your case, but we need to keep Kerryl totally in the dark about you.'

'We don't want anything to happen that might affect the way she responds to the challenges of her situation,' said Gwen. 'And remember, it is only for two months.'

'Don't worry,' said Adam. 'I'll keep an eye on your sister. I'll have to stay in the background because it's vital she doesn't know she's being observed, but I'll make sure she comes to no harm. And each time I go to the farm I'll take photos and videos so you can see for yourself that she's all right.'

The programme began the next day. Lander was collected by a white coated technician and taken along the corridor to a consulting room where Gwen waited.

She started with an apology, of a sort. 'I'm afraid you're going to get bored with this, because we plan to carry out these procedures every time Adam goes to your home to study your sister. Then when he comes back we can compare his observations with what we've learnt from you.'

'When do we get the new viruses?'

'They'll be introduced to both of you at the same time.'

'How?'

'That's still under discussion but it will probably be by means of an aerosol spray, administered to you and Kerryl on the same day.'

'All right,' said Lander. 'What do I have to do and when do we start?'

'You don't actually have to do a lot. We'll need the usual samples – blood, urine, faeces. A technician will deal with collecting those, and we'll need them every time. We'll also need a semen sample.'

'What, really?'

'I'm afraid so. We have to check your sperm count. A technician will deal with that, too. A male one,' she added, enjoying Lander's embarrassment. 'Apart from those, all you have to do is lie back and relax. Right now we're going to do some neuroimaging.'

'What's that?'

'It's using magnetic resonances to build a map of your central nervous system, including your brain and the way it works. You've probably heard them referred to as MRI scans and CAT scans.'

'Will you be doing them?'

Gwen smiled. 'No, I'm not a radiographer. I'm going to love you and leave you.'

'And is Adam going to watch Kerryl?' He almost said 'spy on', because that was still how he thought of it.

'He's already gone,' said Gwen. 'He left at crack of dawn. Enjoy your day, and I'll drop by when the tests are over.'

It wasn't as easy as Gwen said. The first procedure was gruelling. Lander had to change into a hospital gown and was told to lie down on a gurney in front of a long tube. He knew what it was – a scanner – because he'd seen them on the TV, and he'd taken part in a fund-raising event at school as part of an appeal to buy a new one for the hospital in Halifax. What he hadn't bargained for was the loud noise the machine made, and the terrible feeling of being shut in as the gurney rolled into the tube. Claustrophobia had always been a thing with him, and he felt a surge of panic as he was drawn in. But the radiographer was a girl, Janice. She was nice looking, and Lander was anxious not to look a prick in front of her. However, it took him a huge effort of will to overcome the urge to press the help button she'd given him.

Janice had told him to stay completely still so he did, while his mind wandered over the life which, until very recently, he'd taken for granted. He couldn't communicate with Kerryl, that had been made clear, but he wondered if she had any idea of what was going on. Maybe she had a notion of what was happening to him. He was sure she'd know he was alive, just as he knew she was.

What would their future be now, after all this was over? There'd be no Yorkshire cricket team to play for, and he'd not found anything else that appealed to him as much. Earlier in the year Kerryl had been offered a place at Cambridge to study English. He didn't know much about it, but why would anybody want to spend three years reading? He'd looked up Cambridge on the internet and it seemed full of old buildings, not his cup of tea at all. Besides, in the Boat Race he'd always rooted for the other side, the dark blues, Oxford. Kerryl had been keen to go, but would there be any Cambridge anymore?

Not for the first time he wondered where his sister had got her brains. Not from their Mam, that was for sure. Celebrity TV and Hello magazine were her style. From their dad? They'd only been children when he'd had the accident that killed him and so they'd been too young to judge, but he seemed to know a great deal. Granddad read a lot – non-fiction and newspapers mostly. He knew about politics and events, and would launch into monologues on a range of subjects – the way farmers were treated, prices, taxes, the march of the wind turbines over his beloved moors, the management of Leeds United. 'Aye up, he's off on one,' their Gran would say when he started on a diatribe. Now he came to think of it, she was probably the sharpest of any of them. True, she watched rubbish television, but often she'd say something that seemed to be so right that he was left wishing he'd thought of it.

Suddenly the machine gave a rattle louder than anything so far, his bed vibrated and he was rolled out of the tube. He sighed with relief and took the ear protectors off.

Janice came into the room. 'My, you didn't like that, did you?' she said, looking him up and down. 'Your heart was going like a road drill.'

He realised he was wet through. He'd not been conscious of feeling hot but he'd been sweating profusely. His gown and the sheet covering the gurney were sodden.

'Jesus, it looks like I wet myself,' he said.

'And didn't you?'

'Course not.' Lander felt himself redden.

'Says you,' said Janice, with a wink. She pointed to the door. 'There's a shower in there. Help yourself.'

'Will I have to do this again?' he asked as he swung his legs off the gurney.

'Probably, though I don't expect they'll need a scan every time. Gwen will tell you. I don't have the full programme.'

'I'm supposed to give a semen sample. Will you be doing that too?' said Lander.

'In your dreams, lover boy,' said Janice. 'Now get yourself showered and dressed.'

For the rest of the day Lander drifted around his corridor or watched old recordings of soccer matches on the TV. The following morning he was taken to a small room with a single desk. He was told to sit down and a man, who didn't introduce himself, gave him a series of test papers to complete – maths, verbal reasoning, comprehension, general knowledge, logic puzzles. Each took half an hour. Lander thought it worse than being in school.

As soon as he'd finished them he was taken back to the neuroimaging department. For a few awful moments he thought they were going to put him in the MRI scanner again. However, this time it was a different machine. Only his head went into it, and so long as he could move his limbs he was happy. He looked out for Janice but she wasn't there. This scan was over very quickly. After lunch he was given another five test papers to complete on the same topics, and then his head was scanned again.

'How was that?' asked Gwen, meeting him as he left to return to his quarters.

'Terrible,' he said. 'If those were exams I think I failed.'

All the days while Adam was away were similar to this. The tests stopped when he was there and they spent a lot of time together, playing table tennis, cards, PlayStation games, or simply talking guys talk about nothing in particular. Adam introduced him to squash, which Lander liked and was good at. Adam stuck to his promise to keep him informed. He told him that Kerryl was fine, and described what he'd seen her doing – milking the cows, riding Joey, walking Buster, going up to the rocks on the moor. He showed photographs and short videos of her in the fields, working in the farmyard, or simply sitting on a wall looking at the moors.

Lander enjoyed the time he spent with Adam; however, he didn't like the feeling of being a guinea pig, the subject of an experiment, and he found the constant investigation and scrutiny irksome. He disliked the scans and hated the monotony of examinations and tests. In comparison, lessons at King's Heath Boys' were models of excitement.

Over the days the boredom anaesthetised his senses, and it was only slowly that he became aware that the reports from Adam were changing. His accounts of what Kerryl had been doing were rarer and less detailed. There were no videos, and the photographs he was shown were all at a distance and many of them were blurred. Except for one. It was a shot of her crossing the yard. Her hand was bandaged and that troubled him, but worse was her appearance. She was limping, and was noticeably thinner than when he'd last seen her.

'What's wrong with her?'

'You mean her hand,' said Adam. 'She caught it on a piece of machinery.'

'What machinery?'

'The elevator you use to lift hay bales.'

'What was she doing with that? She can't have been making hay.'

'It was an accident. It's all right. It's a clean cut and it's healing well.'

'But she looks to be walking with a stick.'

'She slipped and hurt her ankle. It's just a sprain. Again, it's not a problem.' Adam put his arm around Lander's shoulder. 'She's fine.'

Lander wasn't so sure. 'I need to go and see her,' he said.

Adam shook his head. 'You know you can't do that, and you know why.'

'I can do what you do. I can hide, look at her from a distance without her knowing I'm there.'

Adam frowned. 'I don't think that would work. Your sister's all right, honestly. Anyway, the two months will soon be up and then you can join her.'

Despite Adam's reassurances, Lander was still troubled. Kerryl had not looked at all herself in those pictures. She'd lost a lot of weight and her face was pale. He had a suspicion that Adam wasn't being open with him. What was going on?

He didn't sleep much that night. He lay awake for a long time turning things over in his head. Something was wrong; he could feel it. He had to find a way to see Kerryl and ensure she was safe. If she wasn't allowed to come to him and if Adam wouldn't let him go to her, he would take matters into his own hands. He would go back to Paradise Farm on his own. He would have a quick look, satisfy himself that everything was all right, and then come back.

On impulse he got out of bed and walked across to the door to his room. He tried the handle. It turned, but it wouldn't open. He tugged. No movement. It was locked. It hadn't been before.

He banged on the door with his fist, anger and frustration welling inside him. Why was he locked in? What right did they have to do that? They must have guessed what he was thinking of doing. Had he been talking in his sleep? Had he been dream walking? Adam had some questions to answer. He'd have it out with him in the morning.

ELEVEN
ESCAPE

ADAM WASN'T THERE in the morning, so the tests carried on. Two orderlies collected him from his room, walked him along the corridors to Radiography, and waited while he was scanned. Then they took him back to his room and locked him in. He thought about trying to make a run for it, but the men were big and he didn't think he'd have much chance. He demanded to know what was going on, why he was being treated like a prisoner, and he was told that it was necessary for the programme.

Alone in his room he fretted increasingly over what might be happening to Kerryl, and he thought more and more about escape. But how could he do that? He saw no one except the guards, the orderlies who brought his food and the medical staff who administered the tests. Janice seemed to have gone; the other medics weren't as friendly as she'd been and they avoided talking to him. It was like being back in jail.

Then, abruptly, the scans and the tests stopped. Lander expected that meant Adam was back, but he didn't appear. Instead two days passed when he was left completely alone. He waited but no one came, and he spent his time playing video games or trying to find something worth watching on the collection of moviesticks in the day room. He asked the woman who brought his lunch if he could go out for some air, and she said she didn't know. He said could she ask, and she said she didn't know that either. When the guard came on his evening rounds Lander told him he wanted to see Gwen. 'Don't we all?' was the reply.

On day three he got up early, showered, dressed, and lay on his bed waiting for his door to be unlocked. He had decided when it had clicked shut the night before that he needed to take some decisive action. He'd thought about a hunger strike, but that would take a long time to have any impact, and in the short term would anybody notice? The best course would be to make a complete nuisance of himself until he got an audience with Gwen or Adam; then he could demand to be told why everything had ground to a halt and what the fuck was going on. They'd done this topic at school about Gandhi and passive resistance. He would try that and see if it would get some results. He couldn't shake off the continuous, nagging worry that something had happened to Kerryl.

He waited and waited, but nobody showed up. His watch said it was nearly nine, well after the time he was usually collected for the scans or tests, or let out to try to entertain himself in the day room. Eventually he got to his feet and crossed to the door. He bent to take off a shoe so he could pound on it, reached for the handle to steady himself, and found that the door opened.

He was perplexed. He hadn't heard it being unlocked. Had it actually been locked at all? Maybe it had been like that all night. Perhaps that meant that Adam was back.

He was not in the day room, where they usually met. He wondered if he'd already been in and he'd missed him. A woman came in with a vacuum cleaner and plugged it in.

'Is Adam around?' Lander asked.

The woman shook her head.

'Where's Gwen?' he said.

'She's away.'

Lander looked out of the door and along the corridor. There was no one out there. Could he just leave? He didn't know the geography of the hospital. Most of it seemed to be empty and closed off, but he thought he could probably find his way out. There must be somebody in charge, somebody more important than Adam or Gwen who should be able to give him some answers. Maybe he could find out where they were and see them.

The woman finished her cleaning and went. Lander couldn't sit down or settle. Something was wrong. It was not only that Adam and Gwen seemed to have vanished.

He had a persistent feeling of dismay, a sensation as if a ball of lead had lodged in his gut. He struggled with it for most of the morning. Then he reached a conclusion. He had to go north now. He had to go back home.

But how? He had only the hospital scrubs, a smock and pants, that he was wearing. He had no money, no ID and no transport. And there was the minor snag of getting out of the hospital without being stopped. He looked from the window at the street below. There was no one out there and no traffic in sight. In fact the whole of Oxford seemed dead. Even if he managed to leave the hospital, what would he do?

He went on to the landing. At the end of the corridor were stairs down to a foyer. There were a couple of men in white coats standing by a window marked Reception. They were deep in conversation and took no notice of him as he walked towards the large glass doors that marked the entrance.

An ambulance drove into the car park, reversed up to the building, and two paramedics in biohazard gear got out. Lander hid behind a vending machine and watched them walk slowly, casually even, to the rear of the vehicle and open the door. There was a trolley in there with a covered patient on it. They manoeuvred it out and wheeled it towards the automatic doors, which slid open. They were in no hurry. This wasn't an emergency; it was a corpse.

They pushed the trolley across the foyer and into a lift, and the door closed. The two men who had been in conversation when Lander first arrived had now gone. One of them had left his white coat on the desk by the reception window. Lander hesitated. Could he just walk out? Was it as easy as that? He waited. There was silence. But not quite; the ambulance engine was still running.

Lander didn't think about it. He didn't consider where he'd go. He simply stepped from his hiding place, went to the desk, picked up the white coat and put it on. Underneath it was a stethoscope. Even better. He hooked that around his neck, walked out of the hospital door, climbed into the ambulance, pushed the gear lever into drive, and moved away.

'Not too fast,' he told himself, 'not too fast.' He didn't want to do anything that would attract attention. He was simply a medical vehicle on routine business.

How long did he have before the crew realised that their ambulance was missing? What would they do when they did? Had anyone seen him drive away? What should he do next?

He couldn't go all the way from Oxford to Yorkshire in an ambulance, that was ridiculous. Or was it? The fuel tank was almost full, and an ambulance looked official. Perversely it might arouse less curiosity than a car. He was starting to realise that there wasn't anything like the surveillance that there'd been before the Infection. It would be some time before they worked out who had taken the ambulance and guessed where it had gone. It was time that would be wasted if he stopped to look for some other means of transport. His best bet would be to get out of the city as quickly as he could, then decide how to go on from there.

The street was empty. He didn't know Oxford but he saw a sign for the M40 and he knew that would take him in the right direction. Use that to get clear, and then divert on to minor roads where there'd be less chance of being noticed.

He glanced up at the row of switches above the windscreen. One was labelled 'lights', another 'siren'. Dare he? His hand hovered over them, then he thought better of it. Using them would be cool and it was something he'd always wanted to do, but now was not the time. Now he had to get north without causing a fuss, and find out what was happening to his sister. With the thought of her the awful, corpse-like weight of anxiety settled on him again.

He kept following signs for the M40, ignoring those for Lytham, Wolvercote, Kidlington. They might have led him by a less exposed route, but he didn't know these places and it could be they'd take him out of his way. His plan was to follow the motorway north and look for an opportunity to strike out across country.

He made good progress. There was little to slow him, apart from the fact that none of the traffic lights worked and he had to reduce his speed at each junction so that he could check for things coming the other way. The chances were that there would be nothing but it was best to be careful. A stupid accident at a blind junction was the last thing he needed. He saw only two other vehicles, one a car and the other an army Land Rover. Neither paid him any attention. He supposed that in his hospital clothing and white coat he looked pretty genuine, although they might wonder why he wasn't in a bio suit. When he got to a spot where it seemed reasonable to stop he'd check in the back to see if there was a spare one.

After about twenty minutes he reached a roundabout: the M40. Bicester and Birmingham were one way, High Wycombe and London the other. He took the northbound carriageway, towards Birmingham.

The motorway was as empty as everywhere else, and it took him only five minutes to reach the next junction. Birmingham straight on, Brackley and Northampton by another route. It would be dangerous to get too close to Birmingham, so he took the exit. This new road was duelled, but it was slower than the motorway because there were frequent roundabouts. They were all littered with damaged or dead vehicles which must have been dragged there to get them off the highway. On one there were some people camping; two women, a man and a small child standing in front of a shabby tent. They tried to flag him down and he began to slow, but then something warned him not to get involved and he accelerated. One of the women stood in the road to stop him and only jumped aside at the last minute. He saw them in his mirror, shaking their fists and giving him the finger. It was probably a set-up, an ambush, he thought. On the other hand they might have been in trouble. He should have stopped. It could have been the child, and the mother thought he was a real medic and would help them. But there was nothing he could have done. If he'd picked them up, where would he have taken them? Even so, he felt bad. Kerryl would have stopped, for sure. She thought and expected the best of everybody, and she was always ready to help someone in trouble. She would have called him a selfish pig for driving on. But it was for her sake that he was doing it.

He passed Brackley and saw a sign for Silverstone. He knew about that; there was a motor racing circuit there. He'd seen it on TV. Where was it? Could you drive on to it? It would be a hoot to do that, to go round the Silverstone track in an ambulance, siren screaming, blues flashing. What speed would this thing do? But he told himself not to get distracted, and he pushed the temptation aside.

He didn't know how big Northampton was but he thought it might be quite large and therefore best avoided, so before he reached it he turned onto a side road. Even though he'd had no breakfast he wasn't hungry, but he thought he should eat. The question was, where could he find something? From past experience it seemed that a private house would be his best bet. Apart from the ones in Snaith, all the stores he'd seen had been raided and nothing decent was left. If he could find a house that was hidden away he'd have a better chance. Everything in the fridge would have gone off, but there'd be packets and tins in store cupboards. Finding another Snaith would be terrific, although on reflection that hadn't turned out well.

He came to a tiny village. It was no more than a hamlet really, just a small church and four or five cottages clustered around a green. It was picture postcard England, and it was easy to forget the tragedy laying waste the country and the world.

Nobody was around so he parked the ambulance and set about exploring. The first house he tried had been wrecked. The door had been forced, and it swung loosely on ruined hinges. A window had been smashed, and when he looked inside he saw rubbish and toppled furniture. He moved on. The next house had also been entered, but somebody had tried to repair the damage. Cardboard had been taped over the inside of a broken window pane, and the door was firm. He tapped on it. There was no sound or sign of movement from inside, so he tried the door. It was loose but there was something stopping it opening. He shook it and there was a clatter as whatever had been holding it fell away. He eased it ajar and crept in.

The door gave on to a small sitting room. It was so crammed with furniture he wondered how anyone could possible live in there, but it was clean and tidy, with brightly coloured rugs and cushions neatly arranged. There was a faint scent. Lilac? Gran liked that. There were two other doors. One opened directly to a staircase. The other seemed to lead to a kitchen. He pushed the kitchen door and stepped through into another neat little room.

He was bending at a cupboard to look for food when there was a flash of light, his head exploded, his vision blurred and he fell forward, curling in a ball.

Through his pain he heard a shrill shout. 'I'm not going, you bastards!'

He twisted to see someone standing behind the door. It was waving something, a short wooden cudgel with a bulbous end. That must be what had hit him.

'I'm not going with you. You're not taking me,' it shrieked. The voice was strident and pierced him like an arrow.

The figure wasn't showing any sign of coming nearer and Lander eased himself into a sitting position. He dabbed his scalp and expected to see blood on his fingers, but they came away clean. Nevertheless, he was hurt. He felt as though his head had been split in two.

His attacker was a woman. She didn't move but her eyes never left him. She was elderly. A streak of grey hair hung across her face. He marvelled that she could have hit him so hard. Oh God, not another old crone as nutty as Louise, he thought.

He raised his hand in what he hoped would be taken as a gesture of peace. 'I don't want to take you anywhere,' he said.

'Why are you in my house, then? You're not taking me to the hospital.'

What was she talking about? Who did she think he was? 'I'm not here to take you to the hospital.'

'Then what's the ambulance for?' Her mouth was set in a firm line and her chin jutted forward defiantly.

Ah, the ambulance. Is that what this was about?

'I'm nothing to do with the authorities,' he said. 'I stole the ambulance to escape from the hospital. They were keeping me prisoner there.'

The woman nodded, as if to say, I told you so. 'Prisoner?'

'Yes. They were doing some tests on me. I took the ambulance to get away.'

'But you're wearing hospital clothes. You look like a doctor.'

'These are the clothes they gave me,' said Lander. 'They took my own.'

The woman looked doubtful, wondering whether to believe him. The arm holding the cudgel relaxed a little, but she didn't put it down.

'If you're not from the hospital, what are you doing here?' she said.

'I'm going north, to find my sister. She needs help. I thought these houses were empty. I was looking for food. I've not eaten since yesterday. I don't mean you any harm. If you'll let me pass I'll go on my way and I won't bother you.'

The woman's expression changed, she looked less suspicious. 'Not eaten since yesterday?' she said.

Lander shook his head and immediately wished he hadn't. He closed his eyes and waited for the throbbing to subside.

'Well we can't have that,' said the woman. 'Go through there and sit down. I'll bring you something.'

She stood away from the door. She was calmer now, but she still kept well clear of him and she still had the cudgel. Lander edged around her. She was tiny, not even up to his shoulder. Her face was grey and wrinkled, and her skin had the same soft puffiness as Gran's. She had the same seriousness and determination too. He could easily have knocked her over, but he didn't want to do that.

'There,' she said, pointing with the cudgel to one of the two sofas. It had its back to the kitchen. He chose the other, the one that faced the door; he wanted to see her coming.

He sat down and held his head. He felt sick. Gingerly he examined where he'd been hit. A large bump was forming. His vision had cleared and although he had a headache he didn't think there was any serious damage. From the kitchen there were the sounds of implements being moved around, water running.

The woman came into the sitting room.

'Here,' she said, holding out a damp flannel. 'Bathe it with that.'

He noticed that she hadn't given up the cudgel, she wasn't yet ready to trust him. She went back to the kitchen and there were more sounds of movement.

Lander applied the flannel to his head. The compress helped and the pain became less intense.

After a few minutes the woman returned. This time she wasn't holding the cudgel, it was dangling from her wrist on a cord. She was carrying a bowl and a plate, which she put on a low table beside him. Whatever was in the bowl looked good but the smell of food made his stomach churn.

'Pea soup,' she said. 'I made it myself. I'm afraid it's cold, but it still tastes good.' She pointed to the crispbreads on the plate. 'I've run out of bread. I make my own once a week, on a Tuesday. There'll be some more the day after tomorrow.'

Lander thought he ought to eat, although he didn't feel like it. However, once he'd forced himself to start he felt better. The woman sat on the other sofa and watched him. The soup was tasty and he got through it quickly.

'More?' the woman said.

Lander was improving all the time and would have liked some more, but he couldn't take all this old lady's food. 'No, thank you,' he said.

'Nonsense,' she said, getting up and taking his bowl. 'A fine young man like you, of course you'll have more.' She paused in the doorway. 'My name's Mrs Turner,' she said, 'but you can call me Maisie.'

When she returned to the sitting room it was without the cudgel.

TWELVE
MAISIE

LANDER STAYED WITH Maisie for three nights. She insisted on having him that long to be sure his head was all right. He was anxious to continue on his way, to get home to Kerryl, but he welcomed the relief from the tedium of the hospital. Besides, until well into the second day he felt groggy; he certainly didn't feel like driving – or running into any further problems.

He soon decided that he liked Maisie, despite their violent introduction, and she seemed to warm to him. She told him that everyone else in the village had died from the Infection. The last ones to go had been her immediate neighbours, and she'd nursed them through their final days. After their deaths there had been a couple of visits by vandals. They'd ransacked next door, and Maisie had waited hiding with her cudgel while they'd tried to break into her own cottage. To her relief they'd lost interest and gone away. They'd done a bit of damage but they hadn't stayed long, and more importantly they hadn't come back.

'So you're the last person left here,' said Lander.

'Yes. I was the oldest inhabitant, and it looks as though I'll be the last one to go. I can't think why I've been spared. Perhaps this virus thingumabob doesn't like old meat.'

After his meal on the first day Lander had wanted to go to sleep but she wouldn't let him.

'Not good after a bang on the head,' she said. 'You've got to keep awake. The doctor told me that after my Jimmy fell off his bike.'

Jimmy was her son, a soldier who had been in Afghanistan training the Afghan army. She'd heard nothing from him and she assumed he was dead. She also had a married daughter living in Northampton and she hadn't heard from her either.

The bump on Lander's head was still sore and there was an occasional ringing in his ears but rest, good food and Maisie's care were all helping his recovery. He was soon thinking of her as another Gran; maybe his father's mother, the grandma he'd never known. She was ninety-three, she told him. 'I was born in the village and I've lived here all my life. I've lived in this cottage since I was wed seventy-four years ago.'

Lander didn't at first say much about himself and Maisie didn't pry. In fact she seemed happy to take him at face value, but Lander felt he owed her an explanation of why he'd entered her house and where he was heading, and so he gave an account of what had happened to him. He didn't tell her the real reason he'd left home – he didn't want to spook her – so he just said that it was because he'd gone to find help. He described getting arrested and sent to jail. He said they'd decided to use him for some investigations and taken him to a hospital where he'd been subjected to tests. He'd seen his chance to escape in an ambulance and had taken it. Finally, he said he'd been told his grandparents were dead and he was going back home to be with his twin sister. Maisie had listened in silence and she didn't say anything when he'd finished, but when she got up and passed him on her way to the kitchen she squeezed his shoulder. He was beginning to think that he had a talent for charming old ladies.

Every morning Maisie went over to the church. On days two and three Lander joined her. The building was light and airy, and there were fresh flowers on the altar. Maisie knelt at the altar rail, recited The Lord's Prayer, and then prayed silently for a few minutes. Lander, whose concept of God was something between a rather strict teacher and a football referee, wanted to ask her what she thought He was doing to let things get like this. Perhaps He'd looked away, or nodded off. Could she really believe in a God who would allow the devastation and suffering that were destroying the world? A God who would sit back and let His supreme creation inflict such terrible suffering? Surely if there was a God, He'd do something about it.

But Lander held his tongue. He didn't pray, although he did feel a great sense of peace from being beside this kind old woman in that quiet, ancient place.

'Why do you really think you haven't caught the Infection?' he asked Maisie as they walked back to her cottage. He was wandering whether to let her in on some of what he'd learned from *thetruth* and been told by Adam and Gwen.

'I don't know, dear,' she said. 'The Lord will have a reason for sparing me. He must have something in mind for me. Meeting you, perhaps.'

Lander decided to leave it.

Maisie fed him like a prize fighter. She said he looked peaky, and she loaded his plate three times a day. He felt guilty taking her food and protested, but she said she had plenty.

'I don't eat much,' she said. 'Anyway, at my age I'm not going to need much more, am I?'

It turned out that it was the ambulance she'd been afraid of. When her neighbour had died it had been an ambulance that had come to collect her body. The crew took not only her but her husband as well, even though he was still alive. He didn't come back.

'I thought you'd been sent to get me so I could be finished off,' she said. 'You know, mop up the old ones, clear 'em out of the way. That's why I hit you. I'm sorry.'

'That's all right,' Lander said. 'You thought you were protecting yourself.' He felt his bump. 'That stick you've got packs quite a punch.'

'Yes,' she said. 'That's Titan. That was my husband's name for it. He was called Jimmy, too. He was a gamekeeper at Juniper Lodge, that's a big house just a few miles up the road. He'd had no end of bother from poachers. They'd come four or five times a year and they'd take no end of his birds, and Jimmy would get it in the neck from his boss. One night he caught two of them at it. One got away but Jimmy hit the other with Titan. He didn't hit him hard, but the man fell and hurt himself. He died. The police arrested Jimmy and they took him to court. He pleaded self-defence and got off, but it was a nasty business and it went on for a long time. He lost his job, and some of the people around here were really horrible to him. He decided it would be best to work away for a bit, and he got a job on an oil rig. Good money, but I rarely saw him.'

'That must have been a hard time. Was he on the rig for long?'

'A few years. Two months before he was due to retire there was an accident with a winch and he was killed. The company was found to be negligent and they had to pay me compensation.

'I'm sorry,' said Lander.

'Quarter of a million pounds I got,' said Maisie. 'An absolute fortune. Everybody said how well the company had treated me, although their money couldn't bring him back. I've still got most of it. I'd planned to leave it to the family, but I can't do that now. Anyway, money's no good any more. I'd give it to you but I can't get at it, it's in the bank.'

Lander shook his head. He didn't want Maisie's money.

On her insistence he drove the ambulance around the side of the church and parked it out of sight of the road.

'I shouldn't think there'll be anybody coming here to see it,' she said, 'but then, I didn't expect you, did I?'

On the third morning Maisie came into the sitting room where Lander had been sleeping and gathered up his hospital scrubs.

'This way, young man,' she said, and set off up the steep, narrow staircase. At the top she opened a door. 'Jimmy's room,' she said. 'There's lots of clothes in his drawers. You're about his size. Help yourself to anything you fancy. He won't be needing them. Those you don't put on you can pack in this.' She indicated a plastic hold-all on the bed, and left him to it.

It was the smallest bedroom Lander had ever seen. Most of it was a bed, which filled a raised platform running right across the room from one side to the other. There was just enough space for him to stand beside it. He wondered where everything was; then he saw that there were deep drawers under the bed platform, three of them. One was full of t-shirts, vests and boxers. Jeans, chinos and cotton shirts were in another; the third contained shoes and socks. Jimmy must have been a little shorter and slighter than Lander so some of the clothes were tight, but he managed to find things that fitted him fairly well.

Taking Jimmy's clothes was difficult. He knew that he wouldn't be coming back for them, and if Lander didn't use them they'd just stay in the drawers until they rotted, or somebody came and nicked them. Nevertheless, it was awkward.

'How are you going to get home?' Maisie asked him as he showed her what he'd chosen.

'In the ambulance,' said Lander. 'It's got plenty of fuel.'

'You'll stick out like a sore thumb. You'll be stopped in a jiffy, mark my words.'

'Maybe, but it's all I've got. It's that or nothing.'

Maisie thought for a moment. 'Come with me,' she said, heading for the back door.

At the end of the neat little garden was a rickety old garage. Maisie pushed the door open and Lander followed her in. It was dark and spidery, and in contrast to the rest of the house this place was a tip. There was an old bike, a rusty tool box, tubes, wires, a hosepipe, garden implements; and in the middle there was a Mini Countryman. It was an old one, tiny, not like the more recent Minis which in comparison were huge. It was the colour of putty and had wooden cladding on the rear half. It was covered in dust.

'There,' said Maisie, with a note of pride. 'Jimmy and I used to go everywhere in that. Skegness, Hunstanton, Rhyl. We even went to The Lakes once. He loved that car, but I don't drive so it's not been used in a long time. I was always going to sell it but I never got round to it. Why don't you take that?'

Maisie was right: the ambulance would be very conspicuous. In this he could nip along back roads, dodge trouble. In a lot of places the roof of the car would be below the hedge tops.

'Will it start?' he said.

Maisie put her hand on his arm. 'Now there you have me,' she said. 'It always used to start first go. But that was Jimmy. He used to spend hours on it, cleaning it, servicing it, what he called tuning.'

Lander eased around the side of the car. Somebody had had the foresight to put it on axle stands, so he expected the tyres would be all right. He opened the door. No interior light came on. That was a bad sign. The keys were in the ignition. He turned them. Nothing. The battery was dead. He popped open the bonnet. Everything looked in order. The big question was, how do you charge a car battery when there's no mains electricity? He went to the back of the car, opened the rear doors, and there was the answer: a pair of jump leads. They looked to be in good condition, but would they be long enough? Could he get the ambulance close enough for them to reach?

There was only one way to find out. He fetched the ambulance from its hiding place under the trees behind the church and managed to get it along the rough track that ran past the back of Maisie's cottage. With a bit of manoeuvring he worked the nose into a position where he could just manage to connect the jump leads. He restarted the engine, then went back and sat in the Mini. He waited. Then he turned the key again, just one click. A light came on the dash and the fuel gauge kicked slightly, but it stayed on zero.

'Is it all right?' said Maisie, who'd been watching all this.

'We need some fuel.'

Maisie pointed. There were three large jerry cans against the garage wall. 'Young Jimmy put them there last time he was here. He said he thought that the way things were going there'd be fuel shortages and I might need them.'

Lander couldn't believe his luck. Old fuel, either stored in cans or in the car's tank, probably wouldn't be much good, but if this lot was only a few months old it should be fine.

He got one of the jerry cans and emptied it into the Mini's tank. Then he sat down again in the driver's seat. He took a deep breath and mentally crossed his fingers. His hand was trembling as he turned the ignition key.

The Mini gave a reluctant grunt, then the engine spun, but it didn't fire. He tried once more. Still no luck. If it was really dried out it would take a while for the fuel to get through, he thought.

'Let's give it one more go,' he said. 'This time, for sure.'

Maisie waited, looking anxious. Lander turned the key again. The engine fired, spluttered, and then caught. He jabbed the accelerator and it revved.

'Brilliant!' Lander yelled. 'Absolutely gob-smackingly brilliant!' He got out of the car, leaving the engine running, and gave Maisie a hug. 'Are you sure this is all right?' he said. 'For me to borrow it? I'll bring it back.'

'You're welcome to it,' said Maisie. 'It's no use to me, I couldn't even get it out of the garage, and it just sits there reminding me of better times. Don't worry about bringing it back, although it would be nice to see you again.'

Lander disconnected the jump leads.

During the next hour he jacked up each corner of the car and removed the axle stands. The tyres looked a bit soft but not very, and he was sure they'd be good enough to get him to the farm. He left the engine running all the time to charge the battery, then he got into the driver's seat and turned it off.

'Crunch time,' he said to himself. If the alternator wasn't working the battery wouldn't have charged. He'd still be able to use the car once he got it going, he just wouldn't be able to restart the engine if it stopped. 'Oh well,' he said, 'nothing venture...'

He turned the ignition and the Mini started. He got out and punched the air. Then he put the other two jerry cans in the back of the car and returned to the cottage.

Maisie was in the kitchen, preparing an evening meal for them. She'd been baking that day. There was wood smoke in the air, and the house smelt of fresh bread. Lander's mouth watered.

'Tell you what,' he said, putting his arm around Maisie's waist as she stirred something on the stove. 'Why don't you come with me?'

Maisie stopped stirring. 'Are you propositioning me, young man? Come with you where?'

'Come home with me, to the farm. You'll get on really well with Kerryl and she'll love you. And you say yourself there's nothing for you here.'

Maisie smiled up at him. 'That's very sweet of you,' she said, 'but what would I do in Yorkshire? And you know what they say about two women in a kitchen.'

'Well let me at least take you to Northampton. We can go to your daughter's place and you can stay there, or if...if...' he struggled to find a kind way to say it, 'if there's nothing for you there I can bring you back.'

She shook her head. 'You need to get on your way. It's best for me to stay here. I'm not comfortable anywhere else. I've lived in this village all my life and this is where I'll die.'

Lander meant to set out early the following day, but he and Maisie stayed up late into the night talking. She told him something of her life, of being a young woman in World War II, of Jimmy the elder being conscripted into the army, even though the authorities knew he was a farm labourer. She told of the worry while he was away, of her dread of the postman's visits, and her joy at his sudden and unexpected appearances when he returned on leave. She talked about the younger Jimmy, and her daughter, Jenny, who was a doctor's receptionist. Lander told her more about his life in the valley, his interest in computers, the way that before the Infection he'd felt bored and frustrated because there was so little going on. He told of his dreams of playing professional cricket.

'I hope one day you'll come back here,' Maisie said, 'but even if you don't I know people will hear of you. You're an outstanding young man. You'll make your mark, I'm sure of it.'

Nobody had ever said that to Lander before, and he was so touched his eyes watered. Not even his own mother had expressed such faith in him.

He thought of Maisie's words as he drove out of the village the next day. He was leaving much later than he'd intended, but he had to go. The longer he stayed with this good-hearted old lady the harder it would be to continue his journey, and if he didn't get going today he might just stay for ever. Besides, Kerryl needed him. All his life he'd had a sense of connection with her, even when they'd been apart. He didn't have that now, and it worried him.

He kept to the back roads. He didn't recognise many of the place names and he didn't have a map. It hadn't occurred to him to ask Maisie if she had one, and he could have kicked himself for the omission. However, there was a dash mounted compass in the Mini, and he reckoned that if he kept heading roughly north he'd eventually come to somewhere he'd recognise. The little car went well, and he was near Derby when he pulled in and ate two of the sandwiches Maisie had packed for him.

It started to rain, and it was then that he discovered the only fault he could find with the Mini: the windscreen wipers didn't work. He managed for a while, peering through the drops, but the rain got harder and it was when he almost went into a ditch that he decided he'd have to stop. He pulled into a farm gateway, getting the car as clear of the road as he could. He waited for a while but the rain was hard and it looked as though it had set in for the rest of the day. He'd stay here. The Mini was fairly well hidden, and if he kept his head down nobody who saw it would think there was anyone inside; it would be just another abandoned car. Hopefully he'd be able to carry on when the weather improved.

The Mini didn't make for comfortable sleeping but there was no other option. He'd seen no more than half a dozen other vehicles since he'd left Maisie's, and only one of them was travelling on his road. He'd be all right. There were some ancient tape cassettes in a box – Jethro Tull, Genesis, Abba – none of it really his thing, but he put one on softly and wrapped himself in the rug Maisie had given him. It was hard to settle and he was awake for a long time before he eventually dropped off.

LANDER WAS DREAMING of the farm. He and Kerryl were children. They were at the Bride Stones, an unusual formation of rocks on the moors above the farm, where they would often play. They'd been enjoying a game of hide and seek, taking turns to conceal themselves amongst the wild outcrop while the other searched. The trick was to anticipate the arrival of the searcher so you could leap out and scare them before they found you. Then the dream soured. This time, instead of Kerryl being the seeker, Lander was hiding from a nameless, black shape. He couldn't describe it or avoid it, and it terrified him.

Suddenly there was a loud noise and he fell to the side as the car door he'd been leaning on was jerked open. Before he could react, he was seized by the collar and hauled out on to the ground. A torch shone in his eyes. Was it one person or more? He tried to shout out something but a fist came out of the brightness and hit him in the mouth. His lip split and he tasted blood.

Whoever had him was strong. They dragged him away from the car, rolled him over and put their knee in his back. He thought it was just one person, but he was big and heavy, and Lander couldn't move to fight back. His chest was being crushed against the wet road and he could hardly breathe. It flashed through his mind that the last time he'd been attacked it had been Maisie, and that had turned out well. Perhaps this would be all right too. He tried again to speak but the knee twisted, pressing him painfully into the ground.

His arms were yanked behind his back and his wrists taped together. Then a rope was looped around his neck and something put over his head. It was a sack, a hessian sack. It smelt of the henhouse and made him want to vomit. He had to shut his mouth and his eyes to keep the dust out. He licked his lip and tasted blood.

He thought he was going to pass out when his captor at last got off him, but he had only a second to enjoy the relief because his wrists were grabbed and he was heaved to his feet. The movement twisted his arms behind him and was so excruciatingly painful that he cried out, but a kick on his shin told him he mustn't do that. The rope pulled him forward and he felt himself being led away from the car. His eyes were tightly shut because of the hessian dust, but they ran with tears of rage. The Mini had been a tiny jewel, a symbol of Maisie's warm thoughtfulness and his passport back to Kerryl; being snatched away from it was unbearable.

There was a hard shove in the small of his back and he staggered forward. He had no idea where he was going, it seemed to be along a track. It was rough and uneven, and his feet sloshed into puddles so that his trainers were soon soaked. His foot caught on something and he tipped forward. Without his hands to break his fall he landed hard on his knees and hurt them. Wary of another kick and of his arms being twisted again he choked off the cry that rose in his throat and struggled to his feet as quickly as he could.

His captor said nothing coherent, but he grunted and swore a lot. Lander limped on, each step painful. The rain beat down, and the bag over his head was now so saturated it dripped cold water down his neck. It was hard to breathe. Was this what being waterboarded was like? No wonder people would do anything to make it stop. He was choking and he felt panic rising.

His progress was halted by a jerk on the rope. There was the unmistakable stink of a farmyard, so strong it overrode the chicken-shed stench of the hessian. It wasn't the healthy, wholesome smell of Lander's farm, his home. This was the rancid reek of a poor farm, a neglected farm with over-full slurry pits and ailing animals.

He heard the grating scrape of a metal door sliding open and he was pushed inside a building, an outhouse of some sort. His right arm was seized and what felt like a metal brace was put on his wrist. He winced as it was squeezed tight, pinching his flesh. He could feel the weight of a chain attached to the brace. Then the tape binding his wrists was cut roughly. He was pushed again and he heard the door slide shut behind him. There was the unmistakable rattle of a padlock being fastened into a hasp.

His right arm was encumbered because of the chain but his left was free and he used that to snatch the wet sack off his head. He was in a big room. He could tell that from the way sounds reverberated and from the sense of space, but he could see nothing. It was completely dark, not a chink of light anywhere. Gingerly he fingered his split lip. A couple of his teeth had been loosened too. He rubbed his wrists and picked off the remains of the tape. He'd felt the knife cut him and he pressed on the wound to stop any bleeding.

He had no idea where he was: some sort of farm building obviously, but was it a shed? A stable? The stench of slurry was strong and there was a smell of urine too. Was there a pit for animal waste in the middle of this space? He turned towards where he guessed the door to be but the chain wouldn't let him go in that direction, so he shuffled carefully backwards until his heels came to a wall. He turned and ran his hands over it. It was ribbed metal, cold and damp. The chain would allow him to go in only one direction, away from the door. If he tried to go the other way something held him back, although he didn't get the impression that it was a firm fixing; whatever it was had some give.

He went the way the chain allowed, keeping his back to the wall, feeling along it with his hands and extending his leading foot cautiously, wary of dropping into the imagined slurry pit. The chain became slacker as he moved. His foot came against something fixed to the floor and he bent to investigate. It was a metal ring, with the chain running through it. He knelt down – his sore knees protesting – and pulled at the restraint. Again there was a resistance. He was too shaken up to explore further. His shoulders were painful from where they'd been wrenched and his knees and wrists hurt.

He sat on the floor beside the ring to try to work things out. Obviously he'd been taken prisoner again, but who had done that, and why? Where had he been taken?

The surface of the floor was rough, like concrete. It was also damp. So was he. He was more than damp, he was sodden. He was cold and he was shivering. He'd heard people say they'd been so perished their teeth had chattered, and now he realised what they meant. He drew up his knees and hugged them. His back and his chest ached from where he'd been knelt on. The side of his face was sore from its contact with the road. His mouth hurt from where he'd been punched.

Another shower of rain came, even harder this time, hammering on the metal roof so that it was like being inside a drum pelted with pebbles. He hitched himself forward to get away from the chill of the wall, and felt an obstruction in front of him. He explored it with his fingers. It felt like a bale of hay. Beside it was another. He groped for the binding twine, eased it off the bale, and pulled out handfuls of the sweet-smelling grasses. He spread them to make a bed. He loosened the other bale, lay down on his makeshift mattress, and pulled more hay on top of him until he was cocooned. Within a few minutes he was feeling warmer, although he would still have been hard pressed to name a part of him that didn't hurt.

The rain stopped. The din it had made on the roof had been deafening and now it was gone there was an eerie quiet. He could hear another sound. It was a sort of quiet snuffling. For a second he thought it was a rat, but it was something bigger than that. There was an animal in the shed with him! It was not the noise a cow or a horse would make. What was it? A sheep? A pig? A pig would at least account for the bad smells. He felt the chain move very slightly. Was the animal also attached to it? Was he fastened to one end and a pig to the other? He didn't mind pigs but he didn't like them. They stank and were stubborn.

He was about to give the chain an experimental heave to see what happened when he heard more sounds, this time from outside. There was the rattle of the padlock, the screech of the door sliding back and a light appeared. It was from a hurricane lantern carried by an enormous man. He had a bushy beard the size of a shovel and a huge belly. Lander guessed it was the same man who had pulled him out of the car. No wonder his back hurt from where he'd been knelt on; the guy must weigh a ton! The lantern was in one hand, in the other was a billycan and a plastic bag. He put all three items down against the far wall and returned to the door.

'Dinner is served, your majesties,' he said, with a mock bow. He went out and slid the door shut behind him.

Majesties? Plural? Lander looked around. In the dim light from the lantern he could see that the chain ran through an iron hoop set into the concrete near the wall, and there was indeed something on the other end. It was human. He – or was it she? – was also lying on a pile of hay. It had its back to him and all he could see was a filthy t-shirt. It had short, black hair and there was a red mark high on one arm. The figure rolled over and regarded him. Its eyes were big and dark. There was a bruise on one cheek. It sat up, so skinny and flat chested that he thought it must be a boy, but then he realised it was actually a girl.

The shed was big. At the far end, just discernible, was an old tractor and some other bits of scrap machinery, and there were more hay bales. He was relieved to see there was no slurry pit, but there was a shallow channel running across the middle of the space, leading to a small hole in the wall. The slurry pit would be out there, hence the smell. The concrete floor was pitted, stained with what could have been oil but was more probably animal excrement.

The girl began to move, edging towards the billycan and bag. Lander felt a tug on his wrist and saw that she had reached a point where the chain was preventing her going further. He didn't want to leave his bed, but he realised that she was stuck unless he gave her some slack. He shuffled nearer to the hoop. What now? The girl reached the bag, extracted two plastic bowls and put them on the ground. Next she took out a hunk of bread. She measured this with her eye and tore it roughly in half. She gripped one of the halves under her arm and put the other in one of the bowls. Finally, she filled the other bowl, the empty one, with liquid from the billycan. It was all done mechanically and with precision, and it seemed to Lander to be a routine familiar to her.

She picked up the full bowl and came over to the hoop, and Lander beside it. At first he thought she was intending to give the food to him, although he couldn't think why she'd do that. She didn't. She squatted beside the hoop and started to eat, taking slurps from the bowl and stuffing bread into her mouth. She wolfed for a moment or two and then pointed at the billycan and bowl. She meant him to go and get his own food. That was why she'd come to the hoop, so that there was enough slack in the chain for him to reach it. Lander crawled painfully over the floor to where it was. The shed was lofty and there was plenty of room to stand, but the chain seemed to dictate how he moved.

He investigated what was on the menu. The billycan contained a grey liquid. He sniffed it; it smelt of cabbage.

He poured what was left into the remaining bowl and took that and his half of the bread back to his place.

He wondered if the girl would retreat, now the purpose of her coming to the hoop had been served, but she didn't. She remained where she was, not looking at him but squatting on her haunches a few feet away. Her back was against the corrugated metal of the wall, careless of the cold. She'd finished her ration and was wiping her bowl with the remains of her bread.

Lander sipped the liquid. It was awful, thin and very salty. He took a bite of the bread. It tasted of mould. He didn't want any of it. He put the bowl and the bread down. He thought fondly of the food parcel Maisie had given him for his journey, with sandwiches made from one of her home-baked loaves. It had been in the hold-all in the car. Where was it now? Where was he? He was weary of being imprisoned. What was it this time? Who was his captor? How long would he be held in this unspeakable hole?

The girl was staring at the food Lander had rejected. She looked at him directly for the first time, and an eyebrow twitched. Lander pushed it towards her and she snatched it quickly, as if she was afraid he might change his mind. She ate it quickly, cramming the bread into her mouth and washing it down with the sludge.

Lander studied his companion while she ate. Now he was closer he could see that she was older than he'd at first thought, perhaps in her middle twenties. However, it was hard to tell because she was so emaciated. Her arms were stick thin, her shoulders and elbows bony. She seemed to be wearing nothing under her t-shirt and her breasts were tiny, mere bumps, with hard little nipples. He could see now that the red mark on her arm was a burn, and quite a nasty one. It was fairly recent because there were still blisters.

She finished eating and wiped her mouth on the back of her hand. She got up, picked up both the bowls and walked over to the empty billycan and the lamp. The chain rattled behind her as she went. For a second it reminded Lander of a movie they used to watch at the farm every Christmas, the one where the ghost of a miser has to drag around a chain forged from the bad things he'd done during his life. The memory of happier times was painful. He'd give anything to be back there again, watching the TV with his family. He even missed his chores, and their Mam's nagging.

The girl licked out both bowls, shook the crumbs from of the plastic bag into her hand and lapped them up. Then she returned the bowls to the bag and took that, the billycan and the lamp to the sliding door.

Lander thought she'd be coming back to the hoop but instead she went to a battered bucket in the corner. The chain would only just reach. She turned her back on Lander, let down her muddy jeans, squatted over the bucket and urinated in a steady stream. When she'd done she pulled them up and came back to the hoop. She sat down in her former position and stared at him. Her eyes were wide, dark and steady. The bruise on her cheek looked to be from where someone had hit her, and maybe had once been a black eye.

Who was she? She looked like one of the refugees he'd seen in pictures on the TV. Or somebody from a concentration camp. She was skinny enough. Was she an illegal immigrant? How did she get here? Why were they both chained up?

Lander cleared his throat. 'Do you speak English?' he said.

There was a long pause before the girl responded, as if she was deciding whether or not to reply. All of the time her eyes remained fixed on him. At last she spoke.

'My name is Magda,' she said. 'What's yours?' Her English was perfect.

FOURTEEN
WORK

LANDER THOUGHT THAT learning Magda's name might be an ice breaker, the start of a conversation, but he was wrong.

'I'm Lander,' he said.

Magda frowned.

'It's a nickname,' he said.

'Right,' she said, turned her back on him and shuffled away to her pile of hay. She lay down, still with her back to him, and seemed to be settling to sleep. There was so much Lander wanted to know: Who was she? Where had she come from? Where were they? How long had she been there? Who was the fat man who'd caught him and brought in the food? What did he want?

Some of these things he learnt the next day. For others he had to wait longer.

His bed of hay was surprisingly comfortable, and after some adjustment he got into a position where the chain wasn't digging into him. At last he was warm, and with the rain rattling again on the roof it was strangely cosy. He was hungry and he wished he'd persevered with the sloppy goo and the bread, but despite this he dropped off to sleep.

He was roused by the rasp of the door sliding back and the beam of a torch. He blinked against the light. The fat man was standing in the doorway.

At once he was wide awake. 'Why have you put me in here?' he shouted. 'What have I done to you? Let me go.'

The fat man came towards him. He looked dangerous, menacing, and very bad tempered.

'You shut the fuck up, pretty boy, or I'll bust your lip again.' He stared at him and Lander looked away. Slowly the man went back to the doorway, picked up the bag, the billycan and the lamp and left. The door slammed shut and it was pitch dark once more.

Lander wondered how long he'd been asleep. It was then he realised that his watch was missing. Strange he hadn't noticed it before. Had the fat man taken it? When?

He lay awake for a long time, listening to the rain. At one point he called out. 'Magda? Are you awake?' There was no response. In the end he lapsed into an uneasy doze, almost asleep but not quite, with images of his home, his family, his room, all scrambling around in his head. Why had he left the farm? It had seemed right at the time but he could see now that it was a dreadful mistake. He might have predicted that Gran and Granddad would die from the Infection. That meant that he had left Kerryl to manage on her own. How was she coping? Was she coping at all? He had no idea whether she was well or ill, happy or sad. She might not be immune after all; she might have died, all alone. Was that the reason Adam had stopped meeting him? Because she was dead?

He seemed to have been asleep for only minutes when he heard the scrape of the door again, the usual herald of their jailer.

'Good morning, love birds,' the man shouted, and banged hard with a stick on the metal wall of the shed. 'Rise and shine.'

Magda jumped up and hurried over to him, her chain scraping after her.

He turned to Lander. 'Get your arse over here, you lazy bastard,' he shouted.

He beat on the metal again; the din was ear splitting. Lander saw that what he was using was not a stick but the handle of a whip. He hurried over.

'Hope this little prick hasn't been molesting you, my dear,' the man said to Magda, and winked. He had such a brutal voice, such a heartless manner that even endearments sounded coarse.

'No, he was fine, Mickey. I know how to defend my honour,' Magda said, and she winked back.

The man, Mickey, roared with laughter, but it wasn't real. It was a taunt, a savage, mocking sound. A sound that said he was in control and they were at his mercy. Lander had no doubt that here was someone who was capable of doing him great harm.

He started with Magda. She'd been chained by her right wrist, like Lander. Mickey now put another shackle on her left wrist. This was joined to a lighter chain which ended in a fetter, and he locked this on her ankle. Then he undid her right wrist from the longer chain.

'You wait here, pretty boy,' Mickey said, and he led Magda out of the shed, locking the door behind him.

Lander's heart leapt. With no one on the other end of the chain he might be able to escape. Then he realised what a stupid idea that was. How could he run away, manacled like this? The chain weighed a lot. Always assuming he could get out of the shed, he wouldn't be able to drag it far enough or move quickly enough to find freedom. The only thing he could do was wait to see what happened.

There was a small stack of hay bales close by and he sat on one to wait. Fingers of daylight poked through gaps in the roof and he could see the layout of the shed more clearly. It would be useful to know how things were organised, in case he had to move about in the dark. Presumably Mickey was going to come back for him when he'd delivered Magda to wherever he was taking her. He was right. It wasn't long before the door opened again.

'Come on then, squire. Get your hands off your cock and let's rock.' Mickey laughed once more in his cruel, humourless way.

There was another short chain and fetter on a hook on the wall, and Mickey repeated on Lander what he'd done with Magda. For a second Lander wondered if he could swing the chain hard enough to knock Mickey out, or maybe loop it around his neck and squeeze. But Mickey was strong, and he knew that if he failed and only managed to hurt him, he would be dead.

When the small chain was fixed and the long one lay on the ground, Mickey stood back and looked at Lander. The whip was prominent in his hand. It was a savage looking thing with a thong of plaited leather. A blow from that would rip skin.

'Right then, it's off to work we go,' he said, offering Lander a grim smile. His two front teeth were missing. This was a man for whom violence was the norm. 'You can start with the bucket. I don't think emptying shit and piss is a job for a lady, do you?'

Lander didn't reply.

Mickey leant forward until his face was inches from Lander's. He tapped the whip on his cheek, ominously. 'Well do you, arsehole?'

'No.'

'So answer me when I talk to you, fuckbrain. Go over there and collect the marmalade pot.' He pointed the whip in the direction of the night bucket and Lander crossed to it. It stank so much it made him gag. In the daylight he could see that there was a lid on the floor beside it. Next to that were two short planks, which he guessed were to lay across it to make a rudimentary seat, although Magda hadn't bothered with these the night before. The toilet suite was completed by a few torn newspapers on the floor.

'Pick it up and follow me,' Mickey said from the door.

The bucket was about half full and couldn't have been emptied for several days. Lander carried it to the door. It was heavy, and encumbered by the shackles it was hard to move without slopping its contents. Mickey led the way around the side of the shed. Lander's guess had been right. There was a slurry pit there. It was almost full.

'In there,' said Mickey.

Lander tipped the contents of the bucket on to the slimy surface.

'Any bother from you and you'll go in after it,' said Mickey. 'Now put that shit pot back in the shed and come with me.'

As he followed Mickey, Lander had his first opportunity to look around. They were on a rough track, and he was made to walk towards a small, dilapidated farmhouse at the bottom of it. Behind him was a farm gate which led onto a road. The shed was about half way between the two. The light was raw, and Lander concluded it couldn't be much after 6 o'clock.

As they neared the house he saw that it was in as bad a state as everything else. It was red brick and at one time had been covered in a cream render, but much of that had fallen off, leaving gaps like scabs. There were white deposits on the exposed bricks, and the paint had peeled from rotten window frames. The place was surrounded by rubbish: an old trailer, broken pallets, a rusty washing machine, a bedstead. A few ragged chickens pecked in the yard around Maisie's Mini. Its door was open and one of the birds hopped inside. Lander felt a mixture of anger, frustration and regret. Maisie had given him her car to help him, and look how he'd thanked her. Why hadn't he set out for the north earlier, so he could have done the journey in one go? Why had he stopped beside the road instead of finding somewhere less obvious? He had hung about, left his departure too late, parked carelessly, and as a result here he was.

Mickey took Lander around the side of the house, where there was a tumbledown brick building that might once have been a garage. It had no roof and one wall had collapsed.

'Here,' said Mickey. He picked up a lump hammer and a rusty cold chisel and held them out. 'Well, get hold of 'em!'

Lander took the tools.

'Your job is to clean up those bricks. Knock all the old mortar off 'em so I can use 'em again. When you've done 'em, pile 'em there.'

There was a small stack of smooth bricks to the side of the building, presumably Mickey's work. Or, it occurred to Lander, maybe he'd had a predecessor. He looked at the fallen wall and the jumbled pile waiting to be done. There were hundreds of them. It would take ages.

'Ever done this before?' said Mickey.

'No,' said Lander.

'Well this'll be a fucking first for you, then, won't it? I'll be back in a bit to check on you, and when I do you'd better be fucking working. And remember, I want all the mortar off every brick, every single fucking bit of it.'

Mickey strolled away in the direction they'd come, swinging his whip.

Again Lander thought of escape. How far would he get, manacled the way he was? The chain wasn't long enough to allow proper movement. Walking was hard, running would be impossible. All the land around the farm was open and it would be easy for Mickey to spot him. A better opportunity would surely come. He wondered about Magda. Where had Mickey taken her? What was he making her do?

He picked up a brick and started to chip away at the mortar. Some of the bricks were straightforward to clean because the mortar was brittle and came away easily. Others weren't; the mortar was solid and seemed fused in place. He quickly decided to leave the trickier ones, and he threw them aside. He'd go back to them later, when he'd got better at it. Some of the bricks broke, and he tossed those away too. It was slow work, and hard on his hands, which were soon sore. To make the whole business even more difficult the chain constantly got in the way. The extra weight made his arm ache and that, plus the restriction it imposed, slowed him down. If Mickey needed bricks why didn't he go and look for new ones? There must be millions of them on building sites, there for the taking.

He'd probably been working a couple of hours when somebody appeared around the side of the house. It wasn't Mickey, but a woman. She had a pinched face, and wisps of ginger hair escaped from around a patterned headscarf. She was carrying a plastic dish with a lid. She put it and a plastic spoon on the pile of bricks and walked away. She didn't speak or even look at Lander. The legs below her brown overall were puffy and laced with varicose veins.

Lander took the lid off the dish. It contained a thin, watery porridge, still slightly warm. In normal circumstances Lander wouldn't have touched it, but he was by this time so hungry he would have eaten wallpaper paste. He dipped in his finger and tasted it. It was quite sweet and not too bad. He ate it all, getting what he could with the spoon and then licking out the container, wiping his finger into the corners. He'd felt derisive the night before when Magda had licked the bowls; now he realised that it didn't take much to make a person behave in ways that they would previously have scorned.

He put the bowl and spoon back on the brick pile and carried on. His hands were by now rubbed raw, which made the work even more difficult. The pile of cleaned bricks had barely grown, and when Mickey returned Lander felt a tremor of anxiety. It didn't look much for a morning's work.

Mickey sneered. 'Is that all you've done, Nancy boy?'

Lander nodded.

'What?'

'Yes.'

Mickey sighed. 'Fuck me. A right bloody slacker you are. I'm going to be hard pressed to afford to feed you if this is the best you can do.'

'It's this chain,' said Lander. 'It makes it hard to do the job. If you took it off I could get on more quickly.'

Mickey gave a contemptuous snort. 'Oh yes, and why don't I order you a fucking Uber while I'm at it, so you can get right away? Do I look fucking stupid?'

He did, but Lander couldn't tell him so. 'No,' he said, 'but you could tie my leg to something.'

'Could I? I have your royal permission to do that, do I? Well thank you, your fucking majesty.'

'Anyway, I could do better if I had work gloves,' said Lander, holding up his red hands.

Mickey looked incredulous. 'Work gloves! Ah, diddums.' He reached forward and roughly seized of one of Lander's hands. 'What are you? Some kind of fucking fairy?' He spat on the hand and dropped it. 'You'd better have done a lot more by the time I come back.'

The day wore on and Lander worked and worked. In the late afternoon the sun came out and it grew warm. Lander took off his shirt, as far as he could with the chain on his wrist, and wrapped it around the hand that was hurting most. It was now so sore that it was bleeding, and the makeshift bandage helped.

The sun was well down – it must have been after seven – by the time Mickey returned and led Lander back to the shed. He was bone weary and just wanted to collapse on the hay. Magda was already there, on her own hay pile and attached to her end of the chain. She watched as Mickey removed Lander's shackle, chained him up and left.

Lander flopped down on the bales. There was just enough light coming through the holes in the roof for him to see Magda. She watched him for a few minutes, then got to her feet and clanked across the concrete to him. She stood in front of him and bent down to take one of his hands. He let her. She turned it palm up and examined it.

Without speaking she went to the wall, where there was an enamel jug and a mug. She came back with both, filled the mug, took his hand and gently splashed water on it. At first it stung, but then it felt better. She did the same to the other hand, then returned the mug and jug while Lander sat on the bale and his hands dripped. They felt less angry after the bathing but they were still throbbing.

'Thank you,' he called to her.

She nodded and went back to her hay.

They stayed like that for some time, at opposite ends of the chain, umbilically connected but apart. At last there were footsteps outside, the door screeched and Mickey came in with the lamp, billycan and bag.

'Dinner for one tonight,' he said, putting the lamp and food in the usual place. He gestured at Lander. 'This fucker hasn't done enough work today to earn his.' He spat towards Lander and went back to the door.

It smelt like the same concoction again. There was only one bowl and, Lander guessed, probably only half as much as before. Magda went to the can, filled the bowl and took that and some bread back to her bed in the hay. She drank the soup and wiped the bowl. Then she went back to the billycan and poured what was left into the bowl. She took the rest of the bread and brought them both to Lander. She put them on the floor in front of him.

'What's this?'

'It's your share,' she said.

'No it's not, it's yours. You heard him, there isn't any for me.'

'Don't be daft. If you don't eat you can't work. He knows that. There was the same amount as last night but only one bowl. He was just making a point.'

Lander wasn't sure whether she was telling the truth or sharing with him what should have been all hers, but he wasn't going to argue. He was famished and he ate quickly. Remembering what Magda had done the night before, he put the empty, licked-out bowl in the bag beside the billycan. Mickey clearly ran a regime with routines that he expected to be followed, and Lander didn't need to be told the importance of not upsetting those.

Magda watched him all the time. He thought about going to sit beside her, the chain would have allowed it, but he returned to his own half of the shed and lay on the hay. He was achingly tired but not sleepy. His hands were hurting too much for sleep, anyway. He thought Magda might speak but she said nothing, just watched him. He felt something was expected of him but he didn't know what. Looking at how starved she was, she must have been here for a while. You'd think that given the opportunity she would have taken all the food for herself, rather than sharing.

'Do you want to talk?' he said.

'What about?'

'I don't know. You could tell me who you are.'

'I have told you. My name's Magda.'

'I know that, but I mean who are you? Where are you from? How long have you been here?'

'Why do you need to know that?'

'I don't need to know it. But we're shut in here together and we have to live with each other. I mean, you can't even go for a pee unless I cooperate by moving so you can get to the bucket. Same for me. And the same for reaching the food. We're fixed like conjoined twins. I just think it would be good to know something about you, and you me.'

Lander waited but Magda said nothing.

'All right,' he said. 'I'll start.'

He talked. He began by describing his home on the farm, and the life he'd lived there with Kerryl, their Mam and their grandparents. He talked about what they all used to do, where they used to go. He talked about the virus coming and all their friends dying, then their Mam and, so he'd heard, Gran and Granddad too. He told her about leaving, heading south, being arrested, tried and imprisoned.

He was moving on to being let out of the jail and taken to Oxford when he realised that Magda was asleep.

FIFTEEN
MAGDA

LANDER'S HANDS HURT so much that, exhausted though he was, sleep was out of the question. Several times he dropped off, but then he rolled onto a hand or the chain and woke himself up. Despite the pain and discomfort, morning came too soon.

The next day was the same as the one before. Magda was taken away first, and then Lander was collected, made to empty the bucket, and put to work on the bricks. As he passed the Mini he saw that the door was still open and there were now more chickens inside it. Maisie had treasured the car for years, it was a classic and Mickey was just letting it go to ruin, same as he'd done with everything else he touched.

The state of his hands meant that Lander worked even more slowly than he had on the first day. Every brick was torture. He loosened his shirt and pushed his hands into the sleeves so he could use them for protection, but it was awkward, and soon the fabric wore through. His shirt stank. He was wearing the same clothes he'd had on when Mickey had dragged him from the car. Where were his others? They wouldn't fit Mickey, so why couldn't he have them? He daren't ask. He'd already learnt that Mickey didn't like questions, and he was wary of the whip. He soon discovered that he had good reason to be.

Mickey didn't come to him at all during the day, just the woman with the porridge. The weather was much colder now and Lander would have been glad to put his shirt on properly, but he preferred to use it to protect his hands. The work went slowly because he was having to stop frequently. When at last Mickey appeared around the side of the house he was furious.

'Jesus, is that all you've done? I don't fucking believe it,' he bellowed. 'What the fuck have you been doing all day? Sitting on your arse wanking?'

He swung the whip and the thong snapped across Lander's thigh. It was like being cut, a burning, searing pain, but he managed to avoid crying out. Something warned him that any reaction would provoke Mickey further. He hobbled away from the brick pile, Mickey swinging the whip ominously behind him.

Back in the shed, Magda bathed his hands again. This time she had what looked like an old tea towel and she used it to dab them. Lander sat on a hay bale, his palms and fingers screaming and his leg throbbing from the whiplash. When she'd finished the bathing she went to her own hay pile, rummaged in it and came back with a small jar. She opened the lid and held it out to him.

'What is it?'

'It's skin cream. Take some and rub it into your hands. Gently.'

Lander extended a finger, loaded it with the cream and applied it to his palms. It smarted, but it also soothed.

Magda went back to her pile and returned with something else. 'Here, take these,' she said. Lander was astonished at what she was holding out to him: it was a pair of gloves, made of black leather. He tried one of them. It was small and a tight fit, but the cream helped him slide it on. Once in place it seemed to hold everything together and definitely helped with the soreness. If he wore these he'd be able to handle the bricks more easily. He was touched.

'Where did you get this stuff?' he said.

'I stole it. From Edna.'

'Who's Edna?'

'She's Mickey's woman. The old tart with the ginger hair. My job is to help her in the kitchen and around the house. That's what I do when you're working on the bricks. I found them in a drawer in their bedroom.'

'Won't she know they're gone?'

'Edna? Never. She's rarely on this planet, and if she does notice she'll blame Mickey. Don't let him see them, though.'

'No, of course not. Thank you,' said Lander. 'Thank you for everything – for bathing my hands, sharing the food, and for the cream and the gloves.'

Magda smiled. It was the first time he'd seen her do that. Her teeth were yellow but the smile was warm. 'You're welcome,' she said.

Lander thought it might be a good moment to get answers to some of the things that had been chasing each other around in his head. 'Is there only Mickey and Edna? Does anyone else live here?'

'Do you think anyone else could stand it? No, just those two. And us.'

'Yes, and us. How long have you been here?'

She pointed to some tally marks, scratched in groups of five on the side of the shed near her hay pile. There looked to be a lot of them.

'Sixty-one days,' she said.

'My God,' said Lander. He looked at her. Two months of this and he'd be like her, and she would probably be gone.

'We've got to get out of here,' he said.

'Don't I know it. I've been thinking about that ever since I got here, and I have a plan. I think you arriving might be just the distraction I need.'

Lander wanted to ask her what her plan was but he was prevented by Mickey's evening visit. This time there were two bowls.

'See? I've taken pity on you,' he said to Lander. 'Though fuck knows why. Well, what do you say?' He advanced on Lander with the whip poised.

Lander put his hands behind his back to hide the gloves. 'Thank you,' he said.

'Thank you who?'

'Thank you, Mickey.'

'I should fucking think so. You just make sure you work your balls off tomorrow, else you'll feel my tickler again.' He laughed and turned away. He looked at Magda. 'You'd like to feel my tickler, wouldn't you, sweetheart?'

'Depends which tickler you mean,' said Magda, and winked at him.

'You just be ready and you'll find out,' said Mickey. His tone was heavy with innuendo, and with threat. He stared at her for a minute, then left, pulling the door closed behind him.

It was sickening, thought Lander. How could she behave like that towards someone like Mickey? He waited until he was well clear, then said, 'Does he often talk to you like that?'

Magda laughed. 'All the time. But not when Edna's around.'

'Why do you let him?'

Magda smiled again. 'I have my reasons.'

'Has he, you know?'

'What, jumped me? Don't be daft.'

Was it daft? 'Not in all the time you've been here by yourself?'

'He hasn't got the balls. I've met a lot of blokes like him. Loud. Foul mouthed. They're all the same, all talk. Besides, if he tried anything with me Edna would murder him.'

Lander had a vision of the wispy haired, thread-veined woman alongside her blustering, pig-paunched partner.

'Really?'

'You bet. She has a knife under the mattress her side of the bed, a really sharp one. Now why do you think she's got that? And why keep it there?'

It was hard to think of Mickey as a dominated husband but that was what Magda was suggesting. She sat down on the bale next to him.

'Magda. That's a German name, isn't it?' he said.

'Is it? My family's German but I was born in Swindon.'

She looked across the barn and Lander thought her eyes were watering. 'I was living in a coven, a sisterhood.'

'You mean like a convent?'

She laughed. 'No, not at all like that. It's a community of women. Don't you know about them?'

'No.'

'There are quite a few. Groups of women who've banded together so they can support and look after each other. The groups all have names. They call themselves after famous women, and they specialise in different things. There's the Nightingales, they're into health and looking after people. The Pankhursts, they're very political. The Brontës are mostly creative arts and writing types. They're making a record of everything that's happened. There are others, too. Those are just the ones I've come across.'

'And they're all women?'

'Mostly. I think some of them may have a few men who identify as women.'

'Which of them were you in?'

'None of those. I was in the Bonnies.' Lander looked blank. 'Anne Bonny was a female pirate. A couple of hundred years ago.'

'So your lot nicked stuff.'

'Not exactly. As the Infection has taken hold there's been a lot of looting. People haven't just taken what they needed, they've taken more, much more, and they've trashed the rest, like a fox in a chicken coop. We Bonnies are trying to conserve what we can. We concentrate on saving things that are either unique, or hard to make and repair. We go out looking for anything that's useful and serviceable. We have a big warehouse where we store what we've preserved, so it will be ready for when it's needed.'

'Was it raided, then? Is that how Mickey got you?'

'What, the warehouse? Oh, no. We keep that under armed guard. No, I was in a scavenging party with two other girls. I got separated, somebody banged me on the head, and the next I knew I was here. Mickey's guest.'

'A bit like me really,' said Lander. 'I was in a car, I fell asleep and he dragged me out.'

'That Mini. I know. Mickey told me.'

Lander was surprised. He hadn't thought of Mickey holding a conversation. It seemed that the relationship Magda had with Mickey was very different from Lander's.

They sat in silence on the hay bale. Lander liked Magda. At the start he'd thought she was distant, aloof, but now she was opening up he saw she wasn't like that at all. In reality she was friendly, and kind. She'd looked after him. Bringing the cream and the gloves for his hands was especially thoughtful. She should have been one of the Nightingales. He took a sideways glance, and tried to imagine her in different circumstances. Beneath the surface she was nice looking. Her nose turned up slightly and her eyes were huge and dark. But the toil and inadequate diet had taken its toll. Her face was pinched, her frame scrawny and she had spots. And she was filthy. And she smelt. He expected that he did too, and he couldn't think what he must look like in his dirty shirt, his jeans thick with brick dust and his hands in black gloves.

'Do you know that people started it?' Lander said.

'Started what?'

'The Infection, the spread of the virus. People did it on purpose. It was some kind of germ warfare thing that got out of control.'

'Where did you hear that?'

'They told me when I was in hospital in Oxford. One of the people there said the virus had been developed in a lab and released in Africa to see what would happen. They were going to try it out and then kill it off, but it got loose. It was somebody pretty high up I got this from, so I think they must be right.'

'Jesus. Who would do something like that?'

'The Russians? The Americans? The Chinese? Us?'

Magda sighed. 'People seem to spend all their time thinking up new ways to kill each other. Crazy.'

'It's not the people. It's the politicians.'

'OK, but the politicians do it because that's what the people want. That's what gets the politicians into power, and it's what keeps them there.'

'I don't think people really want to kill each other that much, do you?'

'Don't you? Try being an immigrant. You should hear some of the things my dad's been called. Kraut bastard. Russian arse licker. Fuck off back to where you came from. We had a shop, a delicatessen, and the windows were always getting smashed. A week after the Brexit vote somebody tried to set the place on fire. So some people certainly wanted to kill us. And what about Mickey? Wouldn't you like to kill him?'

Lander hadn't thought about it like that. Mickey was a cruel thief and a slave driver. He had treated him badly, and Lander would certainly like to pound him with his fists, but kill him? Although that was what Mickey was doing to them. If he carried on working them and starving them the way he was doing, they wouldn't last long. Magda was little more than skin and bone already.

There was a pause, then Magda spoke. 'Is your sister like you?

'We're twins, so yes, in a lot of ways. In others we're very different though. I'm into sport and she's not. I like computers and computer games, and that just bores the knickers off her. I'm not good at school and she's a real keeno.'

'Brainy, is she?'

'She's going to Cambridge University. Or she was.'

They sat in silence for a little longer. Lander shuddered. The night was cooler than before and there were lots of gaps in the metal cladding that let the wind through. Magda got up and dragged her chain over to her hay pile.

'You can come over here with me, if you like,' she said.

Lander hesitated.

'Nothing funny,' she said. 'I just thought you might like some company. And we can keep each other warm.'

He walked across to her and they lay down on the hay a little awkwardly, back to back. It took some adjustment to get themselves arranged around the chain. Despite the conditions, despite the ripe smell of his companion, Lander had to admit it was greatly preferable to being on his own.

'You said you've got a plan for getting out of here,' he said.

'Yes.'

'Tell me about it.'

'Maybe later,' she said, 'when I'm ready. It would probably shock you. For now, if I tell you to do something please do it. Don't stop and think about it. Just do it, even if it sounds weird.'

'Yeah. All right, if you say so.' Lander wondered what she had in mind. Mickey never came near them without his whip or a stick, and they were chained all the time. He didn't undo the loop chain until he'd got the shackles on, and vice versa. He dealt with them separately and kept them apart while he was doing so. Overcoming him seemed out of the question. But what she'd said sounded mysterious and indicated she'd certainly got something in mind. He just wished she'd tell him what it was.

He rolled over and put his arm across her. She didn't move away so they stayed like that, a pair of strays cuddling against the cold. They woke each other several times during the night, getting entangled in the chain as they turned over. At one point Lander had to get up and go to the bucket. When he came back Magda had turned over and this time she put her arm around him.

Towards dawn she nudged him.

'Hey.'

'What?' Lander felt he hadn't slept long enough and his head was fuzzy.

'Wake up. It's nearly morning. Better get back to your own bedding. If Mickey finds you over here with me he'll use his whip on you.'

'Why would he do that?'

'Don't worry about why. Just take it from me that he would.'

Lander shuffled across to his own hay on the other side of the shed, the chain dragging behind him.

'Don't forget,' Magda called over to him. 'I may do some things you think are peculiar. Just go with it, and do what I tell you.'

'Very mysterious,' said Lander.

'Promise?'

'All right.'

'Good. Because I think I can get us out of here, but it won't be pleasant.'

A little later Mickey came in to collect Magda.

SIXTEEN

MAGDA'S PLAN

WITH THE HELP of the gloves and the cream, Lander's hands improved. Magda's balm also lessened the pain in his wrists and ankles, sore from the fetters. Best of all, Mickey set him to a different task; he spent the next two days sawing logs. That was hard on the arms and shoulders but gave his hands something of a rest and the chance to heal. And it made a change from the boredom of the brick pile.

The log store was on the other side of the house, so not only did Lander get a change of scene, he was also able to see more of what went on. He caught glimpses of Magda at work. She'd hang out washing, and fetch water from the well and the trough. She opened windows and shook out mats. She waved to him when no one was looking. He also saw Mickey leave in the Mini, his huge bulk crammed behind the steering wheel, and come back a couple of hours later. He was pleased that the chickens had been turned out and that the car still worked, but resentful that Mickey should be using it.

He followed Magda's example of making a mark on the shed wall for each day he was there. He'd made six marks but it felt as though he'd been there for ever. Hunger was a constant companion, a permanent biting ache. He drank lots of water to try to lessen the pangs, but that meant he needed to use the bucket several times in the night so he never got uninterrupted sleep. He was exhausted and he wondered how long he could go on. What would Mickey do if he – if either of them – became too weak to work? He could guess.

On the morning of the seventh day he awoke at what he thought must be the usual time. Magda was snoring gently beside him and seemed dead to the world. He hurriedly got up and returned to his own hay pile to await Mickey. However, Mickey didn't appear, and Lander dropped once more into sleep.

He woke again, and this time he could tell it was late. The light coming through the broken roof was different and the shed was warm from the sun. Magda was still sleeping. He thought he must have missed something and at any minute Mickey would be there with the whip, bawling at them for not being ready. He got up, the chain rattling.

Magda looked up blearily from under the hay. 'What's up with you?'

'Look! It's late! We have to get up. Where's Mickey? What's happened?'

Magda lay on her back and stretched. 'Easy, easy,' she said. 'Don't panic. I forgot to tell you. It's day seven.'

'Day seven?'

'Yes. Sunday. Or I think it must be Sunday. Every seventh day we get the morning off. Mickey likes a lie in and he doesn't get us up till later. I should have said. I'm sorry.'

Lander felt his anxiety drain. He sighed and let himself down on the hay again.

'What happens on Sunday, then?'

'It's very civilised,' she said. 'We're allowed out to wash ourselves and our clothes in the trough in the yard. If Edna's feeling generous we might even get a bit of soap. Then we'll get some of her wonderful oatmeal. We'll be left for a bit to rake up the old hay and put it in the corner over there, and we can break open a new bale. Then we'll be taken out to work for the afternoon. At least, that's what's happened with me so far. I guess it will be the same for you.'

It was. Mickey arrived about half an hour later – it was hard for Lander to know exactly without his watch. He seemed in a buoyant mood, almost jovial, and for once he didn't have his whip with him.

'All right, you lucky people. Enjoyed your lie in? Good good good.' He undid their chain but didn't fit the shackles. 'This way then, campers.'

They followed him out of the shed and down the track to the farmyard. For the first time since he'd arrived there Lander was free of chains. The sense of liberty was wonderful; it felt like walking on air. He was thinking how he might take advantage of his unchained state when he saw, tied to the fence, a dog. It had a mean face and a lot of teeth. Rottweiler? Pit Bull? Lander wasn't well up on dogs. The only one he knew was Buster, but Buster was a lazy old Labrador; this dog looked nasty. Where had it been? He'd not noticed it around before. Mickey untied it and it looked at Lander and licked its lips, as if savouring the possibility of a juicy mouthful.

'This is Bullit,' said Mickey. 'Try anything funny and he'll bite your balls off. Or in your case, sweetheart,' he said to Magda, 'guzzle your tits. Not that you've got that much.'

'Don't worry about that, handsome,' said Magda, cocking an eyebrow at him. 'My other bits work just fine.'

'Do they now?' said Mickey. 'One day I'll have to find out. You're a bit scrawny for me, though. Nothing to get hold of. I like 'em chubbier.'

'Well whose fault is that?' said Magda. 'You'll have to feed me up. Anyway, have you never shagged a skinny girl? You'd be surprised how good we are.'

Once again Lander was uncomfortable at the smutty banter between these two. Magda seemed to encourage Mickey. Surely she didn't really enjoy this sort of stuff.

Magda had a handful of garments with her. Presumably she was going to wash these, but Lander didn't have any clothes other than the ones he was wearing.

'Here,' said Mickey. 'You might as well have this back.' He had Lander's hold-all and he threw it towards him. 'All this clobber's too poncy for me. Won't fit me anyway.'

Lander opened the hold-all. Its contents had been turned over, but it was still full.

'Get your kit off and get cracking,' said Mickey. 'The missus has donated some soap.' There was the slimy looking end of a bar on the edge of the trough. 'I'm going for a shit. Bullit'll be here to look after you. If you try to leave this yard he'll have you.'

He ambled away to the house. From an upper window Edna regarded them, one hand holding back the curtain. She looked angry, her thin face drawn into a beak so she had the appearance of a bird of prey staring down at them. She let the curtain fall back and disappeared from view.

Bullit had been left untied and watched them closely, its teeth slightly bared. Magda patted its head and the dog wagged its tail.

'Do you know this brute?'

'He's all right. He lives in the house mostly and he's supposed to be protection for Edna when Mickey's out. He's right, though. If you do something unexpected he'll go for you. Now I'm going to take my clothes off, so turn your back.'

Lander had lost count of the number of times he'd seen Magda use the bucket, and for the past five nights he'd slept alongside her, so her coyness now seemed unnecessary. Nevertheless, he did what she told him. There was a sharp intake of breath – the water must be freezing – and the sound of splashing, the smell of soap.

'Well you are a good boy,' said Magda. 'You can turn round now.'

She was sitting on the edge of the trough. She'd put on a fresh t-shirt and jeans, and she was drying her hair on a threadbare towel. She held it out to him.

'Here, you'll have to share this. It obviously hasn't dawned on Edna that there are two of us now. I've tried not to get it too wet. Don't get it dirty though, it's me what has to do the washing.'

Lander took the towel. It was a sorry object, the fabric so thin that in places it was almost transparent. He wondered why there was nothing better. He remembered the soft cotton ones their Mam liked so much, and the ones in the house in Snaith. There must be thousands of towels in hundreds of places. Why hadn't Mickey helped himself to some new ones? Why make do with this old thing, even for people he was using as slaves?

He took off his shirt and jeans and dropped them on the yard. There was no point washing them, they were gone. He got into the trough. It was perishing, but the sensation of the water was so good he put up with the cold. He splashed himself with water and lathered himself. He rubbed the stubble on his face. He hadn't shaved since Oxford and wished he could now. He rubbed soap into his hair. Magda didn't turn her back but watched him.

'Do you really like all that stuff?' he said.

'All what stuff?'

'That stuff with Mickey. The way he talks to you. The way you answer him, all that sexy shit. Why do you go along with it?'

'You jealous or something?'

'No, of course not. Although I don't mean you're not attractive or anything. I mean... I...' Lander petered out in confusion.

Magda laughed. 'I'm teasing.' She came closer and lowered her voice. 'Mickey's a slob and he turns my guts, but I'm encouraging him for a reason. Just remember what I said.'

Lander rinsed his hair and climbed out of the trough. He rubbed himself down, put on some clothes from the hold-all, and sat beside Magda. He closed his eyes. It was wonderful just to sit there in fresh clothes, slowly drying off in the autumn sunshine, not having to work, not needing to be fearful of Mickey suddenly arriving and expressing with his whip his dissatisfaction with the amount or quality of what he'd done.

It didn't last long. Too soon Bullit jumped up, wagging his tail, and Mickey came out of the house. He looked even grumpier than usual. He didn't say anything, but took them back to the shed, fitted the shackles and directed them to their labours, Magda to the house and Lander to the log pile.

That evening Lander was taken off work later than usual. He had no way of knowing the exact time but he could tell by the sun that it was well after the time Mickey normally came for him, and he was wondering if he'd been forgotten and, if so, how he'd get through the night.

That's the way it goes, he thought. You get the morning off but you have to work late to make up for it. So much for Mickey being generous.

Mickey did come for him, but he seemed flustered and preoccupied. He didn't take Lander back to the usual shed but instead led him to a smaller brick building on the other side of the track.

'Where's this?'

'It's your new fucking mansion, squire,' said Mickey. 'I can't have you two fuck buddies together anymore, so you're in here now.'

Mickey left Lander's work fetters in place and padlocked them to an iron rod bolted to the wall. Then he left, and locked the door.

Lander stood in the semi darkness, taking stock. Obviously Mickey didn't want him in the big shed with Magda, but why not? He had a nasty feeling that this new arrangement was because Mickey was up to something, and he had a good idea what that might be. He was fearful for Magda. She wasn't strong, and was certainly no match for Mickey.

There were no haybales but there was some sacking on the floor. The arrangement with the fetters and the rod meant that Lander couldn't lie down. The best he could do was lean with his back against the wall, his arms held awkwardly above him. However, after a few minutes they began to ache and he had to stand up again. Then his legs hurt and he needed to squat. Then his thighs cramped and he was forced to keep up a constant fidget to ease the discomfort. How long would Mickey leave him here? Surely not all night. Probably until he'd finished what Lander suspected he wanted to do with Magda. Would she really let him? How would he react if she tried to stop him? He did his best to push these thoughts aside. He was in no position to affect what happened in the shed, but he made a promise that if Mickey hurt Magda he'd make him pay.

Would there be any supper? Mickey's got more than catering on his mind, Lander thought ruefully. He was so hungry that even the cabbage soup and stale bread would have been welcome. Time went by. This place was in better repair than the cowshed and only a little light got in from the outside, but night came and even that faded.

Lander waited in the dark, wondering what was going to happen. Was this part of the plan Magda had mentioned? What was she doing and how was it going to help them? He tried to make himself comfortable on the sacking but there was no chance of sleep. Even if he could lie down, a wind had sprung up and there was a persistent rattle from the roof flapping and the shed door shaking.

It was well into the night when he heard a key in the lock. Supper at last, he thought. Mickey must have finished. But it wasn't Mickey. The wind snatched the door open and it was Magda. She had a hurricane lamp.

'Come on,' she said. 'Hurry up.'

She was trembling and seemed tearful. Her clothing was smeared with dark blotches.

'Is it Mickey? What's the bastard done?'

She didn't answer, but fiddled with some keys on what looked like Mickey's bunch. After three or four tries she found the one that unlocked Lander's wrist, and then the one for his ankle. The chain dropped away and he rubbed his sore limbs. He could barely stand and she helped him up. Then he saw what the dark blotches were.

'My God, you're bleeding. Are you hurt? What's happened? Where's Mickey?'

'Mickey's in the shed.'

'Jesus. How did you get his keys? Is he asleep? Won't he wake up?'

Magda shook her head and her voice cracked. 'No, Mickey won't ever wake up. I've killed him. Mickey's dead.'

MAGDA DIDN'T SPEAK. Perhaps she couldn't. Lander wanted to know what had happened in the shed but she didn't answer. She seemed catatonic, staring fixedly through the windscreen and hardly moving, except that every few minutes she would have a fit of trembling.

When she'd come to unlock Lander's fetters she'd been shaking, but she'd seemed in control. She helped him stand and ushered him out of the door and towards the yard, where the Mini was parked.

'Get in and let's get out of here,' she said, collapsing into the passenger seat and tossing Lander the keys.

He ached all over. His hands, his wrists, his arms and legs, his neck and back were all agonising. He doubted he'd be able to drive. He turned the key and was relieved to see that there was still plenty of fuel in the Mini's tank.

He started the engine and put the car in gear, ready to pull away, wincing at every move.

Suddenly the house door crashed open and Edna came charging out. She had a shotgun and she levelled it at them. Instinctively Lander dived across Magda and braced himself for the impact, but at that moment Bullit rushed from the house and ran at the car, leaping up at the window, claws scraping on the door, barking, snarling. Edna couldn't shoot without hitting the dog and she let the gun fall. Lander saw his chance, put his foot down and gunned the car up the track, the wheels scattering mud and grit. Once on the road he sped up, trying to get away as quickly as possible from the hell that Mickey had made for them.

He kept the car's lights on until they were well clear of the farm, then he slowed down and switched them off. There was a big moon, huge, almost full, and it was easily bright enough to drive by so long as he didn't go too fast. He didn't discuss with Magda where they were going. He'd already decided that; he was taking her to his home, back to Paradise Farm, back to Kerryl. If she was still there.

Magda was drained. He couldn't imagine what had gone on in the shed, or how this slight woman had got the better of the strong, powerfully built Mickey. What exactly had happened? She said Mickey was dead? How did she know? What did she do? Was she sure? He didn't know whether it was best to talk to her or to say nothing. He stole a sideways look at her. The moonlight drained the colours so it was not easy to see whether what covered her was mud or blood, but he suspected it was the latter. He'd seen in the lights from the house the crimson and brown on her face, her hands, her arms, her clothes. One side of her, the side nearest him, seemed to be soaked, with dark patches on her t-shirt and jeans. He had a sudden and alarming thought. He'd assumed that this was Mickey's blood, but suppose it was hers. Suppose she was bleeding to death beside him. He slammed on the breaks and the car slid to a stop.

'Are you all right? Are you bleeding?'

Magda shook her head. Which question was she answering?

'Are you all right?' he repeated.

She nodded.

'Not bleeding?'

She shook her head.

'Tell me what happened.'

That was the trigger. She began to cry, quiet sobs at first, and then it was as if a dam had burst. She let out a shuddering howl and there was a torrent of tears. She cried as though her world had ended. Lander wrapped her in his arms and held her until the shaking stilled and the yowl subsided to a whimper. Gradually, slowly, she became quiet. He stroked her hair. It felt matted and sticky.

She pulled herself away from him and wiped her nose on the backs of her hands. There was a box of tissues Maisie had given him on the back seat and Lander pulled out a handful and gave them to her. She blew her nose loudly and sniffed.

'I'm sorry,' she said. 'I don't usually cry. I'm not one of those girls who blubs all the time.' She sniffed again. 'It's just that I've never killed anybody before. I'm not used to it.' She smiled ruefully.

Lander had expected Mickey to clear out or trash everything in the car, but he hadn't. There was some chicken manure, but that was the only damage. The rug and two big water bottles Maisie had given him for his journey were still there.

'Here, get that shirt and your jeans off. You can clean up and then you can tell me about it.'

Lander helped pull her t-shirt over her head. It was wet and stiffening. He threw it out of the window. She got out of the car, took off her jeans and dropped them beside the shirt. She wasn't wearing any pants and she started to shiver again.

Lander took one of the water bottles. 'Sorry, this'll be cold,' he said.

He tipped water over her, while she dabbed at the bloody marks with the shirt. Then he helped her wrap herself in the blanket and get back into the car. He rinsed his own hands and got behind the wheel again. She was still shaking and he turned up the heater.

'I'm going to need some clothes,' she said.

'Yes. We're going to where you can get some.'

It was easy to find the way. The place names on the signposts were now ones that Lander recognised, and he knew where he was going. Once he saw lights moving along a side road, but apart from that there was no traffic. None of the houses they passed or saw in the distance were showing any signs of life. All the streetlights were out.

There was so much Lander wanted to know, but he didn't want to start her crying again. He couldn't imagine what it must be like to actually kill somebody. He'd tried to when he'd held the gun and looked at Spencer. He'd seen plenty of fictional killings in the cinema and on TV. He'd blasted countless humans and aliens on his XBox, scattering blood, bone and body parts over screen after screen. He'd seen some real deaths on the TV too, news reports from war torn areas. And of course he'd shot animals – pests, an unwanted bull calf, usually as a mercy to end suffering, very occasionally for fun. Mickey was an animal, but could Lander have killed him? He didn't know, and he was in awe of Magda's courage in taking him on.

'I never thought it would be so hard,' she said. Her voice was so quiet that Lander could only just hear her over the noise of the engine and the rumble of the tyres.

'I bet,' he said. 'I don't know how you screwed yourself up to do it.'

She made a sort of hissing noise. 'I don't mean that,' she said. 'I wanted to kill him. He was a bastard. He was brutal, he was working and starving us to death and he was trying to rape me. He deserved it. I've wished him dead a thousand times and I'm glad he is. What I mean is that I didn't know it would be so hard to make him dead.'

Lander waited for her to go on.

'I've been prick teasing him, you know that. That's what all that mucky talk was about. Thanks to his hard rations I don't have the figure I once had so I can't pretend I was mega-tempting, but I figured that if all Mickey had was Edna he wouldn't turn his nose up at an easy fuck. I knew that sooner or later he'd come to the shed. So I stole the knife from under Edna's mattress. I knew I didn't have long because she'd miss it, so I ramped up the tempting. I was hoping he'd try it with you there in the shed, make you watch. Then you could have helped me. But he didn't. He locked you in the other shed and then he came to me. There was no messing, he just took his pants down and got on top of me. I tried to make him stop, told him I needed time, wanted to do it properly, but he wouldn't. I panicked then, because I couldn't reach the knife where I'd hidden it under the hay, but after wriggling around a bit I got my fingers on it. I stabbed him. He didn't stop, though, just kept on pounding, so I stabbed him again. The knife was slippery and my fingers slid down the handle and I cut myself. I think I shrieked and that was when he pulled out of me, so I stabbed him again, three or four times in the neck. He was twisting about and swearing at me and it was hard to hit him properly. He got his hands around my throat and started squeezing. I thought I was going to pass out and I kept jabbing at him with the knife. Then it skidded out of my hand and I thought that was the end, he'd strangle me, but all of a sudden his hands slackened and he went limp. I got myself out from under him and felt for his pulse, but his neck was just a mass of blood. There was no pulse. He was dead.'

'Oh My God,' said Lander. Half way through Magda's speech he'd stopped the car and turned off the engine. It was hard to comprehend the horror of the situation: the two of them wrestling in the shed, then Mickey lying there in a pool of his own blood. 'Jesus, what a nightmare. Are you all right? Did he hurt you?'

'Yeah, a bit, you know, going in when I wasn't properly ready. And my throat hurts, especially when I swallow. And my fingers are sore where I cut them, and I've got some bruises. But no, I'm all right really. Just glad it's over, that's all.'

Lander sat for some time, still struggling with the enormity of what Magda had faced, what she'd done.

'Thank you,' he said. 'For getting me out too. It was a good job he had his keys with him.'

'I knew he would. He always kept them on his belt, he never went anywhere without them. The car keys were a lucky break, though. I thought they might be in the house and we'd have to face Edna and the dog to get them, but they were in his pocket.'

Lander started the engine again.

'Where are we going?' Magda asked.

'I'm taking you to where I live. It's remote, so we'll be safe there. You can meet my sister.'

Lander drove on. Neither of them spoke, and he thought perhaps Magda was sleeping again when she clutched his arm.

'Stop here,' she said.

'Here? What for?'

'I need to pee. Quickly. Here,' she said and shook his arm again.

They were beside a war memorial in the centre of a village, a tall cross with the statue of a soldier at its base.

'It's too conspicuous,' said Lander. 'Can you wait while we go on a bit? I'll find you a field.'

'No,' said Magda, with surprising intensity. 'No. I can't wait. It's got to be here.'

Lander didn't want to seem insensitive. It might be some woman's thing, a reaction to what had happened to her.

'All right, if you must,' he said.

Magda gathered the blanket around her and went behind the memorial. She reappeared a few moments later.

'Better?' said Lander.

'Loads,' she said.

He drove on. It wasn't until later that he realised how significant that stop had been.

EIGHTEEN

HOME

LANDER WAS NOT surprised that Magda slept for the rest of the journey. The driving was easy, even though he had to rely on the moonlight, and the Mini was going well. He loved that little car. In another hour they were entering the bottom of the valley and heading towards Walbrough. They'd be at the farm in half an hour.

He had told Magda that he was taking her to meet his sister, but he was not sure she was there. For as long as he could remember he and Kerryl had always known what was happening to the other. It wasn't telepathy or anything like that; neither could tell what their twin was thinking. It was more a matter of feelings, an awareness of the other's mood, an emotional resonance. When Kerryl was being bullied at school during what Gran called her 'puppy-fat days', he had known she was going through something that was hurting her and he'd helped her to deal with it. And when their Mam had put her foot down to stop him from going to the Yorkshire Cricket Academy, only Kerryl really understood how desperately unhappy that made him. They had a constant, low-level connection with each other, in the background but always there. Except not now. Now it was as if he was on one end of a phone call but he'd lost the connection. It had been like that since Adam had vanished back in Oxford, and he couldn't help thinking that the two things were connected.

The valley road was a narrow funnel with only limited avenues of escape and he'd been anxious about the possibility of running into a patrol, but there was nothing. He felt a moment's trepidation when he reached the spot where he'd met the BMW, but the road was empty.

Day was breaking as they drove into Walbrough. The town was far worse than when he'd left it. The damage then had been serious, but now the devastation was complete. There were signs of the start of a clean-up – rubbish had been bulldozed into piles, a few of the gaping shop windows boarded over – but there was a huge amount still to be done. Nothing seemed usable any more. Would it ever be put right? Granddad would have said not. Lander could imagine it now, him grumbling that 'them buggers in the south' would be too busy mending things in London to bother with a place like Walbrough.

They passed the market square. There was what looked to be a llama by the drinking fountain, abandoned and bewildered. Further on there were goats in the park, and a few sheep were lying in the middle of the main road. They moved grudgingly to let the Mini pass. And there was the usual complement of dogs, bad tempered and starving, worrying at one of the rubbish heaps, tearing at anything they thought they might be able to eat. A single dog ambled over to the car. It was so big it could look at them on a level through the Mini's window. There was foamy, yellow spittle around its muzzle, but it didn't look aggressive. Lander wasn't prepared to chance it, and he drove on.

Magda was still asleep when he turned up the lane to the farm, but the bumpy road woke her.

'Where are we?'

'Nearly there.'

'What, at your farm?'

'Yes. It's not much further, just up this hill.'

'I'm a mess,' Magda said, trying to smooth her hair. 'I should have cleaned up to meet your posh sister.'

'You mean put on something from your wardrobe full of gowns? Anyway, Kerryl's not posh.'

'You said she was going to Cambridge.'

'Yes. Was. Anyway, she might not be here.'

'Oh.' Magda sounded disappointed. 'Why's that?' And then, 'Are you all right?'

Lander nodded, although actually he was feeling a dread that grew worse as they reached the top of the hill. What would he find? Their grandparents were dead; was Kerryl too? Was that why he no longer felt any connection with her? And if she was there, how would she greet him after he'd walked out on her?

At last he could see the farm house across the fields, the grey stone bathed in the amber glow of the rising sun. There was a horse in the paddock. It was Joey! Lander's heart leapt. Kerryl must be there, she must be all right.

He stopped the car by the field gate and whistled. Joey ambled over, looking pleased to see them, and Lander stroked his neck and his muzzle. When he looked at the animal more closely he could see that he needed some attention. In normal times Kerryl brushed Joey most days until his coat shone, but now it was dull, and his mane and tail were tangled. He had an open gash on his leg. It was weeping, and a magnet for flies. Kerryl would never allow Joey to get like this. Lander's sick feeling grew. She couldn't be there.

The dread got worse when he drove into the farmyard. The place didn't look like his home. It was a mess. There were two bin bags which had been tipped over and their contents strewn about. There were empty cartons, tin cans and plastic all over the cobbles. In the corner there was a heap of empty bottles. A couple of windows had been broken and covered with cardboard. Some of it had gone soggy and showed the jagged glass beneath. The clutter and disorder were completely out of character with the tidy Kerryl. There was another oddity: a battered looking Lambretta was propped against the wall of the barn.

'Jesus,' said Lander. 'It's a dump. It's as bad as Mickey's place.'

The back door of the house had been smashed, and crudely repaired with scraps of plywood. They'd not even been sawn to fit, but just snapped off and fixed with duct tape.

'Stay here,' said Lander, getting out of the car. 'There might be trouble. I need to find out what's going on.'

'I'll come too.'

'What, wrapped in a blanket? Don't be daft. Stay here.'

He got out of the car and pushed the house door. It opened, creaking loudly. It was dark inside, but there was enough light from the door to see where he was going. He tried a light switch, but nothing happened. The house was as untidy as the yard, and it smelt. There were spills on the kitchen worktops, dirty pots in the sink, clothes on the floor. Somebody was living here, but it wasn't Kerryl.

The front room wasn't as bad as the kitchen but it hadn't been cleaned in ages. There was thick dust on every surface and a smear of mud on the carpet. There was a black plastic vase on the mantelpiece. He recognised the urn that contained their Mam's ashes. He could remember collecting it from Walbrough after her cremation. It was only a few months ago, but it felt as though it had been in another life. Next to the urn were two white cardboard boxes with something written on their lids. He read the inscriptions; they were the names of their grandparents, the dates of their births, and of their deaths. So here it was, proof that what Adam had told him was right. Gran and Granddad really were gone. But where was Kerryl? Had she been here when they'd died? She must have been, because who else would have collected these boxes and put them there? He felt a stab of anger. Why had these things been left on the mantelpiece? Why weren't their grandparents' ashes in proper urns instead of these tatty boxes? Why hadn't they been laid properly to rest? But then he remembered that he was in no position to complain; he'd walked out, and something awful must have happened to Kerryl to prevent her from dealing with them.

'Oy. What do you think you're doing?'

The shout startled him. There was a figure silhouetted in the doorway to the hall. It was a boy, about his own age and he was pointing a shotgun at him. Lander could see it was one of Granddad's Purdeys. He was worried that the guy might not know what he was doing and might fire it by accident, so he raised his hands and very slowly backed away. The gunman came into the room and looked hard at Lander.

'Hey, I know you,' he said. 'Aren't you Kerryl's brother?' He lowered the gun.

'Yes. And I know you, too. Didn't Kerryl used to go out with you once? Steve?'

'Yeah. Lander. Hey, dude. Good to see you.'

Lander winced as Steve let the gun fall to the floor and grabbed him in a rough hug.

'What are you doing here?' said Lander, untangling himself.

He was annoyed, partly because of Steve treating his Granddad's expensive gun so carelessly, but mainly because he guessed that the mess in the house and the yard was down to Steve.

'Hey, where you been, man?' said Steve, patting him on the arm. 'Nobody was here so I came in. I'm crashing. You don't mind, do you?'

'Where's Kerryl?'

Steve looked uneasy. 'She's not here. The place was empty when I got here.'

Kerryl not here. Then where was she? He wanted to ask but he was afraid of what might be the answer. He went to the window and pulled back the curtain. 'Jesus, you allergic to daylight or something? Anyway, the last I heard of you was that you were partying in Bradford.'

'Oh, yeah,' said Steve. He looked rather shamefaced. 'The "Death's Door" thing.'

'That was it. What happened? What are you doing here?'

'Oh, you know. It was great while it lasted. There was loads of people there and some top DJs – RAM40, Punk Daddy, Dr Acid. We were all chilling and popping pills, and smoking, and there was loads of shagging. Not me,' he added quickly, 'but pretty much everybody else was doing it, right out in the open.'

'Sounds wonderful.'

Steve didn't pick up Lander's sarcasm. 'Yeah, it was, but then people started getting sick, the virus. Some of them got it really bad, right there, and that freaked people out so much they took off. At the end there were just a few of us left and it went tits up, know what I mean? I'd been messaging Kerryl until the system went down, sending her pics and that. I wanted her to come over but she said she didn't fancy it, so when I left Bradford I came to look for her.'

There was a voice from behind them.

'I'm Magda.'

She was standing in the doorway, still in her blanket. Steve did the proverbial double take.

'Holy fuck. What happened to you?' he said.

'A long story,' said Lander. 'What she needs now is a shower and some clothes.'

'There's hot water,' said Steve. 'Loads of it. The solar panels still seem to work fine for that. I expect Kerryl's clothes are where they always were. I've nicked some of yours, but I haven't touched hers.' He sniggered.

Lander didn't know Steve and wondered whether he was going to like him. He'd certainly made himself at home.

Lander showed Magda where the bathroom was, and Kerryl's bedroom. He told her to help herself to Kerryl's things. He was sure she wouldn't mind – if she came back, that is. It was a jolt to see his sister's room again. It was clean and neat, and looked as though she might have only just left it. There were her posters and pictures on the wall, her books on the shelves. There were some magazines, and a box of moviesticks. There was make-up and other goodies on the dressing table, including a bottle of perfume. It was Eau d'Amour, their Mam's favourite. He and Kerryl had given it to her last Christmas.

Last Christmas. How long ago that was. Last Christmas was another life. The Infection had been hardly known then, just a rumour from a faraway land that most of the time didn't even merit a news tailpiece. What would they all have done if they'd known what was going to happen? Lander remembered asking their Granddad this question and he'd said he'd have set off for the Scottish islands, the Outer Hebrides. 'Safest place,' he'd said. 'Pull up the drawbridge and wait till it's all over.' Would they have done that? It's easy to think so now, but leaving everything behind, would they? Is that what Kerryl had done? Had she thought that if her twin could take off, so could she? Should he look for her in Scotland?

'What happened to her?' said Steve as Lander came back downstairs, leaving Magda in the bathroom. 'She looks as though she's been in a fight.'

'She has in a way,' said Lander. 'She had a run-in with an animal.' He supposed that was fairly accurate, and if Magda wanted Steve to know more she'd tell him.

'Fuck, I'd like to have seen that. There's blood all over her.'

'Yeah, well. She's washed some of it off. You should have seen her before. Anyway, you said Kerryl wasn't at home when you got here. Where's she gone?'

Steve looked uncomfortable.

'I need to tell you a few things,' he said. 'About what happened and why I came here.' He sat on the edge of the kitchen table. 'There was this mate of mine at Death's Door, and he said that if anything happened to him I could have his Lambretta. Well it did, happen to him I mean, so I took the Lambretta and I headed here. We, me and Kerryl, got on really well when we was going out – I don't know why she dumped me, but she got off with that big jerk Mark Radshaw, the one with the flash car. Anyway, I was at Death's Door and we was messaging, and neither of us seemed to be getting the Infection, so I thought we could get together. Like I said, I wanted Kerryl to join me but she wouldn't, so I thought I'd come here. Know what I mean?'

Lander knew why Kerryl had dropped Steve. She'd told him it was because he was a knob head. But maybe she'd changed her mind. Or perhaps she was just lonely. When most of the friends you've known are dead your standards are bound to drop somewhat. He wanted Steve to get on with the story.

'So you came here, and smashed the door in,' he said.

'No, easy, man. I didn't do that. That was not me.'

'Who was it then?'

'Well, I was on the Lambretta and I was just coming out of Walbrough when a helicopter came over, real low. I thought it might have spotted me but I was under the trees and it went straight over. Know what I mean? Anyway, I watched it go up to the edge of the moor and it landed. There's a load of big rocks up there, and it landed near them.'

'The Bride Stones,' said Lander.

'Yeah, well, it landed there and some guys got out, but I couldn't see what they was doing so I carried on up the hill. When I got nearer to the farm I could see there was something kicking off. There was a couple of army vehicles in the yard. There was a Toyota Avatar, like the patrols use, and another, much bigger, like an ambulance but khaki. Anyway, I was watching them when this car came flying up the track. It was a low sports jobby, and it was bouncing on the bumps like tits on a trampoline. I bet he fucked his suspension right royally, know what I mean? Anyway, it was a good job I'd got the Lambretta off the track or he'd have seen me.'

Lander was getting impatient. 'So where was Kerryl?'

'I'm getting to that. I hid the Lambretta and went up the side of the field and when I got nearer I found a spot where I could see what was going on. The helicopter took off and went off in the direction of Manchester. Then a bunch of dudes came down from the moor and went off in the Avatar. After a bit some more came out of the house, all in bio gear, and they went in the ambulance. The sports car was still in the yard but there was no sign of the driver so I moved in. It was unlocked, and the dumb dude had left his briefcase on the passenger seat. So I took it. I mean, he'd smashed your door in, hadn't he? And anyway, it was the fucking government, wasn't it?'

Steve paused, as if waiting for Lander's approval.

'For Christ's sake, what has this got to do with where Kerryl's gone?'

'Ah, well, this briefcase. There was nothing much in it, a few government papers, all official like, and some personal stuff. And these.'

Steve opened a drawer and took out two notebooks. One was purple and one was green. 'They'll tell you what's happened to your sister,' he said. 'Better than I can.'

Lander knew the books were Kerryl's. He'd seen them before, seen her writing in them.

'You might want to read them on your own,' Steve said.

'Why?'

'You just might, that's all.'

Lander felt a twinge of anxiety. Steve was hiding something. He took the notebooks upstairs.

His room was very much as he'd left it, except tidier. His clothes had been put away and the shelves straightened. The USB stick he'd taped to the wall was gone, so Kerryl must have found it. His laptop was on his bedside table. He'd told her she could have it because he thought it might be useful to her, but she'd not taken it. She'd once told him that she liked the physical process of writing things out by hand. Really? Nuts! Writing was a pain, and anything that made it easier got his vote every time.

He sat on his bed and put the two notebooks beside him. He knew they were diaries, and because of that he knew they'd be special. One of the worst rows he'd ever had with Kerryl had been when she'd caught him looking at one of her diaries. He hadn't meant any harm, he'd done it without thinking. But she'd accused him of prying and had said what she'd written was private, and the row had gone on for a long time. So he was wary of these books now, and of what they would tell him about his sister.

He opened the green notebook. It was filled with Kerryl's handwriting, page after tumbling page, all in her neat script. At one point she'd changed the colour of her pen, but apart from that the pages were all the same. There were no doodles, no sketches, just words. Pasted into the purple book were some of the press cuttings he'd given her about the Infection.

On the flyleaf of the purple book Kerryl had written 'You should read this one first'. So he did.

LANDER SKIPPED MOST of the purple book which covered the build-up to the Infection arriving at their home because he'd been there, although he remembered some of what had happened differently from the way Kerryl described it. He felt guilty when he got to the part after their Mam died. And the feeling of loneliness that came through from her account after he'd gone brought a lump to his throat.

It was as he went through the green diary that his anger grew. He reached the end and read Kerryl's last words, and slumped forward on his chair. The notebook dropped from his hand. He stayed there immobile, while rage built inside him until the dam burst and he exploded. He jumped up, tipping his chair over. He let out a howl, picked up his laptop and brought it down hard on the stone window sill; and again – three, four, five times – demolishing the case on the granite. He looked at the mangled wreck and dropped it. He picked up one of his most important treasures, the ball from the cricket match with Derbyshire. He looked at it for a moment, then ran down the stairs, taking them two at a time, out into the yard and hurled it, as if throwing in from the boundary. He watched the scarlet sphere rise in an arc, hang for an instant, then fall. It hit a rock and bounced into the heather. He wiped his eyes with his sleeve and walked back towards the house.

It was Adam. Adam had done this. Adam was the reason why Kerryl wasn't here.

'The fucker,' he snarled. 'The total, complete bastard.'

He went to the front room and slumped down on the sofa, facing the urn and the boxes of ashes on the mantelpiece. There should be some for Kerryl. Where was she? What had they done with her?

He tried to piece together exactly what had happened. At first in Oxford Adam had kept him up to date with events on the farm. Then his accounts became more vague. Lander pressed him for details, and he had confessed to setting-up "little puzzles" for Kerryl to solve to see how she would respond. But sabotaging the turbine that provided her electricity? Letting out her chickens so she lost one of her food supplies? Come on! And then there was what Lander could plainly see was an eating disorder. Kerryl had had problems with food before. At one time she'd been quite tubby. As she'd grown older she'd become more conscious of her figure, but she always found managing her weight difficult and she would see-saw between obsessive dieting and letting herself go. It seemed that the strain of extreme loneliness had driven the whole business completely out of hand and she had become totally fixated on her weight.

Why hadn't Adam done anything about what he must have seen was happening? He'd promised he would look after her. Lander couldn't work out from the diary exactly how Kerryl had died, but he was damn sure something could have been done to prevent it. Might she have imagined some of what went on? Did Adam really do all the stuff she described? No wonder he'd scuttled off like a rat, rather than face Lander with the news.

He lay back and took deep breaths, forcing himself to calm down. Smashing things wouldn't achieve anything. He needed to compose himself, and focus.

Magda came in. 'Penny for them,' she said.

Lander shrugged. 'Maybe they're not worth that much. I was thinking about that fucker I was with in Oxford, the one I told you about who was conducting the tests.'

She sat down on the couch beside him and tucked up her legs. He caught a whiff of Eau d'Amour; She smelt very different from the way she had in the shed. She looked different too.

'Adam, you said his name was.'

'Yes.'

'What about him?'

'I want to kick the shit out of him.'

'Why?'

Lander raced upstairs, got the green notebook and tossed it on the sofa beside her.

'Read that. Then you'll see why.'

———

It was well into the following day before Lander saw Magda again. During this time he continued to seethe. His sister had been used, and so had he. Adam was responsible for her death; would he have got rid of him too? His first impulse had been to go to Oxford and beat Adam to a pulp. He still wanted to do that, but he also wanted to know why he'd done what he had. What sort of a sick pervert would stand by and watch a girl kill herself?

Then he had some more thoughts, and these were extremely uncomfortable because they concerned his own behaviour. He, Lander, was guilty too. If he hadn't left, if he'd not become obsessed with some internet garbage but stayed at the farm with Kerryl so that they faced the isolation together, there would be no Adam, either real or imagined, and his twin would still be alive.

Whatever, he needed to get to Oxford and confront Adam. The problem was, how? He had only the vaguest idea of the situation nationwide. He'd seen evidence of some attempts to tidy up and get things working again, but they were few. There was chaos everywhere and repairs would take a long time. And who would do them? Most of the people you'd expect to be working on this sort of thing were dead. He'd been held by Mickey for two weeks and nothing seemed to have changed in that time. There was still no mains electricity. Lander could charge his phone from the power generated by the wind turbine or the solar panels, but he couldn't find a cellular network and there was no internet. He checked these obsessively, because he assumed that whatever government there was would give the highest priority to things like that. The only sign of anything organised was a single FM radio station, all bland music, with a recorded announcement every few minutes saying that the Provisional Government was working to restore services as soon as possible, and listeners should remain where they were and stay tuned for further information and instructions.

The big issue in getting to Oxford was transport. It must still be illegal to travel. The Infection had petered out but the authorities wouldn't want people going around and risking spreading it again. If he were simply to set off down the M1 he was sure he'd be stopped. He might find himself back in jail. He guessed the powers that be would want to keep a handle on who went where, at least to begin with.

On the positive side, Steve had laid in a good stock of provisions. Or perhaps that was Kerryl. Or maybe even their Gran, who never liked to see an empty larder. There wasn't any fresh stuff, but there were lots of tins and packets. The turbine had kept the fridge and freezer working, and there was cheese (but no milk), and frozen sausages, burgers, pizzas, lasagne, peas, and various vegetables. Naturally, he couldn't take the cold provisions with him, but he could stoke up before he left.

He went out to the yard and examined the Mini. It seemed none the worse for its stay at Mickey's, although there were a few feathers around and chicken shit on the rear seat. Thankfully the two petrol cans he'd got when Maisie had given him the car were still in the back and still full. The Mini was frugal, and there would be easily enough in the cans to get him to Oxford. That was good, because filling up on the way probably wouldn't be possible.

He went into the barn. The stalls where their few cows had been were empty, but the honeyed smell of hay remained, a bitter-sweet reminder of past times. When he and Kerryl were kids they used to play in there, jumping from the loft onto the soft piles of fodder. It was here that their Mam had died. When she got ill she had insisted on moving into the barn so as not to infect the rest of them. Granddad had fixed up a bed for her. Lander could remember looking at her from the doorway, and sounding off at Kerryl for getting too close. Maybe it was Kerryl who had carried the germs into the house and infected their grandparents. He couldn't bear that idea and he forced the thought away.

Their Land Rover was at the far end of the barn. The keys were under the seat where they were always kept. It was almost empty of fuel but it didn't matter, he wasn't going to use it. What he was after was Granddad's battered old road atlas. He found it rammed at the bottom of the front scuttle.

He took the atlas back to the house and began to work out a route which would stick to minor roads and avoid towns. It would take much longer, but it would be far safer.

'You're going to Oxford?' It was Magda, who'd come in and was standing behind him.

'Yes.'

'Good. I think that Adam guy's a bastard. What he did to your sister was murder.'

Inexplicably Lander found himself defending Adam. 'Yes, but I don't think he meant her to die.' Lander had liked Adam and got on really well with him during the short time they'd been together. He didn't seem like a killer. But then, neither did Magda.

'All I know is that if he'd treated my sister the way he treated yours I'd be after him with a hatchet. I think you should go.'

'I am. I'm going to go find him. It's just that for now I'm giving him the benefit.' Lander was surprised. He was certainly going to challenge Adam, but why was Magda pushing so hard?

'I'll come with you,' she said.

'What?'

'I'll come with you to Oxford.'

'Why?'

'How many reasons do you need? I'm an excellent map reader. I've travelled about a lot and I'm good at finding my way around. I can do some of the driving. And despite you being such an arse, I like you. So I'll come. If you want me to, that is.'

Lander did. He'd assumed that Magda would have plans for putting her life back together and he'd expected to be going to Oxford on his own. He'd be delighted to have her with him. He put his hand over hers on his shoulder and looked up at her. Something in her eyes reached out to him. He stood up, and there was a moment's pause before she stepped into his arms. He held her. She was so bony, so skeletal there was hardly anything of her. A good squeeze would break her. He wondered again at how she'd managed to overwhelm a brute like Mickey. He turned his head and their lips met.

It was not great, but she was the first girl he'd kissed for many months. After a moment she pulled back.

'This doesn't mean anything,' she said. 'It's just for now.'

He didn't really understand her message but he said, 'Okay.' He let go of her and moved away. Then he said, 'You can show how good you are with maps by working out a route that gives a wide berth to Mickey's farm.'

'Oh, I can do that. There's no way we're going anywhere near that place. When are you planning to leave?'

'As soon as we can. As soon as we're ready. There's no point hanging around here.'

'Right. We'd better warn Steve. We'll need to take some of his food.'

Lander thought that the food would have been there before Steve arrived so wasn't actually 'his', but he let it go.

Steve was out. When he came back, his reaction to the news of their trip to Oxford was a surprise.

'I'll come too.'

'What?'

'To Oxford.'

Before Lander could answer, Magda said, 'Great. Join the party,' and gave him a hug.

Lander was torn. There was no doubt of Magda's fire and spirit, but after her imprisonment and ill treatment she was physically fragile; whereas Steve was beefy and strong. That could be useful. But there was a worry. Steve hadn't caught the Infection. What if that meant he was a dream walker? That was a worrying possibility. Steve would have to be watched. Nevertheless, it would be good to have another male with them.

'Welcome aboard,' he said.

'Great,' said Magda, and she kissed Steve on the cheek.

It was Steve's idea that they should go by boat.

'People don't realise it, but you can get almost anywhere in this country on the canals, and they're in much better nick than the roads. There'll be lots of places to hide – in tunnels, under bridges, in cuttings – and there won't be anyone else using them. There's still a ban on travel, there are notices about it all over the town. But the army and the police will be watching for vehicles, they won't be thinking about the canals.'

Lander wasn't sure. 'But don't the canals go right alongside the roads in places? I know the one in the valley does. If there was something on the canal you'd see it from the road. And what about the locks? There are hundreds of them. Won't it be obvious we're using them? Anyway, going by canal will take ages.'

'We'll travel at night mostly,' said Steve, 'and we should be able to keep up a fair speed. We'll take the Rochdale Canal and then go on to the Ashton. There are not many locks at all on the Ashton, so we'll be able to make good time there. The worst bit will be Marple locks. There are fifteen of those, but once we're through it'll be plain sailing again, straight down the Trent and Mersey to Birmingham, and then to Oxford. If we can do some of the less exposed sections in daylight too we should get there in just over a week.'

'Sounds good to me,' said Magda.

Steve's estimate was lower than Lander had expected, but even so a week was a long time. He wanted to track down Adam sooner than that if he could. Steve was making it all sound too easy, and he was suspicious. 'How come you're such an expert?' he said.

'My Mam and Dad used to do a lot of canal cruising. We even had our own barge.'

'Great,' said Magda, 'where is it?'

Steve shook his head. 'It's moored in the basin at Rochdale, but we can't use it. It's too big and noisy. There'd be much more risk of being seen in that. We need something smaller, something lighter and more manoeuvrable.'

'Right,' said Lander. Where were they going to find a boat like that?

'One good thing,' said Steve, 'is that we've got a really good engine, and it doesn't make any noise.'

'Have we?' said Lander. 'Where?'

'That bloody great horse out there in the field.'

'What, Joey?'

'Is that his name? He looks strong, and once he gets the boat moving it will be easy for him. Canals are flat. It's not as if he'll have to pull us up hills.'

'Cheap on fuel, too,' said Magda. 'He runs on grass.'

Steve left the room and Magda said, 'He seems to have this all figured out.'

Lander was more doubtful. 'I hope so. I was meaning to get to Oxford in less than a week, but I can see the sense in what he's suggesting.'

'Sounds the best way to go to me,' said Magda. 'And it will give you time to think through what you're going to do when you eventually meet up with this Adam guy.'

Steve came back with an armful of beer cans, Final Reckoning, a strong lager that was one of Lander's favourites.

'I found these in the off licence in town and I've been saving them,' he said. They popped a can each.

It seemed to be all settled. The atlas showed the canals as well as the roads, and Magda, with Steve's help, started working out a route. Lander was happy to leave them to it. He took his lager and ambled around the house and the yard, revisiting things he'd never taken much notice of when they'd all lived there. He had a sad moment behind the barn when he looked at the remains of a fire and saw charred animal bones. He knew from Kerryl's diary that they'd belonged to Buster. He also came across a board with the name Paradise Farm still just legible on it. So little had changed, but then so much had too.

He returned to Magda and Steve. They had got as far as the route around Birmingham. He took another can.

He had another lager after that. Then he and Magda found some lamb chops in the freezer. He had another lager while they thawed them out, and then another while they lit a fire in the grate and cooked them in Gran's old frying pan. Then he had one more to accompany the meal. Then he lost count.

Later he was vaguely aware of Magda helping him to bed. When he woke in the night his throat was parched and his head felt as though there was an imp inside his skull hammering to get out. He was in his mother's double bed. Magda was asleep beside him.

LANDER FELL ASLEEP again, and when he next awoke Magda had gone. He found her in the kitchen, washing up. He sat down at the table and put his head in his hands.

'Did we drink all that?' he said, surveying the litter of empty cans.

'You and Steve did.'

'Come on, Miss Goody. I saw you having some too.'

'A couple of cans, that's all,' Magda said. 'There was no way I could keep up with you two. Drinking for England, you were.'

Lander groaned. 'Did you put me to bed?'

'I did indeed.'

'Thank you. Did you have your wicked way with me?'

'Fat chance. There was absolutely nothing about you that was capable of standing up last night. Now, how about a full English breakfast? Sausages, greasy bacon, fried eggs, fried bread, black pudding...'

'No, don't,' Lander protested, his stomach heaving at the thought.

'OK.' She laughed. 'We don't have any of that stuff anyway, so instead you can help me clear up this mess.'

Lander began to gather the empty cans and drop them into a plastic sack. His head was pounding and each can landing on the others was like a blow. He tried to place them gently, but that meant bending into the sack, which was just as bad. It was the same whenever he had a hangover; the unanswerable question, why did I do it?

He couldn't recall much of the previous evening, but he had a recollection of getting into an argument with Steve.

'Was I obnoxious last night?'

'No more than usual.'

'I seem to remember yelling at Steve.'

'You did.'

'Why?'

'Don't ask me. You and Steve are the ones who were shitfaced.' Magda came away from the sink and dried her hands. 'You asked Steve if he and Kerryl really were planning to get together again, and he said he'd been hoping so because your sister was hot, despite looking like you, and you said he didn't deserve her and he had better keep his filthy hands off her, and he said you were only saying that because you wanted to shag her yourself, and you took a swing at him and missed and fell over, and so did he. I don't think I've left anything out, except that you both seemed to have completely forgotten that the poor girl isn't with us anymore.'

Lander was ashamed. He'd decided he didn't like Steve. He was aggrieved at the way he'd made himself at home in their house and helped himself to anything he fancied. He suspected him of wanting to help himself to Magda too. He hadn't liked the notion of him being with Kerryl, and what Steve had accused him of had been way out of order; he'd been quite right to take exception to it. But on the other hand Steve was trying to help them, and he probably didn't mean any of what he said. He was thick, that was all.

'Sorry,' he said.

'It's probably Steve you need to be sorry too, he's the one you tried to lay out. But I think he owes you an apology too.' Magda came beside him and put her arm around his waist and her head on his shoulder. 'It's all right. I guess you both needed to let off steam.'

'Is he still in bed?'

'I expect so. Unless he's run away. I haven't seen him, I slept with you. Not that you would have noticed.'

'He must have been up, though. There are two mugs on the table. One's yours, the other must be his.'

For an instant Magda looked confused. Then she said, 'Well you've got it wrong this time, Sherlock. They're both mine.'

'Really? One's got white dregs in it and you take your coffee black.'

Magda looked irritated and moved away. 'I poured it by mistake. There was milk already in the mug and I didn't realise. Anyway, what are you? The coffee police?' She tossed him a tea towel. 'Dry those things on the draining board.'

The cutlery and pans on the stainless-steel made a noise like a foundry, and the scraping of the crockery was like tectonic plates moving, but he stuck at it.

In the earlier, pre-lager part of last evening they'd agreed that Lander and Magda would spend the next day getting together everything they'd need for the trip, while Steve would go down the hill to search the canal for a suitable craft to take them there. Steve didn't think this would be a problem because he had an idea of where to look. But he didn't get up until late afternoon, and after his efforts with the tea towel Lander needed a rest, so none of this happened.

However, the following day it did. All three of them were up early. Lander felt better and so, it seemed, did Steve. They shook hands.

'Okay?' said Lander.

'Okay,' said Steve.

'Right then,' said Magda. 'Let's get to work.'

Steve went off on his Lambretta, and Lander and Magda started on their own jobs. Magda took control. She was very methodical. She packed food into plastic crates while Lander raided the kitchen drawers and Granddad's tool bench for anything that he thought might come in useful – torches, knives, cable ties, duct tape, basic tools, rope, and so on. When they'd got it all together, Lander backed the Land Rover out into the yard and they loaded it with the things they'd gathered.

Next, they both went into the field to find Joey. Lander was worried that he might have wandered off because the fence was broken and there was nothing to stop him, but there he was, in the middle of the pasture, grazing. He was wary of them but Magda had some carrots she'd found in the cellar and they drew him over. They'd started to sprout but Joey didn't appear to mind. Magda seemed to have a way with horses, and while Joey ate she got a halter around his neck. They led him up to the yard and put him in his old stable. He seemed happy to be home.

'Here,' said Magda, 'you hold him steady while I look at that gash on his leg.'

The wound was nasty but it was healing. Magda bathed it gently and applied some antiseptic cream. Joey stamped and tossed his head, but he seemed to know they were helping him and he stayed calm.

'What did your sister use when she groomed him?' said Magda.

'It's all there,' said Lander, 'in that bag on the shelf.'

Magda took the brushes and the combs and got to work on Joey. She brushed him until his flanks began to show some of their previous gloss, and she combed his mane and tail.

'You've done this before,' said Lander.

'Yes. I used to have a pony. Before the Infection.'

'What happened to it?'

'I don't know. Somebody broke into our stable and she ran away.'

By the time they'd finished, Steve was back. He was excited.

'Good news,' he said. 'Top good news in fact. I've found the perfect things to get us to Oxford. Just behind that big factory on the main road, the one that backs on to the canal...'

'Yes, Masham's, I know it.'

'...whatever, anyway there they were, inflatables, two of them. Good sized ones, really tough and in good nick. They'll be perfect. They've got a shallow draft so they don't need much water.'

'Why is that good?'

'The canals might be low in some places, too low for a standard barge but fine for these. We can hook them together, put our gear in one and ride in the other, and the horse can pull them both. We can take turns leading Joey along the towpath. And the best bit is they have, like, these wooden runners fixed to the underneath. Know what I mean? Some of the locks have, like, grass ramps up the sides, and with the runners we might be able to haul the boats up instead of using the lock, and that could save time.'

It sounded good news, and over coffee they told Steve what they'd achieved.

In the evening all three of them sat at the kitchen table and they ate cheese on toast, using the last of a loaf and some cheddar that Magda had found in the freezer. Over the meal they talked about the journey. Lander felt a mixture of excitement and caution. Magda had written down the route in detail and marked it in the atlas, so that when they got to junctions there would be no confusion and it would be clear which way they were to go. What they didn't know was who or what they might meet on the way.

'There are bound to be patrols around,' said Lander. 'They seem to be checking on everything. I expect they'll be made up of arkies.'

'What?' said Steve.

'Arkies. It's the word they use for the people who have sat out the Infection in the government's protected areas. They call them arks. They'll have been isolated for weeks. They won't have much idea of what's been going on and they might also be a bit scared.'

'From what I've seen the patrols are around only during the day,' said Steve, 'so if we travel at night we should miss them.'

'And they'll mainly be interested in the towns,' said Lander. 'We need to avoid those as far as we can.'

'Can't avoid them all,' said Steve. 'The canals run right through them, that's why they were built. But in the big places, like Manchester and Birmingham, they go through the industrial areas and there won't be anything going on there.'

'Some of the survivors could be a problem,' said Lander. 'You'll remember from my letter in Kerryl's diary that some people, men, who thought they were immune weren't really. They'd caught the virus but in a different way, and it damaged their brains.'

'Yes. And that can make them unpredictably violent,' said Magda.

'You mean they take a swing at you for nothing at all,' said Steve, looking hard at Lander.

Lander rounded on him. 'It wasn't nothing, what you said about me and Kerryl...'

'Now now, you two,' Magda said sharply.

'Sorry mate,' said Steve.

'All right,' said Lander. 'All I'm saying is that it's not only the patrols we'll need to watch out for. We could come across some of these other weirdoes too.'

'There might be kids as well,' said Magda.

'Kids?' said Steve.

'What about them?' said Lander. 'I thought most of the kids had caught it.'

'Most did,' said Magda. 'Children were particularly vulnerable to the Infection and not many of them survived. But a few did. Some of them are on their own and they're slowly starving to death. That's mainly the younger ones. The older ones have formed into gangs and they're completely out of control, they'll do anything. They'll be watching out for the PG too, and they might well be keeping away from towns and roads, like we plan to. So we could run into them, and they could be dangerous.'

'What, kids? Dangerous?' said Lander.

'You'd be surprised,' said Magda.

'How come you know all this?' said Steve.

'The covens are trying to find lost kids so they can take them in and look after them. I came across a few when I was with the Bonnies. We were caring for about a dozen kids and I talked to some of them.'

'Bonnies? Covens? Are you a witch or something?' said Steve.

Magda laughed. 'Coven just means band or group. It's usually used for witches but it doesn't have to be.'

'Magda was a member of a women's group before we met,' Lander explained. 'There are several of them.'

'What, gangs of women? Where? Lead me to them.'

'They call themselves covens in memory of all the innocent women who have been victimised in the past,' said Magda, icily.

'Will they help us?' asked Lander.

'I don't know,' said Magda. 'I think my lot, the Bonnies, would but they're not near where we're going. Some of the others might. I can't speak for all of them, they're not all the same. And just because one would doesn't mean the others will. Some covens don't get on with some of the others.'

'Typical women,' said Steve.

Magda glared at him. 'Those "typical women" are doing useful things the authorities are neglecting. Things that could well save your life.'

Steve looked chastised, and changed the subject.

'If we're trying to spot trouble, there are the stray animals too,' he said. 'Some of the dogs are insane. One nearly went for me today in the town. Got me in a doorway and stood there growling. Luckily there was a brick I could chuck at it. There's other stuff too – wildcats, boars, all sorts, know what I mean? I think we should take the guns.'

Lander could see the sense in that, but he could also see a problem. 'I don't know,' he said. 'The patrols will be armed, and they'll probably be jumpy. If they see us with guns they might think we mean trouble and take a pot at us.'

'That's a risk we'll have to face,' said Magda. 'I think Steve's right. We don't know what we're going to come across. We should take the guns, but we must keep them out of sight and only use them if there's a real emergency.' Magda, pushed her plate aside and replaced it with a note pad. 'Right,' she said, 'let's check. What have we got and what else might we need?'

They spent the next half hour brainstorming, while Magda's list grew. It was hard to get Steve to focus because he kept making suggestions that he thought were funny but were really just irritating: Xbox, condoms, bubble bath, dartboard. Lander and Magda tried to ignore him, and eventually he took the hint. When the list seemed complete, Lander read it out.

'I think we've got everything pretty much covered,' he said.

'Yes,' said Magda. 'But we don't have enough food to last us for the whole trip. Maybe we should add some more.'

'I don't think the inflatables will take it,' said Steve. 'They're not very big, and we need room for all our personal stuff – clothes, sleeping bags and that.'

'In that case we'll just have to forage on the way,' said Magda.

Lander was doubtful. He'd seen the state of some of the stores he'd passed. They'd be fine if most of them were like the ones in Snaith, but if they were more like the ones in Walbrough, where everything decent had been taken or trashed, they might find nothing. However, there seemed to be no other option, so that's what they agreed to do.

'We're OK for bedding,' said Magda. 'You've got your sleeping bag, Lander, I've got Kerryl's. Steve, think you'll be all right with just a duvet?'

'Sure. The nights are getting colder but we can huddle together, know what I mean?' He nudged Magda. Lander tried to ignore it.

'One more thing,' Steve said. He got up and went to pick up a large canvas bag he'd left by the door. 'When I was in the town today, not only did I solve our transport problems, I also got these.' He unzipped the bag and tipped out its contents with a flourish. 'Ta-da!'

What Steve had found were army fatigues in brown-green camouflage.

'Where did you get those?'

'In the discount store. There's been a fire and not much is left, but there's a store room at the back that's untouched and there are piles of these on a table. I reckon they look close enough to the uniform of the patrols to pass, don't you? I hope I've got the sizes right.'

Lander's irritation with Steve evaporated. He may be stupid, he may be irritating – in fact he was both – but he did have some good ideas sometimes. He could forgive him a lot for finding the inflatables, and now these. He clapped him on the shoulder.

'Hey, dude, that is fucking brilliant,' he said. 'Let's get 'em on.'

A few minutes later and they were in the fatigues and ready to go. Lander took a last look at the cosy kitchen. It was tempting to put off leaving for another day, to open the bottle of Vodka he'd seen in the sideboard, maybe light a fire against the late summer chill, but he knew that the sooner they left the sooner he could catch up with Adam. And the sooner he did that the easier it would be to put to rest the thoughts that plagued him about the fate of his twin.

BEFORE LANDER HAD finally dropped out of school he had started a course in Sociology. It involved more essay writing than he was happy with, but the ideas were interesting and he'd liked the discussions, and especially the practical assignments. One of these was when the teacher divided the class into small groups and gave each a task to complete. There were only two rules: one was that there were to be no leaders, the other was that each member of the group was to undertake a different job. The teacher videoed it and the class watched the videos and talked about them. One thing that came out clearly was how quickly and easily the group members assumed roles, picking them up without direction. And once they'd taken on responsibility for a function they stuck with it, even defending their right to it.

Lander was thinking about this as they settled into their journey towards Oxford. Without any debate Magda took charge of map reading and navigation. She sat in the front boat and alerted them to what lay ahead, particularly places where the canal came close to major roads and built-up areas. Steve had taken on controlling the boats, including handling the locks and dealing with some of the intricacies of the canal system. Lander managed Joey. This involved leading him along the towpath, making sure that when morning came he had access to good grass, that he was comfortably but securely tethered so he couldn't run off, that the harness wasn't chaffing him, and that the gash on his leg was healing. Each of them had their own work and they got on with it with minimum reference to the other two.

Steve's idea of hauling the boats up the grass banks beside the locks was a non-starter. Without unloading them they were far too heavy to lift out of the water, and it would have taken longer to take all their stuff out and reload them than it did to pass through the locks in the conventional way. However, it meant that during these times they were exposed and at their most vulnerable.

Travelling by night was easy, even when there was no moon. It wasn't as if they could stray off their route; they just followed where the waterways took them, and when they came to a fork or junction it was usually obvious which way they should go. Sometimes there were even signposts. They'd stop every hour or so for Magda to study the maps by torchlight and alert them to what was coming.

Travel by night, sleep by day; it should have been a simple recipe but it was not. The idea was that as dawn approached they'd find a suitable tunnel or bridge, and Steve would check the boats and make them fast while Lander saw to Joey and Magda sorted out their rations. Then they would settle down in the boats to sleep the day away. And there lay the problem. Steve and Lander took one boat and Magda the other, but the cold from the water struck through the flimsy hulls and chilled them to the bone. After an hour or so of this Magda came from her boat to theirs and lay between them. The three huddled together, but even so they were cold and sleep was fitful.

On the second night, when he realised he was never going to get warm, Lander crept out of the boat and lay down on the canal bank. It was not long before he was joined by Magda.

'You can't sleep either,' she said.

'No, too cold. It's fucking freezing under that bridge and the water's like ice.'

'Right. How do you think it's going?'

'What, the journey? Not bad. Actually I'm quite enjoying it. It's restful really, just the clop of Joey's hooves, the gentle splashing of the water and the slowly unrolling landscape.'

Magda gave him a nudge. 'Get you. Who would have thought you had a poetic streak?'

'Not you, obviously,' said Lander. He looked around. 'What do you think of Steve?'

'How do you mean? He's all right. A bit of a laugh really.'

'I mean his behaviour. Have you noticed anything funny about him?'

'No, should I?'

Lander wondered whether he should tell her what he knew of the dream walkers. All sleeping together in the boat, they'd know if anything happened. Perhaps the dream walking only occurred during darkness, and if Steve was a walker he might be escaping the symptoms by being awake and busy then. He decided to leave it.

'Thank goodness there's nobody much about,' he said.

'Yes. We seem to be on our own. There were lights on in a couple of the houses in a town back there, but all the others were dark.'

'Yeah, and there were emergency beacons on the M62.' He remembered looking up and seeing blue flashing lights on the hillside high above them, then realising they must be on the motorway. 'Heaven knows what they were about. There can't be enough traffic for a motorway pile-up.'

'Mm.' Magda thought for a moment, then she said, 'We're not getting on fast enough.'

Lander agreed. He wanted to get to Oxford and sort Adam out, but he hadn't set the pace they were following. 'It was your idea to stop early,' he said. 'You thought we oughtn't to get caught in the daylight in the middle of

Manchester, and it would be best to leave it till tonight and get right across the city in one go.'

'Yes, I know I did, but even so we're going more slowly than I expected.'

'Well, poor old Joey can't gallop!' Lander laughed at the vision of the horse galumphing along the towpath, dragging the boats behind him. 'All we can do is take the risk of doing some of the journey in daylight.'

There seemed to be no alternative. When they put it to Steve he was against it, but Lander and Magda overruled him. They agreed that they would push ahead across Manchester the next night, and once they were clear of the city and in open country they would carry on for a couple of hours after daybreak.

'A lot of the Trent and Mersey goes through Staffordshire,' said Steve. 'From what I remember that's fairly rural, so there won't be many people around. We should be all right.'

Lander's main concern about the new plan was not that they might be seen, it was overworking Joey. 'He's got to have time to rest and eat,' he said. 'He's a big horse and he needs a lot of grass.'

'We've got paddles,' said Steve. 'Some of the time we'll use those and he can take breaks.'

When Lander had been in Oxford he'd asked what things were like in London. He'd been told that it was a no-go area, an anarchic nightmare choked with the dead and the barely living, impossible to enter safely. He'd expected that Manchester would be the same, but the city was quiet. They saw hardly anyone, and those they did see paid them no attention. That included a patrol that cruised by quite close to the canal but ignored them. The result was that they got through the city quickly and without mishap.

On the other side of Manchester the canal went under a railway line. They were moving towards it when they heard an approaching rumble and saw an enormous train of fuel tankers. They hid under the bridge while the train passed overhead. Lander was cheered by the sight. This stuff was going somewhere. The fuel would be used to power vehicles, generate electricity and contribute to the long process of restoring normality.

'Wish,' said Magda.

'What?'

'Wish. My Nan used to say that you should wish if you were under a bridge when a train crossed over it.'

Magda closed her eyes and screwed up her face. Lander didn't know what to ask for. Before the Infection he might have dreamt of playing for Yorkshire, or scoring with Charlene Brooker, a really hot girl at Kerryl's school. But now? There was no Yorkshire cricket any more, and all the girls he'd known were probably dead. Nevertheless he said, 'Okay,' and shut his eyes too. But nothing would come and all he did was pretend, while he listened to the thunder of the waggons overhead.

They kept going, even though it was now broad daylight. The land was flatter here and consequently there were fewer locks. The countryside was open and there was no sign of life. The villages were deserted but they always knew when they were getting close to one because of the unmistakable odour, the stench of things rotting. Manchester had reeked of smoke and chlorine; that had been unpleasant but this was worse. It was a unique smell, sickening and pervasive.

There was a brief scare when they went into a short tunnel and found a man there. He was leaning against the wall and mumbling. He watched them as they passed him.

'Horsey, horsey, I've got a horsey,' he called after them. 'Horsey, keep your tail up. A wail of a tale. I've seen a horse fly. Bet yours can't.' He cackled with delirious laughter.

'Mad fucker,' said Steve. 'Been on the zombie juice I expect.'

'More likely it's the Infection,' said Magda. 'He's a dream walker. He's survived the fever and the virus has got into his brain and tipped him over. We're lucky that at the moment he's in happy land and not violent.'

'Doesn't look as though he could do much,' said Steve. 'He looks a wimp to me.'

'You'd be surprised,' said Magda. 'Men who get affected in this way develop a sort of nervous strength. They can be very difficult to deal with.'

'Men,' said Steve. 'Don't chicks get it too?'

'Not so far as we know.'

Lander said nothing, but what Magda was saying surprised him. Where had she learnt about dream walking? As far as Lander knew it had been discovered by *thetruth* people only when the Infection was well established. Adam had known about it, but nobody else he'd met seemed to. Magda was talking as if she was an expert on it.

They kept going until around midday, and stopped when they found an inviting looking barn close by a bridge. The bridge offered scant protection, but by tying the boats side by side they were able to conceal them from a casual sighting. A bonus was that there was plenty of hay and straw in the barn.

'We can sleep on that,' said Steve.

Lander remembered the last time that he and Magda had slept on hay.

'Joey's happy,' said Steve, as the horse attacked a bale.

'Good for him,' said Magda. 'Better watch he doesn't eat too much, though, or too fast. Come on, gutsy.' She took Joey's bridle and nudged him away. 'It's a pity we humans can't eat hay. We're getting low on food.'

'What, really?' said Lander. 'Already? But we had loads.'

'Yes, and you've eaten it. You two are like bloody vultures. We're getting short of water, too.'

They'd been prepared to wash in canal water, and so long as they chose the spot carefully that had been all right, but none of them fancied drinking it.

'What shall we do?' said Lander.

'Well, Einstein, I think we'd better get some more,' said Magda.

'OK, Ms Einstein,' said Lander. 'How? Oh, I know. I'll just pop along to the shops.'

'There are fish in the canal,' said Steve. 'My dad used to catch 'em.'

'What are they?' said Lander.

Steve shrugged. 'Carp? Roach? I dunno.'

'Did you eat them?'

'No, he used to throw them back. But I expect you could. Eat them, I mean. I'll try to catch some tomorrow.'

'I don't want to be rude,' said Magda, 'but I don't fancy eating anything that might live in this water. I've seen some of the stuff people have thrown into it. The next town we come to we'll go on a raid.'

Steve picked up the atlas. 'There's one not far ahead,' he said. 'It'll be best to go while there's still some light, so we can see what we're doing, know what I mean?'

'That's a good idea,' said Magda. 'We don't want to be trying to find our way around a strange place in the dark.'

'We can't all go,' said Lander. 'Somebody should stay here with Joey and the boats. Why don't I go with Steve?'

'Why?' said Magda. 'You think this is a job for the men and a mere girl couldn't manage?'

'Course not,' said Lander. 'But I do think we can carry more than you can. I'm not being macho, it's just that you're still not fully recovered from your holiday with Mickey. Anyway, if somebody comes along the canal bank you'll be better than Steve or me at talking your way out of any problems.'

Magda didn't look convinced but she agreed. 'Oh, all right,' she said.

'You'd better have a gun,' said Steve. 'You never know who could turn up and you might need to defend yourself.'

He left the barn and returned a few minutes later with one of the shotguns. They'd been well hidden in the bottom of the boat and this was the first time on their voyage one had been brought out.

'Do you know how to use this?'

'Yes,' said Magda, rolling her eyes.

'Don't be afraid to, and if you do, wait until whatever you're firing at is fairly close. Squeeze the trigger, don't snatch it.'

'Thank you,' said Magda, fluttering her eyelashes. 'You're such a big strong man. Can you show me which is the trigger? Is it this little bit sticking out here?'

'All right,' said Steve, resentfully. 'I was just saying.'

'You might leave me the box of cartridges too. In case I miss first time, being only a girl and that.'

'All right, all right,' said Steve.

'Yes,' said Magda, 'it's a good job that I thought to bring them, seeing as neither of you two geniuses did.'

It looked from the map as though the small town they had in mind was about two miles away, a brisk walk along the canal towpath, and Steve and Lander set out at the end of the afternoon. They thought they would be able to get back well before dark. On the way they decided that they'd hide whatever they found and pick it up when they came along the canal that night with the boats, rather than try to carry it back.

Ever since they'd left Walbrough Lander had been concerned that the roads, the railway and the canal were often close together.

'It's because they were all built to follow the easiest route,' said Steve.

'Yeah, but it means it's hard to keep out of sight of the road. We've been lucky so far but I'm bothered somebody official might see us. We haven't got any ID, or at least I haven't.'

Lander's fears were realised when they still had half a mile to go. They were on a straight part of the canal with the road only a few metres away and absolutely nowhere to hide when they became aware of movement beside them. It was a bus.

'Shit,' said Lander. 'Act normal. Just keep walking.'

They did, marching along as if they had every right to be there. The bus slowed, and they could see that the passengers were wearing army uniforms. There were about twenty of them, in full battle kit, and armed. They were all looking at Lander and Steve, and several of them were holding rifles at the ready.

The bus stopped and one of the soldiers stood in the open doorway. He had a sergeant's stripes and was talking into a field communicator.

Steve gave a wave.

'For fuck's sake, what are you doing?' snarled Lander, horrified. 'Do you want to get shot?' He was trembling. He'd heard tales of patrols firing on people suspected of being vagrants.

'Nothing to lose,' said Steve, calmly. 'Act normal, you said.'

'I didn't say stick your fucking neck out. You're out of your mind.'

They kept walking, Lander expecting at any moment to hear a shouted order to halt, or perhaps even the staccato stutter of gunfire. Neither of these things happened. The figure in the doorway went back inside, the bus moved off and disappeared down the road, away from the direction they were heading.

Lander let out a huge sigh. 'Jesus, that was scary.' His legs were trembling. 'I never thought we'd get away. Why didn't they stop us?'

'Maybe acting normal worked,' said Steve.

'More likely they got another call. They left pretty fast.' Lander's heart was still racing, and there was a cold patch of sweat in the small of his back. 'Where did the bus come from? I never heard it till it was on us.'

'It must be an electric one,' said Steve. 'I'd heard they were using them, and it makes sense if petrol and diesel are short. They must be able to get power, though.'

'What, really?' said Lander.

Steve didn't get the sarcasm. 'Stands to reason,' he said. 'They'd need electric power to charge it, know what I mean? There were a lot of them on it. I wonder how far they can go between charges.'

Lander didn't care. The technical specifications of the bus were an irrelevance. What mattered was that they'd been seen. What would happen now? Surely the unit would know that despite the fatigues the two of them were wearing they weren't in the army. Somebody somewhere would check who was authorised to be in the area. He had no doubt they'd be back.

'We'd better move,' he said. 'Magda and Joey are in the direction they've gone. Let's find what we came for and get back as soon as we can. Then we need to get the hell out of here.'

They saw no one else. The visit to the town was a success, although Lander was still too keyed up to do a proper job and forgot some of the things Magda had told them to look out for. The town reminded him of Snaith. There were no people, neither was there the reek of death that afflicted most other towns, but there were signs of damage and destruction. They found a store which still had bottled water and plenty of tinned food, and, to Steve's delight, beer.

'Dancing Vicar,' he said, picking up a can and looking at the leaping clergyman on the label. 'My dad used to like this. It's an old man's drink but it's better than nothing.'

On the edge of the town they'd passed a deserted cottage and Lander had spotted a wheelbarrow in the garden. They'd taken it and now they loaded it up. Steve was for pushing it all the way back to the boats but Lander insisted they stick to their plan, so they left the barrow hidden where they could pick up its contents later. They each took a Dancing Vicar and one for Magda, and jogged back along the towpath.

TWENTY-TWO
CHALLENGES

'FOR FUCK'S SAKE, how many's that?' said Lander, heaving on yet another lock gate. 'You said it would be easy once we were through Manchester.'

'I'd forgotten this bit,' said Steve.

'*The Trent and Mersey is one of the earliest canals built by Brindley,*' Magda read from an information board at the canal side. '*Passing through pleasant countryside it climbs from the Cheshire plain through a series of locks.*'

'Too bloody right about the locks,' said Lander. 'But this is not what I call pleasant countryside.' Every bit of him ached, legs, arms, shoulders, back.

'It says here there are thirty-one of them,' said Magda, 'and the series is sometimes referred to as "Heartbreak Hill".'

'Great. More like back break hill. It's the last time I listen to you,' he grumbled at Steve as they dragged the boats into the next lock. 'I thought you knew these canals.'

'I didn't remember this part. It was ages ago we were here. I was just a kid.'

Lander made a noise somewhere between a snarl and growl.

'At least all these stops mean Joey's having a good day,' said Magda.

It wasn't worth harnessing the horse to pull the boats from one lock to the next so they were doing it by hand, which meant that Joey was redundant and could enjoy the waterside grass, ambling amiably from one lock to the next as they rose through the tier.

'Cheer up,' she went on. 'Only two more and then it's the tunnel.'

'The what?'

'It says here there's a tunnel,' she said, reading again from the board. 'It takes you under Harecastle Hill towards Stoke. How's your claustrophobia? Because apparently it's over a mile and a half long and it's narrow. Better hope we don't meet anything coming the other way.'

'I suppose you don't remember that, either,' Lander said to Steve.

'Oh yes, I remember that. It's creepy. My dad told us there's a ghost in there. Some woman who was murdered in the tunnel and now she haunts it.'

'Great. Now you tell us.' Lander didn't believe in ghosts but he disliked cramped spaces, and the idea of having to go through a tunnel was worse than any threat of haunting.

'Yeah, it's all coming back to me now,' said Steve. 'Her head was cut off and she walks up and down on the water looking for it. My dad said that some boatmen take long detours to avoid having to go through the tunnel. He said as well that sometimes more boats go in than come out.'

Magda was still reading. 'It doesn't say anything about that here, but it does say there's no towpath, so how are we going to get through?'

'Same way as we've done the bridges and the shorter tunnels,' said Steve. 'We'll paddle. Two of us can take the boats through while the third goes with Joey over the hill to meet us at the other end.'

It was inevitable there would be an argument about who the third would be. Steve said he should go through the tunnel as he was the canal guide, and besides, he'd done it before. Magda said that if they thought she was going to look after the horse just because she was the girl in the group they had another think coming. As for Lander, although the last thing he wanted was to go into a pitch-black hole, he would seriously lose face if he looked to be hanging back, so he had to pretend to be keen on going in the boats too. They settled it by tossing a coin. Magda lost, which meant that she took Joey.

Lander and Steve picked up a paddle each and began to move the two inflatables along the narrow approach to the tunnel entrance. It looked like the wall of a house and the mouth was a rectangle, but as soon as they'd gone through this the roof became arched in the way Lander had expected.

His stomach felt unsteady as they exchanged the brightness of the day for the damp, cold dark. Steve rested a torch on the prow of the boat so that it shone ahead and they could see where they were going, but all it showed was a dull, straight passage boring into the hill. The walls were lined with bricks, millions of them, stained with brown from the ores that oozed through the earth. Periodically there were numbers sprayed in yellow paint on the wall; Lander guessed these were distances, probably in yards. What had Magda said? More than a mile and a half? How many yards was that? It would take for ever.

As far as he could tell the tunnel seemed to be dead straight, but he couldn't see the exit. It was too far away, he supposed. The paddling was hard work and despite the chill he was soon sweating. He thought about the ghost, but there was no sound apart from their laboured breathing and the lapping of the water.

'Stop a minute,' said Steve. 'I just want to cool down.'

Lander took hold of Steve's paddle while he pulled the top of his fatigues over his head. He turned to put it behind him and a sleeve flapped the torch. Lander saw what was going to happen an instant before it did and lunged to save it, but he was too late. The torch rolled off the edge of the boat and plopped into the water.

'Shit,' Lander shouted. The word bounced around the tunnel and echoed back to them.

They both leant over the side. There was a faint light below, where the sunken torch glowed through the brown water. Then it went out. It was like a switch being thrown, like having your eyes suddenly covered. Several hundred yards behind was the tiny bead of daylight that was the tunnel's entrance; ahead of and around them was inky dark.

'Fuck,' said Lander. 'What did you do that for?'

'I didn't do anything,' said Steve.

'You caught the torch with your sleeve, you idiot.'

'It was you trying to grab it. You knocked it off.'

'I fucking didn't, I was trying to save it.'

The row reverberated in the confined space.

'We'd better head back,' said Lander.

'Don't be daft,' said Steve. 'What good would that do?'

'We can't go on in the dark.'

'Course we can. It's a straight line. We just keep paddling till we see daylight.'

It was Lander's worst nightmare. He'd been locked in a small cell, but there had been daylight. He'd been wheeled into a scanner, but Janice had been there and he'd had a panic button that would have got him out in an instant. He'd been chained in a lightless shed, but there had been space around him. Here he was in a narrow space, and the darkness was total. His arms trembled so much it was hard to hang on to the paddle. A clammy sweat soaked his back. His pulse raced.

Bizarrely, it was the difficulty of what they were trying to do that kept his fear under control. Steve had said that all they had to do was to keep the inflatables going in a straight line. That sounded easy, but how could they establish that line when they couldn't see anything ahead? They collided with the brick walls of the tunnel again and again, bouncing from side to side, the boats slewing. At one stage the rear boat, the one they should have been towing, got in front of the one they were in. Steve's response seemed to be that the greater the disorder the harder he should paddle, and it was impossible to undo the tangle until it occurred to Lander to use the pinpoint of the tunnel's entrance, behind them, as a marker to realign the boats. Once this was done they managed to straighten themselves out and resume their progress. At one stage Lander allowed himself to look back over his shoulder. The tunnel mouth was barely visible. He forced himself to slow his breathing and concentrate on the rhythm of paddling to keep the claustrophobia at bay.

Suddenly there was a wailing sound. It was obvious at once that it was Steve, but even so it made Lander jump.

'I'm a headless ghost,' Steve warbled in a quavering voice.

Lander sighed. 'Fuck off, will you?'

'All right,' said Steve. 'I was only trying to cheer you up by adding a bit of drama.'

'Well don't.'

Lander didn't need any phantom to chill his spine or curdle his blood: the thought of the millions of tons of rock and earth heaped over their heads did that on its own. Were they half way through yet? A quarter? How long would this torture last?

The end of the tunnel was at first so indistinct that Lander couldn't be sure that he was seeing it. It was faint as a distant star. Was that it? Was that the exit? He strained into the blackness. Yes! There it was. No more than a speck, but definitely, definitely daylight. His spirits rose and he began to paddle harder.

'Steady,' warned Steve. 'You'll tangle us up again.'

It probably took no more than twenty minutes to complete their ordeal, but it seemed much longer. As they approached the end of the tunnel the light seeping in increased, growing brighter and brighter until at last they burst into the glare of glorious day. There was green, there was birdsong, and there were Magda and Joey, waiting for them on the canal side.

'My God, you really did see something in there, didn't you,' said Magda as Lander slumped over his paddle and Steve made the boats fast. 'You're as white as a sheet.'

They rested just long enough for Lander to calm down, to tidy up the boat and harness Joey, and then they carried on towards Stoke.

Joey was refreshed and pressed on willingly, and they got on well. However, there seemed to be more going on here than they'd seen before. There were troops, vehicles and machinery clearing the streets. The air was thick with dust, and with smoke from piles of burning rubbish. Although all the working personnel seemed to be occupied and weren't looking in their direction, they were worried they'd be spotted.

'What do you think?' said Steve.

'Best to hole up,' said Magda. 'Go back to travelling by night until we're through here. I suggest we find somewhere to hide till nightfall and get some rest, so we can crack on once it's dark. What do you think, Lander?'

Lander had been in a stupor since emerging from the tunnel.

'What? Oh, yeah,' he grunted.

Magda gave him a long look. 'Well thank you for your contribution,' she said.

They found a bridge under which they could hide. This time, because of all the additional activity, they decided that rather than bed down on the bank it would be more sensible to go back to their original plan of sleeping in the boats. Or trying to. They all three huddled together against the cold. Lander swaddled himself in his sleeping bag and wrapped a blanket around him, tucking it under his feet, but to no avail. Another obstacle to rest was that in his imagination he kept returning to the terrifying, sightless confine of the tunnel. He pictured roof falls, things lurking in the water, simultaneous pursuit from both entrance and exit trapping him in the cloying, stifling blackness. He looked at his two companions. Steve had dropped off immediately. Magda, too, seemed now to be sleeping. They were in each other's arms. He felt a twinge of jealousy.

Carefully, so as not to rock the boat, he disentangled himself from his bedding and crawled out. He sat on the grass bank beside the canal and put on his trainers; no shoes in the boats was Steve's only rule. He needed some exercise to stretch his legs, so he left the canal and went towards what looked to be a public park. He knew there was a chance he'd be seen, but he would rely on his uniform fatigues and a suitably confident air to deflect any casual enquiry.

There were no signs of life in the park but there were none of death either. To warm himself up he jogged over to some trees on the far side, then turned to run back.

He'd just started the return when there was a thwack, and he felt a sharp sting on his arm. At the same time he heard laughter. He turned around but could see nothing. Then he heard the sound again, and felt another impact, this time high on his thigh. The trees formed a thick copse in a horseshoe at the corner of the park. Whoever was shooting at him, because that's what it was, was in the trees.

'Oy!'

He spun towards the sound, and as he did so there was another blow, this time followed by jeering and sniggers. Then a figure came out of the trees, followed by another. Lander sensed danger and turned to move away, only to find two more blocking his path.

He judged they were eleven or twelve. He counted six of them, but maybe there were more in hiding. Two were clearly girls, the rest boys or indeterminate. They surrounded him, the closest a couple of metres away. He remembered what Magda had said about gangs of older children.

One of them was holding a catapult, obviously the source of the stinging missiles.

'What're you doin' 'ere?' he said. The voice was harsh, and surprisingly deep.

Lander didn't reply and the question was repeated more aggressively.

'I'm talkin' to you, shitface. This is our spot. What're you doin' 'ere?'

Lander knew he couldn't take them on. Although he was bigger than any of them he was well outnumbered. All he could do was bluster.

'Are you talking to me, you little pillock?' he said.

One of the girls giggled and one of the smaller boys shuffled up to his larger neighbour and made to pull him away. Lander pressed ahead with what he took to be an indication of advantage.

'I'm securing this park for the army,' he said. 'Now you lot clear out, or I'll have my unit bring you in.'

There was a pause but none of the children moved. They were clearly weighing him up.

Then the catapult holder said, 'He's full of shit. There's no unit here. He's on his own.'

There was a relieved surge and they moved closer, tightening the circle.

'Tek another shot, Nev,' said another one. 'Bet yer can't get him in the nuts.'

Nev raised his weapon and aimed it at Lander's groin.

'Empty 'em,' he said.

Lander didn't move.

'Empty yer pockets or I'll knock yer nuts off.' He tensioned the rubber.

'We'll have yer neck chain too, and yer trainers,' said another.

Lander thought fast. He had his Bowie knife on his belt. If he could jump aside and dodge the projectile, he could maybe draw the knife and get the catapult holder in the same move. He seemed to be the dominant one; with him down the others would probably run. But it was a long shot, and there was an older girl on the periphery of his vision who looked dangerously detached. Maybe she was the true leader.

'Warned yer,' Nev sang, and lined up for the shot.

Lander braced himself and was poised to jump when there was a shrill whistle and a shout from behind.

'Pigs at five o'clock,' one of the children yelled.

Two women, both in uniform and armed, were running towards them. The group scattered. One of the women raised her weapon and fired. The rubber bullet bounced and hit a child, who shrieked and fell. The rest melted into the copse.

The shooter went to the edge of the trees and grabbed the stricken child, who was rolling on the floor and wailing.

'Are you OK, pal?' the other said to Lander. The name Holmes was written on her tag.

Lander nodded. 'Yes. No thanks to this lot, though.'

'Attack you, did they?'

'They were trying to. One of them, name of Nev, is a crack shot with a catapult. Who are they?'

'Ferals,' said the woman. 'They live in the woods. Get by from raiding and general thievery. They're a pain in the arse.' Her radio issued a burst of static, which distracted the two just long enough. There was a blur of movement and the injured child twisted free and dashed into the trees. The woman who'd been holding him didn't bother to follow.

'We know who they are. We'll get 'em sooner or later,' she said.

'You on the clean up?' said Holmes.

Lander improvised. 'Yeah.'

'Where's your unit?'

Lander thought fast. With everything in turmoil, communications wouldn't be good. Even in the relative order before the Infection one branch of officialdom couldn't be relied on to know what another was doing. He took a risk.

'We're on a five-two-five,' he said.

'Oh.' The other woman, whose name tag said Hussain, nodded. 'A five-two-five. And what might that be?'

There was a hint of suspicion in her tone. Lander had hoped they would just accept it as something else that was going on, but unfortunately they were curious. He improvised some more.

'Don't you know?' he said. 'Haven't you been briefed?' The women looked momentarily disconcerted and he might have got away with it, but he pushed too far. He adopted what he hoped was an authoritative frown and said, 'Perhaps you don't have the necessary clearance.'

'Oh, I think we do,' said the woman called Hussain, 'but I'm not sure you do. Where's your field equipment? You look a bit young for a patrol unit, anyway. Where are your insignia? You've got no name tag or unit decal.'

Lander wondered if he could make a break for it. But a bullet, even a rubber one, would be a lot worse than a catapult pellet. He might get into the copse, it looked pretty dense, but then he might run into the children again. He could only go on.

'But five-two-fives require anonymity,' he said, and tried to sigh as though battling with an impossible fusion of ignorance and incompetence.

'Call it in,' Hussain said to her companion, and she unhooked handcuffs from her belt.

Holmes tilted her lapel mic. 'This is SU7,' she said. 'We have an unidentified in Rollins Park. Male, late teens-early twenties, no ID.'

There was a pause. Then the gods of fortune smiled on Lander. The speaker crackled and a tinny voice said, 'Abort that, SU7. We need you back here, sharp.'

Hussain gave Lander a long look.

Holmes put the handcuffs back on her belt. 'It must be your lucky day,' she said. 'Vanish. I don't want to see you here again.'

'And lose that fucking uniform,' said the other. 'Impersonating army personnel is a criminal offence.'

Both women turned and marched quickly away.

Lander was shaken. It was not safe to be out. On the whole he thought that the children might have turned out to be worse captors than the two patrol officers, but he didn't want to test either. He hurried back to the boat. As he approached it Magda and Steve disentangled themselves from each other.

TWENTY-THREE
BRAVE NEW WORLD

AS SOON AS it was dark they moved on.

They had now left the more built-up areas and were back in open country. It had begun to drizzle and Lander was not happy that he had to walk with Joey on the towpath instead of sitting under a waterproof tarp in the boat. Steve sat with Magda, one arm working a paddle which he used to fend the boat away from the canal bank. His other arm was around Magda. Lander was glad he was in front with the horse and they were behind him, so that he didn't have to witness their petting.

There weren't as many locks to delay them on this stretch of the canal and they got on well. The only interruptions were the few bridges where there was no towpath. At these Lander would unhitch Joey and lead him over the top, while Steve and Magda paddled the boats through the bridge to meet him on the other side.

After an hour they came to a fork where the canal branched. The rain had stopped and the broken clouds allowed a quarter moon to give just enough light for them to see the junction.

'I remember this,' said Steve.

He took the maps and traced their passage with a finger. Magda looked too, her chin on his shoulder and her cheek against the side of his head. Lander walked away and left them to it. He felt shut out.

'We take the right fork,' said Steve. 'That will get us to Birmingham. I'm sure of it.'

'What about the other?' said Lander. 'Where does that go?'

He didn't fancy Birmingham. He knew that the canal went right through the middle of the city and he was worried it might be like London. He'd also noticed that as they got further south there were more parties cleaning up the streets and repairing the buildings. He figured that the chances of them being seen and stopped in Birmingham were significantly greater than they had been further north.

Steve pursed his lips. 'Well, we could go that way, but it's much further. It will take us longer.'

'How much longer?'

'Quite a bit. Here, look.' He offered Lander the map.

'I think it has to be Birmingham,' said Magda. 'I'm sure we'll be all right. If anyone sees us they'll simply think we're army and take no notice.'

Lander was doubtful. He hadn't told them about the incident in the park, but that had proved that their 'uniforms' weren't near enough to the real thing to bear close scrutiny. However, he said nothing. Steve and Magda seemed to be organising this between them, so let them.

Besides, he didn't really care what happened. If they got caught, well so be it. He still had a serious score to settle with Adam over what he'd done to Kerryl, and he was looking forward to an opportunity for that, but the passing days had tempered his sorrow; the anger and grief were still there but their intensity had eased. Revenge is a dish best served cold,' he'd heard somebody say once.

Taking the right fork meant getting Joey to the opposite side of the canal to pick up the towpath, and Lander led him back and over a bridge. When they came down the ramp, Magda was waiting. As she bent to attach Joey to the boat's line, Lander was struck by how much better she was looking. When they'd left Mickey's barn she'd been wasted, a walking corpse. Her skin had been slack and pale, her hair greasy, her face spotty and sallow. Now she was showing the benefits of rest, fresh air, and a nourishing – though often unconventional – diet. She was still thin, but no longer starved-looking. Her hair was untidy but cleaner and healthier. She had colour in her cheeks and her spots were mostly gone. Lander supposed he must be looking fitter too. Heaving all those bricks and logs had been an extended work-out, and the bad treatment hadn't continued as long for him as it had for Magda. He felt strong and well.

Joey now knew the drill and he no longer needed to be led. As soon as the rope was fixed to his neck he resumed his casual stroll. Lander walked behind him, in a position to keep an eye on the rope and guard it from snags.

Instead of getting back into the boat with Steve, Magda fell in beside Lander. They walked side-by-side in silence, just the plod of Joey's hooves on the paved path and the slapping of the boats in the water. Magda had asked Lander if she could take the bottle of Eau d'Amour she'd found in Kerryl's room, and she was wearing it now.

After a while she moved closer, and Lander felt her arm on his waist, her thumb hooked in the back of his jeans. He didn't know how to respond. Was she trying to indicate that although she might have a thing going with Steve, she and Lander were still friends? He ignored it. There was a lock ahead. It was in their favour, the gate open. Lander disengaged himself, loosened Joey, and pulled Steve and the boats into the lock. He closed the downstream gate, and Magda opened the sluice at the other end. They stood together watching the lock fill.

What happened next was unexpected. Magda tugged him back so they were out of sight of Steve, who was still at the bottom of the lock. Then, more quickly than he could register what was happening, she was facing him.

She pulled him into her and her face lifted towards his. He couldn't help it, his arms wound around her and their mouths met. It was a quick peck, then deeper and more enthusiastic. He realised how long he'd been wanting to kiss her, ever since they'd clung together for warmth under the hay in Mickey's barn. But this wasn't right. Not twenty minutes ago she'd been snuggling in the boat with Steve.

He let go of her and pushed her away. She looked puzzled.

'What?'

'No,' said Lander.

'Why not?'

'Steve. You were with Steve. I mean, I thought you fancied Steve.'

'I was and I do, but I fancy you as well.'

Lander hesitated, trying to take this in.

'I can fancy both of you, can't I?' Magda said.

Lander had no answer. Ever since he'd become aware of the mysteries of mating, since before that really, the rule had been one person to one other, usually one female to one male. If you wanted somebody else, the decent thing was to finish with the person you were with first. Among his group at school there had been admiration for a boy who had more than one girl 'on the go', but girls who were guilty of 'doubling up' were called sluts. Some of the young men he knew in Walbrough had been involved in serious fights when one thought another had even looked at 'his' woman in the wrong way.

'Things aren't like what they used to be,' said Magda. 'The old ways of people owning each other don't work anymore. It's time for something new.'

She leant towards him again, but the lock was now filled. Steve and the boats were almost level with them and Lander pulled back.

'But you were with Steve,' he said. 'You were making out with him. I saw you. I mean, I wasn't peeking or anything but I couldn't help it.'

'So? I can fancy both of you, and I can have both of you. Same for you. You can have all the girls you like, but you can still have me.'

Steve had pulled the boat to the side and jumped out. He joined them.

'You see that, don't you, Steve?' she said.

'Yeah,' said Steve.

Lander didn't share Steve's enthusiasm. The women in the Shaw household – his mother, Gran, Kerryl – had all held monogamy and faithfulness in high regard. He could remember when Kerryl had been going out with a boy called Mark. She really liked him, but she discovered he was at the same time dating one of her friends. She'd broken with him even though it hurt her to do so, and she'd cried for days. Like most young males there were plenty of girls he fancied, but he'd always made a point of regarding any girl who seemed committed to somebody else as off limits. Magda presenting herself to him in this way was something his brain couldn't handle. And the fact that Magda knew he'd seen her and Steve and was completely open about the situation made it worse.

'Life has changed,' said Magda. 'Previous generations, with their male dominated moral systems and their rules and restrictions, totally screwed things up. All that's gone. We have an opportunity to reboot the planet, in every way. Actually, it's more than a reboot, it's a complete rebuild because there's the chance to renew everything. I mean everything. Now that almost all women are infertile we need to think again about how the genders interact.'

'What?' Lander wasn't sure he had heard her right. 'How do you mean almost all women are infertile?'

Magda looked puzzled. 'Didn't you know? I thought they would have told you that in Oxford. It's another outcome of the Infection. All the women who contracted the virus and didn't die of the fevers and the gripes have stopped producing eggs. Their ovaries have just dried up. It's like the menopause but quicker, and sooner.'

Lander hadn't heard this. He was astounded. 'And that's happened to you? You can't have kids?'

'Yup. I stopped having periods months ago. I thought I must be pregnant, but when I got to the Bonnies they told me the truth. The authorities are trying to keep it to themselves because they're afraid there'll be a mass panic, but of course they can't do that for long.'

'But how are we going to survive? How are we going to repopulate the country? The world?'

'Exactly. That's one for the boffins, but there are also social implications. Monogamy is a system designed to support the family unit and provide for the raising of children. If there are no children it becomes irrelevant. Generations of women have been brought up to believe that breeding and looking after children are the most important things in their lives. That's not true now, even if it ever was. And there are advantages to being infertile: no more condoms, no more pills, no more coils, no more morning after, no more unwanted kids, no more abortions.'

Even though he had a twin sister, Lander had never really thought about the woman's side of the sex equation. There was a lot more to it for them.

'So while the politicians and the white coats figure out what to do about it, I'm going to enjoy myself.'

Steve got back in the boat, they hooked up Joey again and moved on. Magda put her arm around Lander, and after a few steps he, tentatively at first, put his around her. She gave him a squeeze and he squeezed her back.

'Were you jealous when you saw me and Steve?'

'No, 'course not,' said Lander.

'Bet you were, really. I'm just trying to keep him on our side, that's all. You don't like him, do you.'

'He's an arsehole.'

'Agreed,' said Magda. 'And if he says "know what I mean?" one more time I think I'll kill him.'

Lander laughed. It was a mannerism that irritated him too.

They moved on; past locks, under bridges, towards the city. Little by little the urban environment became more dense. After a while Magda left him and got back in the boat with Steve. When he took a peek they were kissing. He was reminded of a phrase the lads at school had had for loose girls: they "spread the honey". The attitude of his contemporaries at King's Heath to them had been complicated. They'd been reviled, but at the same time they'd been desired. Was that how he felt about Magda?

The voice of Steve roused him from his thoughts. 'It's getting lighter. We'd best look for a place to hide.'

They didn't have to look far. Ahead was a short tunnel. Magda unhitched Joey and removed his harness. 'I'll take him back there along the bank,' she said. 'We passed a meadow where he can graze.'

Lander was doubtful. He didn't like Joey being out of their sight for long. He might stray, and there was the constant threat of feral animals. Or he might simply be taken by somebody. He was a tempting target, a strong, fine-looking horse which, at a time when powering machinery was a problem, could be made to work. But there was no choice, Joey had to eat and there was nothing for him here.

While Magda led him away, Lander and Steve pulled their bedding out of the boat and spread it on the bank. Lander noticed that it was starting to smell. He hoped they'd be in Oxford soon.

'What do you think about this?' said Lander. 'All this stuff Magda was saying?'

'You mean about chicks doing it with anybody?' said Steve. He grinned. 'If that's what they want, it's all right with me. Know what I mean?'

Lander sighed. This was, after all, somebody who's response to the end of civilisation had been to go to a massive rave where sex and drugs had been the palliative.

'Kerryl told me once about a book she'd been reading,' said Lander. 'I think it was called Brave New Life. No, *Brave New World*, that was it. There was free sex in that, and the state kept everybody quiet by giving them drugs. Do you think that's what we're heading for?'

'I dunno,' said Steve. 'Could be worse.'

'Do you like Magda?'

'She's all right. I prefer blondes really. And a bit more curvy, know what I mean?'

'I mean, do you like her as a person?'

Steve looked surprised, as though this had never occurred to him. 'I suppose.'

'Because I do. I like her as a person.'

Steve gave him a long look. 'Look, she told you what she thinks, how it's going to be. The scientists are going to have to come up with some way of getting more sprogs, aren't they. Till then we all do our own thing.'

Lander wanted to take the discussion further, to explore what the future might be for them all, but he wasn't sure Steve was capable of doing that. He sat on the bedding in silence. There was a plastic bottle floating in the water and he started to throw pebbles at it. Steve joined in and it became a competition between them.

It dawned on Lander that Magda had been gone for some time. The field he thought she'd meant was only a couple of hundred yards back. She'd had plenty of time to take Joey, secure him where he could graze, and return to their tunnel. She should have come back by now.

He was about to go looking for her when he saw two figures stumbling through the early light. One was clearly Magda, and she was helping somebody else along. He jumped up and ran towards them. Steve stayed put.

Magda's companion was another young woman, and she was in a bad state. Her face was drawn and she had a hunted look. She could hardly walk and was in the sort of hospital gown Lander had worn in Oxford, except that this one was filthy and stained with blood. She reminded him of how Magda herself had looked when they got away from the shed, and for a second he thought this woman must have been Mickey's prisoner too, but of course that was impossible, Mickey was dead.

'Help me get her to the boats,' Magda said.

Lander took the girl's other arm and she collapsed between them. She tried to walk but she could scarcely put one foot in front of the other, so they half carried, half dragged her.

Lander's mind was racing. Had the pair of them been attacked by strangers? By a patrol? Surely they'd not run into some more feral kids.

'What happened?' he said. 'Are you okay?'

'Yes, I'm fine.'

'Who is she?'

'I don't know.'

'Where did you find her?'

'I led Joey into the field and I was tying him to the fence and she came out of the woods. She ran towards me and fell flat on her face. She won't say anything. Let's take her to the tunnel and see if we can get her to take some food. Then we need to work out what to do with her.'

'How do you mean? We can't take her to Oxford with us.'

'We can't leave her on her own.'

'Why not?'

'Take a look at her.'

Lander glanced down at the slight figure dangling from their arms. She was obviously undernourished and she seemed shattered, but despite the stains on her hospital gown she didn't appear to be injured and there were no broken limbs. Then he noticed the unmistakable swelling of her belly.

'Oh My God. She's pregnant.'

TWENTY-FOUR
LISA

HER NAME WAS LISA. She was exhausted, and it was some time before she could speak, let alone tell a coherent story. Magda persuaded her to try to eat some crispbreads and tinned ham, and she sorted out some clothes from the things she'd taken from Kerryl's room. Gradually as the day progressed Lisa's story emerged.

She and her twin sister, Becky, had lived in a small village near Hereford, with their elderly parents and a much older brother. The others caught the Infection, but Lisa and her sister survived.

'Everybody in the village died of it. Everybody. People we'd known for years were gone, just...just...gone,' she told them. 'All our friends. We tried to call them and we went round their houses, but nobody answered and nobody was in. Then all the phones went dead. And the TV. We was real scared at first, being on our own and that, but after a bit we got used to it. It sounds bad to say it, but in a way it was good. Nobody bothered us and we had enough to get by. I was expecting and Becky was there to see to me. We was all right.'

Lander understood what Lisa was saying. Parts of her story were like his own and Kerryl's; twins surviving, the rest of the family and all their friends being struck down. The way they had felt detached from everyone else, even those closest to them, echoed his experience too. Was there something about twins that made them better able to resist the virus?

Lisa had fallen silent. Steve prompted her to go on.

'So what went wrong?'

'A lot. One day a patrol came to the village. It was sunny and me and Becky was in the garden sunbathing, and we heard this noise. It was a car engine. We was so excited we rushed out into the road, jumping up and down because we thought we was being rescued.'

'And you weren't,' said Magda.

'Well we was in a way,' said Lisa, 'but then not. Or not what we expected it to be. They said we was lucky to be alive and we needed to be taken in for some tests, to make sure we was all right. I was hardly showing then and I didn't see why they'd got to test us, but we had no choice. They took us to this hospital in Wrexham. When we got there we saw they had some other girls too, and a few older women, and we heard children but we never saw them. There was no blokes, apart from some of the doctors and these people they called nurses, but who was really guards. They told us that more women had survived the Infection than men and that we was particularly useful to their research because we was twins. But that was a lie, because they split us up. They took Becky away.'

Lisa stopped and Magda gave her a tissue and put her arm around her. They waited until she felt able to go on.

'At first I was all right,' she said. 'They just left us alone and I spent the days talking with the other girls. It was great to know we wasn't the only ones left. They had electricity at the hospital so we could watch videos. They'd said there'd be tests but there weren't none. It was all right. Then they found out I was pregnant. I think one of the other girls must have told them.'

'How far on were you?' said Magda.

'About three months, I think. I hadn't been to a doctor but there was only one time it could have happened, at a party with a boy I hardly knew. Anyway, they got very excited then, and they did start to do tests. They took blood, and they did scans, all sorts. They took some bone marrow from me too. That hurt. Not at the time, they put you out, but afterwards I had back ache and I felt stiff all over, and I got headaches. I couldn't sleep and I lost my appetite. They said all this was normal and not to worry. Then they started to do tests on Becky too.'

'She wasn't in the club too, was she?' said Steve.

'No, don't be daft. But they did the same tests on her. It all calmed down after that. And then Becky disappeared.'

'They took her away?' said Magda.

'They said they wanted to check on her results, but she didn't come back. I asked them where she was and they said they'd taken her to another clinic because she'd volunteered for some extra tests. I knew that wasn't right. She wouldn't have done that without telling me first. They said she'd be back in a day or two, but she wasn't. She'd vanished. I started to get worried then. I said I wanted to see her but they brushed me off. I knew the baby was really important to them, so I told them that if they didn't take me to see her I'd abort it. 'Course I never would, but that's what I told them.'

'Can you do that?' said Lander. 'Abort yourself? Is it possible?'

'Maybe,' said Magda. 'Desperate women have tried all sorts of methods: knitting needles, doing belly flops on to a hard surface, starving themselves, douching with chemicals. They all can work but they're painful, and dangerous.' She turned back to Lisa. 'What happened. Did they take you to Becky?'

'No. But they got really worried, though. They took me away from the other girls and locked me in a room on my own. There was nothing there except a bed and a chair and a telly. There was nothing sharp, not even a tea spoon. So I stopped eating, and after a few days of that they took me to this really important woman.'

'Do you know who she was?' said Magda.

'Another doctor, but a top one.' Lisa frowned. 'A black lady. She said her name was Gwen something or other.'

'Gwen Matthews,' said Magda.

'Yes, that's it,' said Lisa.

'You know her?' said Lander. He was surprised that Magda would.

'I know of her. Anyway, what did Gwen Matthews have to say to you?'

'She said that Becky was all right but she'd had a negative reaction to one of the tests and it would take her a few days to get over it. Then she said that the authorities had a responsibility for repopulating the country. They wanted to do that as quickly as possible and people like me, women who was pregnant before the virus attacked, was very important. They wanted to take some sort of cells from me. They said they'd be for an ovary pool.'

'Stem cells,' said Magda. 'They must have been intending to harvest oogonial cells.'

'What are they when they're at home?' said Steve.

'They can be used to produce oocytes, immature egg cells. They could freeze them and preserve them for fertilisation later.'

'Like a baby bank,' said Steve.

'Yes, kind of,' said Magda. 'What did you say?' she asked Lisa.

'Well they said it was my patriotic duty to cooperate and I couldn't say no. I asked her what would happen if I didn't do it. There was a bloke with her and he said that to refuse cooperation would be treason, and anyone who did that would be turned out with no money, food or ID. Also I should think about the effects on Becky. So I said fair enough, but I wanted to see Becky first. They didn't seem to like that, and that was what made me realise that there was something wrong. I got upset then and I yelled at the woman, and they took me away.'

Something occurred to Lander. 'This bloke who was with Gwen Matthews, was he young, good looking, curly blonde hair? Name of Adam?'

Lisa looked surprised. 'Yes,' she said. 'I don't know his name, but that's what he looked like.'

Lander had almost forgiven Adam for what had happened to Kerryl. The experiment had gone wrong, but sometimes they did. It was heart-breaking, but it was understandable. However, he was coming to see that Adam wasn't just the affable, squash-playing mate he'd pretended to be in Oxford. He was driven to find ways to rebuild the population. That was praiseworthy, but in pursuing it he would go to any lengths, and that included sacrificing others. The individual was expendable if that led to the greater good, and there wasn't a pie safe from his probing fingers. Lander's anger returned.

'Tell us how you escaped,' said Magda.

'That was weird,' said Lisa. 'And easy, really. When they took me away from this doctor woman I was struggling and kicking and they must have knocked me out. I felt a jab in my neck and I went down. I came to in my room, and the door was open and there was a terrible din coming from down the corridor. Shouting, screaming, furniture – those metal chairs – being thrown about, whistles. I had an awful headache but I had to see what was going on. There was another girl in the corridor and she was scared, trembling like a leaf. "What's going on?" I said and she said there'd been a lecture about how they were all going to help repopulate the country and there was no choice and they had to do it and some of them said they weren't going to be no baby farmers and some of the guards started to get heavy, and then people started throwing things. I could see into the big room at the end of the corridor and there was like a real big fight going on. I saw one of the guards get his helmet pulled off and he was hit with a bottle. Just then something rolled towards us and it started to fizz and smoke, so we ran, right out of the door at the other end. Two of the guards come after us and they grabbed the other girl but I got away.'

'Wow,' said Lander. 'Some escape!'

'What did you do then?' said Magda.

'I hid in a drain in the grounds. I heard people searching, and dogs, but they didn't find me. I was there all day, I was perished. When it got dark I came out. One of the other girls had told me there was a women's group near Stafford, like a refuge where people could go. They call themselves the Nightingales. I thought they might help me with my baby so I decided I'd try to find them. But I had no food and I didn't know the way to go and I got lost. I must have walked miles and I'd reached my limit when you found me.'

TWENTY-FIVE

LAKE MANOR

'HOW COME SHE KNOWS so much about all this?' said Steve.

'How come who knows so much about all what?' said Lander.

'Magda, all this baby stuff. Oomegoolie cells, or whatever they're called.

'Oogonial. I've no idea. Perhaps she's had some medical training.'

'I thought you'd know.'

Lander thought maybe he should have, but when he considered it he had to admit he knew very little about Magda. They'd been confined together, shackled at opposite ends of the same chain; they'd eaten together and slept together, in the literal sense; they'd each had to use the same lavatory bucket in full view of the other; they had jointly murdered a man, or rather Magda had with Lander an accessory. Yet the flow of information had been one way. He'd told Magda about Kerryl, the farm, his family, his dream of playing cricket for Yorkshire, *thetruthwillmakeyoufree*, everything. She'd listened, she'd asked questions, but all she'd given him was a very brief account of being in the Bonnies and getting caught by Mickey. He knew nothing of her life before that. Was she hiding something?

Magda had said that Lisa was too weak to travel and needed several days rest and food before she could. Lander was frustrated, impatient to carry on to Oxford, but there was no choice.

'She needs help,' said Magda. 'We can't just leave her, and we can't take her with us. It's best we get her better and then point her in the direction of the group she wants to join.'

Although they were well into an urban area and there were frequent sounds of human and machine activity, their hiding place under the bridge was a good one. No one was using the canal or the towpath, and they'd only once heard traffic on the bridge. Joey had plenty of grass in his field and he could get water too, sop he was happy enough.

It should have been a good opportunity to rest but it didn't work out like that. It was hard to get back to sleeping at night again after being used to doing that during the day. Lander had never experienced jet-lag, but he supposed this disturbance to his body clock must be what it was like. Noises from Steve and Magda in the other boat didn't help. Eventually he got up.

They'd made a bed for Lisa on the embankment but Lander found her sitting beside the bridge, her face pale in the thin moonlight. He sat beside her. He wanted her to tell him about her plan to seek out the women's group.

'You know this place near Stafford that you're trying to get to? Do you know anything about it?'

'Not much,' she said. 'Only what one of the girls told me. It's supposed to be a big house, in the country, and there's a bunch of women living there. She said there are women's groups all over the place, and all of them go in for different things. Some make stuff, some do studying, some look after kids and teach. They have different names. The one I'm looking for is called the Nightingales. They're supposed to specialise in medical things and in curing people. I thought they'd be the people to go to to have my baby.'

Lander agreed. It sounded as though these women should help. But where were they?

'Do you know any more about them? I mean, a big country house near Stafford is a bit vague. I expect there are a lot of those.'

Lisa rummaged in her pocket. Lander noticed that she was wearing a pair of Kerryl's jeans, he recognised the butterfly embroidered on the thigh. The grief was not as intense as it had been, but occasionally seeing something that had been hers gave him a little stab, like now.

'This is all I've got,' she said, handing him a piece of paper.

It was grubby and folded and almost illegible, but Lander could make out the words Lake Manor, which he supposed was what the house was called, and below that the name of a village and a post code. The post code was no help, the house name not much better, and he'd never heard of the village. Lander had expected a stately home, somewhere like Shugborough, where the Earl of Lichfield lived and which he and Kerryl had been taken to visit when they were kids. A place like that would be easy to find. Lake Manor didn't sound anywhere near as grand.

Steve was asleep and Lander enjoyed waking him up. He shook his shoulder.

'Where are the maps?'

Steve blinked and looked blank, so Lander repeated. 'The road atlas. Where is it?'

'I've got it.' Steve was still bleary.

'Where is it?'

'What do you want the fucking atlas for at this time of night?'

'I need to find a place.'

'What place? Why do you want to know?'

Lander got exasperated. 'It's my atlas and I want to use it. Where is it?'

'What's going on?' said Magda, emerging blearily from under the shared duvet.

'All right, all right,' said Steve. He told Lander where he'd stowed the atlas in the lead boat.

Lander soon found the village. It didn't seem to be too far away, only a few miles, and it should be easy enough to reach. It didn't look to be very large, so once they got there finding Lake Manor ought to be a doddle.

When he got back to Lisa she'd fallen asleep. Lander took off his fleece and covered her with it. He sat beside her for a long time, until the chill of the night forced him to go back to the boat.

In the morning he talked to Magda. She had gone for a stroll along the canal bank, making her regular check on Joey, and Lander went to meet her. He started straight away with what was on his mind.

'You know this place that Lisa's making for?' he said. 'Well, I talked to her about it. She says it's run by a bunch of women like the lot you were with, except these specialise in medicine and care. She wants to have the baby there. She gave me the address.' He offered Magda the paper but she didn't take it. 'It's in a village and I've looked it up on the atlas. It's not far away, and easy country,' he continued. 'I'm sure it would only take a couple of hours to get to it. I thought I might go check it out, you know, see how the land lies. If we can find out exactly where it is, as soon as Lisa's strong enough we can take her straight to it.'

'Good idea,' said Magda. 'I'll come too.'

The whole thing was settled very quickly. Steve and Lisa would stay with the boats and keep watch on Joey while Magda and Lander would locate Lake Manor, see if the Nightingales really were there and, if they were, tell them about Lisa.

'It's only a few miles,' Lander said to Steve. 'It won't take us long. We'll suss the place out and come back.'

'Knock yourselves out,' said Steve.

'Look after Lisa. And Joey.'

'You bet.'

Lander wondered if it might be better to go at night, but Magda pointed out that it would be harder to find their way, and what would they do if they arrived at the place and everyone was asleep?.

'Besides,' she said, 'it's the same old problem. Travel at night and there's less chance of being seen, but if we are spotted we'll be much more suspicious. If we look as though we know what we're doing we'll be fine.'

Magda said she'd half a mind to ride Joey but she didn't fancy going all that way bareback. She abandoned the idea when Lander said he wasn't going to be the one to walk.

They each packed a rucksack with things they thought they might need – some food, extra clothing, and a sleeping bag in case their quest turned out to be futile and they had to spend a night in the open. While they did so it started to rain, hard. Lander went to the end of the bridge and looked at the torrent lashing the towpath and splashing into the canal.

'Not good,' said Magda.

'Granddad used to glue himself to the weather forecasts,' said Lander. 'He never missed the Farmers' Forecast on the TV. I never bothered, but I could do with one now. This might go on for ages.'

A drop of icy water fell from the bridge and found the nape of his neck. He shivered. He'd commit murder for a hot drink. He couldn't remember when he'd last had one. They'd only managed to find a few cylinders for their camping stove and they'd not lasted long. As soon as they got back from this trip a top priority would be to find some more. And some drinking chocolate.

They agreed that there was no point waiting for the weather to clear up; they might as well go.

'Looks like we'll be walking in the rain,' said Magda.

Lander grunted. An earworm, an old song their Granddad used to play, started up in his head. *Just walking in the rain, Getting soaking wet, Torturing my heart, By trying to forget.* He remembered the album. It was called Johnnie Ray in Las Vegas. The cover had a picture of the casino where Johnny was performing, as well as his photo. Their Gran had quite fancied him and Granddad used to make fun of her about it. What a lot of daft stuff people used to spend their time on, he thought. Silly, trivial, useless, time wasting stuff. He'd give anything to have it all back.

After ten minutes they were wondering whether they'd done the right thing. They were drenched, the water trickling off their waterproofs and soaking their fatigue bottoms.

'We'd be better off without these,' said Magda, tugging at hers.

'You mean take them off?'

'Yes. The material just makes a soggy poultice. It's rubbing my leg sore, and the rain won't feel as bad on our bare skin. Might be a bit cold but it will be OK if we keep moving.

They took off their bottoms in a field gateway. There was a bad smell. Lander was conscious that his underwear was far from clean, but it wasn't that.

'What's over there?' he said, seeing a shapeless lump in the field.

It was the body of a dog. Its coat was drenched and rills of dried blood ran from a gunshot wound. The body had started to decompose. Lander poked it with his foot and revealed that it hosted a colony of maggots.

'A wild one,' said Magda, wrinkling her nose. 'The army are shooting them.'

'How do you know that?'

'I've read the PIRPs.'

'The whats?'

'The PIRPs. Post Infection Reconstruction Papers. It's the term for the government's plans to put the country back together again. It's their bible. It covers everything, including culling animals that have gone wild.'

Lander was amazed. It was logical for there to be something like that, some strategy for coping with the chaos and rebuilding the country, but he hadn't imagined anything sensible truly existed. His opinion, and it had been widely shared, was that when the Infection came the government didn't have a clue how to deal with it and thrashed about trying to shut stable doors long after the horses had fled. And once again he was surprised at the amount of information Magda seemed to have.

'How do you know about this "bible"?' he said.

'It's a long story.'

'We've got plenty of time.'

'All right.' She smiled and they started walking again. 'Stop me when you get bored. When the Infection came I was at medical school, in my third year. I wanted to be a doctor. At first none of us had a clue what was going on, but all the students agreed we should try to do something

to help. I mean we were medics, after all. We weren't
fully trained but we knew quite a bit – or we thought we
did – and we were sure we could be of some use, so we all
volunteered. I thought we'd be sent to work in hospitals.
Perhaps some of us were. Not me, though. I was selected
– ordered, actually – to join one of the arks. You know
about the arks, I heard you telling Steve about them.'

'Yes. Adam told me. Places where groups of people were
kept behind protective barriers to isolate them from the
virus. He didn't say where they were, though.'

'They were scattered all over the place: in some of the
Oxbridge colleges, at military facilities, in stately homes.
In some places whole villages were taken over. The one I
was sent to was at Hampton Court Palace. Very grand,
except I spent most of my time in the cellars.'

'Why?'

'The team I joined was there. We were working on AI.'

'Artificial intelligence?'

Magda laughed. 'Artificial insemination. It was part of a
breeding programme. The objective was as soon as the
Infection was over to get as many women as possible
pregnant.'

'Wow. Better not tell Steve.'

She laughed. 'On the face of it what we were doing isn't a
bad idea, but it assumes that all the pre- and post-natal
services – the midwives, maternity units, health workers

– would be in place to support it. Not to mention the later need for nurseries and schools. But of course, all that had gone, blown away by the superbug. What really killed it, though, was that all the women in the arks turned out to be infertile. Like I told you, all of us exposed to the virus got our ovaries blasted, and while everybody thought the arks would be virus free and foundations for the future, it seems they weren't.'

Lander listened for a touch of emotion in Magda's tone but none was there. It was all very matter of fact. It took a moment, but then it dawned on him what Magda's explanation was implying. He said one word. 'Lisa.'

'Yes,' said Magda, 'Lisa. Can you understand how important she is? Can you see why the authorities will be so keen to get her back? Lisa is a rarity, a woman who conceived before the virus struck. There can't be many of those left. Of course, there are loads of questions. Will her baby be born without any disabilities? Once it is born, will her ovaries resume normal egg production or will she be sterile like the rest of us? And if her ovaries are working, will she be able to conceive again? Will the baby be immune to the virus, like its mother? They'll want to get hold of her so that they can discover the answers to all those.'

By now the rain had stopped. It seemed that one effect of the downpour was to inhibit activity elsewhere. There were no patrols or working parties, and there was no sign of anyone else either. They kept up a brisk pace, and soon both were steaming. They came to the first signpost for the village and then they saw it, a small group of houses and a church spire two fields away. They'd have to go around three sides of a rectangle to get there by the road. Lander wanted to take a short cut, but Magda thought that would be too conspicuous.

'We're hoping the Nightingales will be friendly, if they're there, but we can't rely on it. We'll be better off keeping a low profile.'

Lake Manor was easy to spot. There was a large building on a low hill a little way out of the village.

'That must be it,' said Lander. 'There's the lake.'

'Looks like it.'

They headed towards it.

The house was impressive. There was a classical façade above a sweeping flight of steps, with a wing on either side. In front was the lake which gave the place its name, and to the rear was open parkland and a grove of trees. It wasn't exactly a stately home, but it wasn't far off.

'Not bad,' said Lander. 'If Lisa ends up here she should be very comfortable. I can't see anybody about though. Let's go take a look.'

Magda put a restraining hand on his arm. 'Hang on a minute. I think we should take our time.'

Lander frowned. 'Why?'

'Reason one,' Magda said, 'is that even though our fatigues are scruffy they might take us for army, in which case they'll probably hide. Reason two, if they find out I'm a Bonny I don't know how they'll respond. Not all the women's groups get on well with each other. I don't know what relations are like between this lot and us, but I don't want to risk it until we're better acquainted.'

'How would they know you are a Bonny? You're not wearing a badge.'

'Oh yes I am.' Magda pointed to her lower leg; there was a tattoo of a skull and crossbones. Lander had seen it before, but not thought it was anything beyond body art.

'That's the emblem of the Bonnies?' he said. 'I didn't realise.'

'I told you, Anne Bonny was a pirate. You didn't make the connection? Anyway, I think we should put these back on first.'

She tugged her damp fatigue pants out of her backpack, Lander did the same, and they put them on. They were cold and clammy.

'Hold me,' said Magda, and they clung together shivering. After a moment or two she spoke again. 'All right, we can't stay here. Better move.'

They approached the house with caution, but they didn't hide. Magda had pointed out that sneaking up under cover might look threatening, so they walked slowly down the middle of the drive.

The closer they got the more Lander thought their journey was futile. Although the house had looked imposing from a distance, from closer up it was not so impressive. The white paint on the window frames and doors was dirty and flaking, and in many places it was missing altogether. A drainpipe was hanging off the wall. There were signs of neglect in the garden. There was no smoke from the chimneys, no signs of activity outside, and – the clincher – every window was blank, all the shutters closed. The house was abandoned and empty.

'Looks like nobody's home,' said Lander.

'Mm. I'm not so sure,' said Magda. 'Let's get a bit nearer.'

Lander took a step forward, and heard a sound like the crack of a whip. He felt a sharp sting on his buttock. Even as his hand reached down to examine the cause, everything went out-of-focus and he sank into a black hole.

The last thing he thought as he fell was, oh no, not again.

TWENTY-SIX

THE NIGHTINGALES

LANDER WAS NOT sure when consciousness returned. He had faded to black, and it was black when he opened his eyes. For some time he stared into the dark. Then he felt an ache in his thigh muscles. It built until it became severe and demanded relief. He must move, but he couldn't. He was fastened to an upright chair, bound round with duct tape so tight that it was hard to breath.

'You awake?' It was Magda.

'Yes. I'm tied up.'

'Me too. Are you all right?'

'I think so. I can't move and I'm getting a cramp in my leg.'

'I'm getting it too. It must be something to do with whatever drug they've given us.'

'What's going on? What happened?'

'I think we were shot with tranquilising darts.'

'Fuck!' Lander spat the word. 'Fuck, fuck, fuck! I can't believe it. Not again.'

'Again?'

'I've been got by one of those things before. I told you. In Snaith.'

Suddenly the convulsion in his leg returned, like a vice squeezing his calf.

'Jesus, it's back,' he snarled through clenched teeth.

'Take deep breaths,' said Magda.

'I can't. I'm strapped too tight.' He gritted his teeth. Gradually the pain retreated. 'Where are we?' he said, panting.

'I don't know, but we must have been captured.'

Lander let out a howl like a stricken dog. 'First jail, then Oxford, then Mickey, now this. I just keep running into people who want to lock me up. Who is it this time? Who's got us?'

'I don't know,' said Magda. 'It could be the Nightingales but it might be somebody else. Anyway, your yelping will have told them we're conscious so we'll soon find out.'

Lander's head throbbed and his throat was parched. 'It can't be the Nightingales,' he said. 'People who are supposed to care for people wouldn't do this.'

'Don't be so sure.'

'When they got me with a tranquilliser in Snaith it was the army. I bet it's them again. We've walked into a trap.'

'It's not the army.'

'How do you know?'

'I just do. Trust me.'

Lander didn't feel like trusting anyone. Anger and frustration boiled.

'Aaagh!' The pain in his leg struck him again, this time worse. His leg muscles contracted and he sucked at the air. 'Oh my God my God my God, it's back. The tape's so tight I can't move to ease it. It's agony. Aaagh!'

Lander writhed and twisted until the attack receded, leaving him sweating and breathless.

As Magda predicted, they soon met the people who had taken them. There was the noise of a door opening and somebody, several somebodies came into the room. Two of them carried torches, which they directed straight into Lander's face. That meant he couldn't see their captors. Another moved behind him, tied a covering across his eyes and knotted it tightly at the back of his head.

'You can put the light on,' somebody said.

Lander saw a fringe of yellow appear around the edges of his blindfold. What was happening was so like what he'd gone through before that he wondered for a crazy moment if this was some kind of fantasy, a ground hog experience, or if he was in some incomprehensible hell where Mickey had been resurrected.

These thoughts were disrupted by the cramp returning, this time in his thigh. It was excruciating. He groaned and tried to move to ease the agony. His leg stiffened and his teeth clamped as his whole body contracted. Their captors seemed to know what was happening because they did nothing, simply waiting until the attack passed. Then one of them spoke.

'I'm going to ask you some questions. If you give me honest answers, truthful ones, then all this can be over very quickly.' It was a woman's voice, without accent and formal, like a BBC news presenter. It didn't sound cruel or even hostile, but it was firm. It was a voice that was used to giving orders and to them being obeyed. It was not the sort of voice you argued with.

Lander heard the scrape of a chair. The questioner must have sat down in front of him, because when the voice came again it was closer.

'I'm going to start with you, the male,' it said. 'What is your name?'

The old routine, he thought. There was nothing to be gained from hiding who he was. He knew from previous experience that his name was the first thing an abductor wanted to know, and that they would go on until he told them.

'Lander,' he said.

'Lander?'

He always had this trouble. 'It's a nickname,' he explained. 'Short for Alexander. Alexander James Shaw.'

The echo of the cramp was still there, lurking beneath the surface and ready to pounce again at any moment. It made it hard to concentrate.

'Good,' said the voice. 'That's your name settled. Now what about your rank and number? Oh, and it would help us, and you, if you told us your unit too.'

She must think we're army, thought Lander, part of a patrol or something. Magda's right, it's not the army that's got us.

'There's no rank or number,' he said. 'Or unit. I'm nothing to do with anything official.'

There was a long pause. Then the woman spoke again. It was very quiet and very patient, as if she were addressing a small child of limited understanding.

'This can take as long as you like,' she said. 'Just so you're fully aware of what's going on, I'll explain. Then you can decide whether you're going to co-operate with us or not.'

Lander let out a strangled gurgle. His whole body tried to arch but the binding meant he couldn't move. The spasm seemed interminable, and when at last it eased he was breathless and soaked in sweat.

'There you have a demonstration of the problem you face,' said the woman. 'You see, we shot you with a tranquilising dart. It's like the ones that are used for rendering wild animals unconscious. The ones used on animals are harmless, but this particular variant has a serious side effect: severe cramping of the muscles. There's an antidote that stops the contractions very quickly, but without that they will get worse. And worse. And worse.'

She paused, as if giving Lander time to take all this in, but he had got the message; he was at this woman's mercy. His pain was her pleasure, its relief in her gift.

'It's rather like tetanus,' she continued. 'The cramps will become more frequent and the spasms will last longer. Eventually you will reach a point where us questioning you will be pointless, because you won't be able to speak. Soon after that you won't be able to breathe either, and then you'll die. But that will be many painful hours down the road. And of course, we won't let you die. We'll give you the antidote before that. And then, if we don't have the information we seek, we'll start the whole process again, as many times as we need. Now, we have no desire to cause you pain so let's get this over with. We want to know your number, rank and unit.'

There was a choking sound to Lander's right and he realised that Magda too must be experiencing the cramps.

'Yes,' said the voice, 'in case you are in any doubt, you are both being subjected to the same treatment. We shall see who co-operates first.'

Magda spoke. 'We don't have any of those things you want,' she said, and her voice was tight. 'We're not from the army. We came here because we have a friend who needs your help.'

There was a scraping as the questioner's chair was turned towards Magda.

'Why didn't this "friend" come himself?'

'It's not him, it's her. And she didn't come herself because she's pregnant.'

Lander sensed rather than heard the effect this information had on their torturer.

'Tell me more.'

'Our friend became pregnant before the Infection, which she's survived. She was taken by the authorities for a breeding programme. She escaped and ran into us,' Magda said. 'She'd heard about a group called the Nightingales and was told they were at Lake Manor. She thought they would help her when the time comes for her baby. We said we'd find them.' There was another strangled sound, and a long pause before Magda was able to continue. Then she said, with savage bitterness, 'It's a good job we came alone, because if you'd shot her like you shot us you'd have killed her baby.'

There was no immediate response from the woman. Eventually she said, 'What do you think, Christine? Do you go for this, or is it just so much bullshit?'

Another voice spoke, presumably Christine's. She sounded older, and thoughtful. 'I don't know. They're in army uniforms but they have no badges of rank, no decals, and no ID. That's very suspicious. And they give us a yarn about a pregnant woman, which they know is a story we would want to believe.'

Lander got most of this, but another convulsion wiped out some of it. The attacks were more frequent now.

'If we were army,' said Magda, 'do you really think we'd come here in uniform?'

'You might,' said the woman who wasn't Christine.

'Hiding in plain sight,' said a third voice. 'Often the best form of concealment.'

'I can show you I'm not in the army,' said Magda. 'I belong to one of our groups. I'm a Bonny.'

There was an intake of breath.

'Oh yes? Can you prove that?'

'Of course,' said Magda.

'Look at her leg,' said Christine.

There was the shuffle of movement and then the third voice, now low down on Lander's right said, 'It's there. She has the skull and crossbones.'

The first woman spoke. 'That doesn't mean anything. There's nothing to stop an army infiltrator having that tattoo done as part of their cover, so they can deceive us.'

There was a long pause. The women weren't sure. Lander went into another spasm, the most severe so far. He felt as though his limbs were being pulled apart, each joint dislocated from its neighbour. It was the worst pain he had ever known, far worse than the previous record, which was when he broke his collar bone falling off his bike.

The woman made up her mind. 'Give them the antidote,' she ordered.

Somebody fumbled with Lander's sleeve and he felt a jab in his arm. The effect was almost immediate. There was blissful relief as the drug ran through his body and the pain receded, but every muscle was wounded, affronted by the assault it had suffered. His head fell forward onto his chest. He knew he was drooling, and he sucked in saliva.

'Now listen,' said the woman. 'We are indeed the Nightingales, and for now we're going to give you the benefit of the doubt. However, if anything you tell us turns out not to be true, we'll hit you with the tranquilliser again and this time there will be no antidote. We'll simply shut the door and walk away.'

'Lie and you die,' said one of the others.

'It's easy for us to prove that what I've told you is the truth,' said Magda. 'Let us go, and we'll bring the mother-to-be to you.'

And that's what happened, but it was a long process. First their blindfolds were removed, and when his eyes got used to the light Lander saw that they were in a cellar. There was a heavy, brown door and walls of a dingy white. There were three women with them. The one who'd spoken first and done most of the talking told them she was called Carole. She looked to be older than Magda but not much, and she had the manner of a school teacher. The one called Christine was considerably older, more Maisie's vintage. Her grey hair was done in ringlets, which to Lander looked incongruous. The third woman was the youngest of the three, about Lander's own age, he guessed. Her name was also Christine but she'd shortened it to Chrissie.

'The three Cs,' said Carole. 'Charity, chastity and chocolate.' They laughed, for the first time since they'd come into the room. 'But we won't tell you which is which.' They laughed more.

While this was going on Chrissie was releasing them from the tape that had held them in their chairs. Magda was able to stand but Lander couldn't.

'We gave you a heavier dose,' Carole said to him, 'being as how you're a big feller.' She got her shoulder under his arm and gently raised him from the chair. His legs were like jelly and wouldn't hold him up. 'Come on, lean on me,' she said. 'Don't be shy. Most men lean on women all the time.'

They were taken out of the cellar, up some stone steps and along a short passage into what must once have been a drawing room. The furniture was grand but faded, and there wasn't much of it. The space was dim because the shutters were closed and the only light came from a couple of oil lamps on tables. They were given drinks of water and a sweet, scented cordial that they were told was elderflower.

'Drink plenty,' said Carole.

'Yes. In effect we poisoned you,' said Christine cheerfully. 'The tranquilliser is toxic, and even the antidote is really just another poison. You need to wash them both out of your systems as quickly as possible.' She refilled their tumblers.

Another woman brought in a plate of what, rather incongruously, looked like vol-au-vents, but Lander couldn't face any food. Whatever they had given him had made him nauseous.

The next hour resembled a game of chess; they swapped information like pieces, each side taking turn to release one item in exchange for another. They learnt that there were currently eighteen Nightingales – 'But our number grows almost daily,' said Christine. All of them were trained medics, or were in the process of undergoing training when the Infection struck. There were four GPs and a couple of consultants – one an obstetrician, the other a rheumatologist. There was a dentist, an optometrist and a trainee dermatologist. The rest were nurses, midwives and health workers of various stages and ages, and there was one girl with a background in alternative medicines and therapies. They were interested to hear that Magda, too, had had some medical training, and wanted to know why she'd joined the Bonnies and not them.

'I didn't know where you were,' said Magda. 'Anyway, the Bonnies seemed to suit me.'

'We Nightingales, named after Florence, you know,' Christine pointed out rather unnecessarily, 'dedicate ourselves to doing good. We try to heal those who are suffering, or at the least to help them if we can't cure them. We're pledged to try to save and preserve lives. All of us have taken an oath to do that.'

'But we also take another oath,' said Carole. 'That is to defend our community and each other from attack by outsiders, by any means possible. Unfortunately that oath can conflict rather with the first one, as you've found out.'

In return for all this Lander – who was now feeling better and wishing that the vol-au-vents might reappear – and Magda each told them a little about themselves. They added to this where they were going, how, and why. Finally they told them how they'd encountered Lisa and what they knew of her.

'Travelling on the canals? In broad daylight? And you weren't caught?' Carole sounded incredulous.

'We think the imitation army uniforms did that,' said Magda. 'I mean, they fooled you.'

'You were lucky not to be arrested for vagrancy,' said Christine. 'You know that now carries an indeterminate jail sentence? Very lucky indeed.'

It was perhaps because they found this part of their story hard to believe that the women placed strict conditions on the arrangements for fetching Lisa. They agreed that Lander would be allowed to go back to the canal to get her. While he did so Magda would remain with the Nightingales. She wouldn't be locked up, she would be expected to work in the community. However, she would be watched. If Lander didn't return in three days, either with Lisa or with an explanation of why he didn't have her, they would administer the tranquilliser to Magda.

'End of,' said Chrissie helpfully.

GETTING BACK TO the canal was quicker than Lander had expected. He was not surprised that one of the Nightingales was going with him to keep an eye on things, and he'd been pleased when it turned out to be the girl. She was attractive, and he was sure he could chat her up; she wouldn't be any trouble. That was before she showed him a device like a knuckle duster, with finger holes and four spikes.

'This is a stun gun,' she said. 'It may be small but it packs a punch. Want to try it?' She slipped it over her fingers and made a demonstration lunge towards him.

'No thank you,' said Lander, dodging away.

'I should also warn you that I used to be the All-England Under 16 Girls' Taekwondo champion. And I can run too. So no funny stuff.'

'Oh. Right.' Lander had no intention of any funny stuff. Chrissie had made her point.

They walked on in silence for a little way. Then Lander said, 'Are you a student? I mean, were you?'

'No.'

'It's just that you seem a lot younger than the others. You don't look old enough to be a doctor.'

'I'm not. Lake Manor used to belong to my father. Now it's mine. Christine was a family friend. She told me she was starting the Nightingales and asked if they could use the house.'

'So if you're not a medic, what's your job?'

'I help them. And I work on God's plan.'

It was not an answer Lander was expecting and he was thrown. 'God's plan?'

'Yes,' she said. 'His scheme for making a better world.'

Lander was even more bewildered. He'd met two crazy old women. Now it seemed he'd found a crazy young one.

'What scheme?'

'The Infection, of course.'

'You think that what's happened is part of some grand design?'

'Don't you? You've heard the Bible story of the flood, haven't you?'

'Noah and the ark, and the animals going in two by two?'

'Yes. Well it's not a story. It really happened.'

Lander had an image of a wooden ark and pairs of toy animals that he and Kerryl had played with when they were children. Was she serious?

'You're having me on.'

Chrissie looked hurt. 'No, I mean it. Not the ark and the animals, that's just a myth, but the flood itself was an actual event. It's not just Christian and Jewish scriptures that refer to it. Babylonian, Mesopotamian, Ancient Greek and Hindu writings all mention a great flood, and there's evidence from excavations too.'

Lander had heard something like this before, in fact he thought he might have seen a TV documentary about it, but it was a long time ago and he'd not paid it much attention.

'Why does the Bible say the flood took place?' said Chrissie.

Lander shrugged. 'God made it rain a lot. I think He was supposed to be pissed off because humans weren't doing what He wanted.'

'Exactly. And it's happened again. Think of the world before the Infection. A few people were obscenely wealthy while billions of others had barely enough to get by. Some people starved while the greedy continued to hoard. There were the homeless, who had to sleep on the streets. There were wars that killed not just soldiers but thousands of civilians, many of them children. Terrorists slaughtered people they didn't even know and who had nothing to do with the causes they were pursuing. Countries attacked their neighbours for no reason. We were progressively destroying the planet, our only home, and most people didn't seem to care. They were out for themselves. It was a world of inequality, misery and cruelty.'

'Yes, but there was a lot of good stuff too.'

'There was some, but not enough of it, and we kept missing the opportunities we were given to make things better. Think about it. The lives of some people were so terrible that they had to give up everything and leave their homes. They went on long and dangerous journeys searching for better lives, except when they got there they found that those they were looking to for help turned them away. And lording it over all this were world leaders, strutting around and showing off, more interested in their own wealth and power than in improving the lives of others.' Chrissie's eyes burned with zeal. 'God sent His son to show us how it should be done. It's dead simple: be kind to people; don't take more than you need; feed the hungry, heal the sick, look after those in trouble. It's not rocket science. But we couldn't hack it, so the only thing God could do was press the reboot button.'

'You mean make the human race start again.'

'Yes. Not surprising, is it?'

Lander was appalled. Did she really think this? If so she was madder than he'd thought. On the other hand, he sympathised with her analysis of the world before the Infection. If she knew what he did, that it was human beings themselves who had created the Infection in their endless quest to find more effective ways of killing each other, she would be even more convinced. But he was not sure that he believed in God, and if he did it wasn't a God who would do that.

'So what happened?' he said. 'How did God start the virus?'

'Some people think that it was spread deliberately by some very rich and powerful people in order to slim down the world population.' Chrissie thought for a moment, then she added, 'God works in mysterious ways.'

They continued the rest of their journey in silence. Lander noticed that the stun gun remained on her hand.

They found Lisa sitting on a box at the mouth of the canal tunnel. She was sewing, and the sight of her performing such a simple and homely task in this context seemed incongruous. It was symbolic of the disorder they now endured. She was working on a skirt. It was bright blue, with a butterfly pattern. Lander recognised it. Kerryl loved butterflies and it had been hers.

'It's one of Magda's,' Lisa said. 'She give it me. 'I'm letting it out,' she smiled, shyly.

'It used to be my sister's,' said Lander.

'Oh. Do you mind?'

'No. Help yourself. She won't need it.'

'Where is she?'

Lander told her. He was now getting quite good at telling their story, reducing it to its salient elements to produce a condensed version that he could give without emotion and cover in a few sentences.

Lisa looked at what she'd been doing to the skirt. 'It seems a shame she'll not be wearing it no more,' she said.

'Yes, it is, but I'm sure she'd have been happy for you to have it.'

He turned to Chrissie, who had been waiting behind him, and introduced them.

'Chrissie is one of the women's group you're looking for, the Nightingales. We found them, and they are at the house where you thought they'd be. Magda is still with them.'

She looked both anxious and excited. 'Will they have me?'

'That depends,' said Chrissie, 'but we'd definitely like to talk to you.'

Lander described the house, the set-up and the composition of the group. He didn't go into their hostile reception, the tranquilliser darts, the questioning and the threat that would hang over Magda until he took Lisa to them. He didn't tell her either that Chrissie was a nut case.

Lisa wanted to set out for Lake Manor straight away, but Lander insisted they wait until the following day. There was not much daylight left, and although Lisa was looking better she was not strong. Even the shortened route to Lake Manor was some distance, and she needed to be fresh when she tackled it.

Steve had gone along the canal trying to fish. He came back with nothing but a frown. They dined on tinned luncheon meat, some rather bruised apples, and cream crackers. Steve had found some cider in an abandoned restaurant. He and Lander drank some but Lisa and Chrissie declined. Steve didn't hide his disappointment. It was obvious to Lander, and he guessed to Chrissie too, that he fancied her. Her response was to sit some distance away from him. She still held the stun gun. Steve said nothing about it, but he probably knew what it was because he kept glancing at it.

Now the year had moved on it was getting dark earlier. They didn't want to show a light so they sat in the dark. Eventually, after more of the cider, Steve started telling jokes. They were all bad and many of them were crude. Lander said he was going to kip down, and he got his bedding out of the boat. Magda had taken her sleeping bag with her, but there were some spare blankets and he gave those to Chrissie. He left it to her to decide where she was going to make her bed.

'What do you think?' Steve said in his ear.

'What do I think about what?'

'The bint, Chrissie. Reckon she's up for a bit of pussie, like Magda?'

'I don't know,' said Lander. 'There's one way to find out. Why don't you have a go?'

Lander hoped he would. He had a good idea of the response he would get.

He intended to go along the bank, away from the boats, but it looked like rain so he stayed in the shelter of the tunnel. He fell asleep to the muttered voices of Steve and Lisa. Chrissie was nowhere to be seen.

He woke early, like he always did now, and sat with his back against the brick wall of the tunnel looking at the arch of grey daylight at the mouth. He was cold.

What had happened to him? When he'd been at school he'd developed getting up, dressing and catching the bus into a fine art, reduced to twenty minutes and timed to the second so that he could spend the maximum amount of time in bed. Kerryl had been the early bird, rising before anyone else to do the milking. She'd been praised, while Lander used to get no end of aggro from their Mam for what she called his laziness. Actually, the real problem was he'd always been tired. True, he used to stay up far too late using his computer, but going to bed earlier didn't seem to make any difference; he'd still be unable to function effectively before midday. Nowadays, though, he was up before the lark. He sat wrapped in his blanket, watching the mist rise from the water as the drab dawn spread.

Steve had been sleeping further into the tunnel, beside the boats. He stood up, stretched, and came towards Lander.

'A brew?'

'I wish.'

'I mean it. I found a charity shop a bit further along. It had pretty much been stripped but there was a camping stove and some gas cylinders. We've only got tea bags and sugar though, no milk powder.'

They sat for some time listening to the soothing hiss of the stove and waiting for the water to boil.

'You get anywhere last night? With Chrissie?'

Steve didn't say anything but his expression gave the answer Lander had expected. 'Fuck it,' he said, rubbing his eyes. 'I've got cider head.'

'I won't say it serves you right,' said Lander. 'Better get a grip, though. You've got a long walk today.'

'I'm not coming,' said Steve. 'I'm not coming with you and Lisa to this women's place.'

'Why not?'

'No point. You don't need me, and there's nothing for me there. I'd rather get on,' he said.

'Get on where?'

Steve shrugged. 'No idea. Anywhere. See what there is. I fancy being a rolling stone, sort of a gypsy, know what I mean?'

'If you go on without us how will I get to Oxford?'

'You'll manage. It's not that far.'

'It's fucking miles. It must be at least a hundred. How will we cover those?' Lander was annoyed. It was selfish of Steve to carry on without them, and what was worse he seemed to be assuming he would take all their equipment and supplies with him.

Steve shrugged again. 'You'll have Joey. He's a big horse, he'll take both you and Magda. You can ride him along the canal bank.'

'What, and all our stuff too?'

'I'll leave you one of the boats.'

'Kind of you,' said Lander.

'We'll divi up. Split the stuff we've got. You take some and I'll take some.'

Lander wasn't as annoyed as he pretended to be. He would be happy to be rid of Steve. He didn't think he would get on at all well with the Nightingales. More important, though, was that with Steve gone he would have Magda to himself.

Something caught his eye along the bank. It was Lisa, coming towards them, wrapped in a blanket and looking bleary.

'Did you sleep in one of the boats?' Lander asked.

Lisa grunted a yes and sat down beside them.

'I don't know how you do it,' said Lander. 'Weren't you cold?'

She shook her head. 'No, I love it. It's great so long as you're well wrapped up. It's like a water bed.'

'Rather you than me,' said Lander. 'When I tried it I was perished.'

Steve gave Lander and Lisa a mug of hot water and a tea bag each. The tea tasted wonderful.

'I suppose now we can heat water we can use those camping meals,' Lander said.

'Oh yeah,' said Steve. It obviously hadn't occurred to him.

Lander fetched them and they made their selection. Steve and Lander chose an all-day breakfast and Lisa went for a chocolate pudding.

'Anybody seen Chrissie?' said Lander, when their food was ready and they were settling down to eat.

'She's gone,' said Lisa. 'She said she was done here and she was going back to Lake Manor. She said you knew the way, and she'd see us both there.'

Lander was surprised, but he reminded himself that Chrissie was well aware that Lander had an important incentive to return. He assumed she had decided that having checked his story and seen that there really was a pregnant woman, this part of God's work was done and she could leave them to follow.

As soon as Lisa had finished eating she and Lander put some clothes in a rucksack.

'Okay,' Lander said when they'd finished. 'The parting of the ways.'

'I suppose,' said Steve. He looked thoughtful. 'Hey, you know what I said about you and Kerryl? Well I'm sorry. I didn't mean it. I was just mouthing off.'

Lander punched his arm. 'Don't worry about it. I'd forgotten it.'

'She was a great chick, your sister. Know what I mean? I liked her a lot. I'm sorry she didn't make it.'

'Me too.'

Lander sighed. How could the death of someone like Kerryl be part of any divine plan? He pulled himself together. He was neglecting his purpose. He was supposed to be going to Oxford, confronting Adam and facing him with what he'd done; and, if it seemed appropriate, making him pay for it. He'd let himself become distracted. As soon as he'd delivered Lisa to Lake Manor he would be off.

'How are you going to move your boat without Joey?' he asked Steve.

'I'll pull it. Maybe sometimes paddle. It won't be hard.'

'Take Joey,' said Lander. 'Me and Magda won't be riding him to Oxford. We need to get there quicker than he can manage, and I don't want to leave him in the field in case something gets him. If you want him, take him.'

Steve grinned. 'What, really?"

Lander nodded. 'He was Kerryl's horse, so look after him or I'll come after you.'

'Right,' said Steve.

'And he's only on loan. Someday I might want him back.'

'Right.'

They bumped fists, Lander shouldered the rucksack and they left.

Lander had expected that Lisa would find the journey hard but she didn't. She was remarkably lively. The result was that they polished off the few miles to Lake Manor more quickly than he'd expected.

Coming back to the commune was for Lander like returning to a different place. Previously the women had treated him and Magda with a mixture of hostility and suspicion. This impression came not only from the initial reception from the three Cs, it was also the way the other women had watched them, sneaking sidelong glances and whispering comments to each other. This time, however, he was greeted like a celebrity. They made even more fuss of Lisa, treating her like royalty. They crowded around her, asking questions, offering her rest and refreshments. Her nascent bulge held an irresistible fascination for them and they all wanted to touch it. Lander watched in the background until Lisa was led away to a room she'd been given in another part of the house.

'Where's Magda?' he asked one of the women.

'In the library. It's across the hall, at the end of the passage.'

If Magda was ready they could start for Oxford straight away. The sooner they left the better.

The library was a large, oblong room, entered through double doors, which were open. Magda was at the far end. She was deep in conversation with another person. Lander was surprised to see it was a man. He had his back to the door and he was wearing a hoodie, but there was something about the hunched shoulders and the angle of the head that were familiar. They were standing close together, and their positioning and body language said that they were well acquainted. They were friends; good friends. Magda was looking steadily into the man's face and at one point she put her hand on his arm.

However, it was not the intimacy of the gesture that shocked Lander, it was the identity of the person she was treating in this manner. He half turned and lowered his hood. There were blond curls, a squarish head. Even from the back he was easy to recognise him. It was Adam.

TWENTY-EIGHT

REUNION

LANDER TOOK THREE steps back along the corridor, his head whirling. Magda with Adam? Why? Did they know each other? They must. How? Why hadn't she told him? What did it mean? And what was Adam doing here with the Nightingales anyway? Bewildered, he retreated back towards the hall, and then out through the main door.

He stood on the terrace and looked at the house, struggling to find the meaning of what he had seen. Perhaps the Nightingale women didn't know that Adam was from the authorities. Perhaps he had simply arrived from nowhere and they'd sent Magda to talk to him. But why would they do that? Why Magda rather than Christine, say, or Carole, or even the crazy Chrissie? And why was Adam there?

Another possibility was that Magda was somehow in on this,. Maybe she was betraying the Nightingales to the authorities. Is that what she'd been doing with the Bonnies? Infiltrating? She'd lied to Lander before, by omission if in no other way. He'd often had the feeling that she knew more than she was telling him. Could he trust her?

He was angry, and he was hurt. He and Magda had been through a lot together. He liked her, he thought she liked him, and part of him had wondered if they might have some sort of future together, despite her unconventional approach to relationships. He had been jealous when he'd seen her with Steve, and happy that he might now be able to keep her to himself, for a short time at least. And now this. Whatever was going on, Adam seemed to be at the heart of it. Lord Fraud himself.

He turned back towards the door in time to see the hooded figure rounding the edge of the building in the direction of the car park. He was leaving!

Lander raced across the terrace, his feet kicking up the gravel. When he reached the corner, he stopped. Adam was unlocking his car. He looked up, questioningly. There was a beat's pause, then recognition, then an an embarrassed grin.

Lander let out a cry of rage. It was a distillation of all the hurt and anger and frustration he'd suffered since he'd left the farm, the days and nights on the road, the times he'd been held by the authorities, Mickey, the Nightingales, his anguish at his sister's death. It was an animal howl, and with it Lander rushed him, hitting

Adam so hard that he fell against the car and his head struck the door panel.

They both tumbled to the ground and Lander punched him on the side of the face with a force that jarred his knuckles. Adam tried to defend himself, but Lander was like a thing possessed. He punched and kneed and grabbed, getting his hands around Adam's throat while his enemy writhed to get him off.

'You bastard!' he screamed, shaking Adam's head, his spittle spraying his face. 'You bastard! You fucking, fucking bastard!'

His fingers bit into Adam's neck and he squeezed hard, crushing the windpipe like wringing out a dishcloth. If he'd been left alone he might have killed him, but it didn't get that far.

The explosion was deafening. It jolted Lander and Adam squirmed aside, holding his neck. Magda stood over them. She was holding an automatic pistol.

'Are you crazy?' she yelled at Lander. 'Get yourself together.' She looked at Adam. 'I'll shoot the pair of you if you don't stop this. Don't believe me?' She fired again, into the ground between them, showering them with earth and stinging pebbles. 'I bloody will.'

'You lied to me,' Lander shouted back at her. His ears were ringing from the pistol shot. He pointed at Adam. 'You told me you didn't know this bastard.' He put his head in his hands. He could barely hear anything.

'No I didn't. I just didn't tell you that I did know him.'

'Fucking hypocrite!'

'All right. But remember I saved your life. I could have gone off on my own after I'd done for Mickey and left you to rot in that shed, but I stayed and helped you. I'd no idea then who you were, but if I'd left you behind crackpot Edna would have killed you.'

'What do you mean, you didn't know who I was?'

'You'd given me your name and told me about your sister, but I'd got no idea that Adam was looking for you.'

'In that case why did you come to Walbrough with me? Why didn't you just piss off to Oxford or Bicester or wherever the hell else it was you came from, so you could be with your slimy friends.'

Magda stuffed the pistol in her waistband and sat on the patch of earth between them. Adam was still massaging his neck. The ringing in Lander's ears was subsiding. He was pleased to see that Adam had an angry looking red mark on the side of his face. He hoped it would turn into a proper black eye.

'I had to come with you,' said Magda. 'I had no choice. Where else would I go? I was in the middle of nowhere with no transport and no way of getting in touch with anyone. I'd been starved for three months, I'd just been raped, and I'd stabbed a man to death. I was more than half dead. I needed time to get myself together, and going with you was the easiest option. You might remember that I was barely conscious for most of the way back to your home.'

'How did he know where we were?' he said, jerking his thumb at Adam.

'He's known all the time, all the places we've been. On the way to Walbrough I picked up this.' She took a slim phone from her pocket.

'On the way? Where? Anyway, mobiles don't work.'

'Enough questions,' said Adam. 'It's make your mind up time.' His voice sounded strained, constricted and he was still holding his throat. 'You've got to decide whose side you're on.'

'No,' said Magda. 'If he's to make this decision he needs the full picture.' She turned her attention back to Lander. 'Can you remember on the way to your place we went through a village with a war memorial in the middle? And I told you I needed a pee? That was where I got this phone. It uses a completely different protocol and network from the phones you know. It's a system that's been around for a while, reserved for government and emergency use. It was kept going during the Infection to allow communication between the arkies and it's been used since by the army. Spare handsets were hidden in locations all over the country, to be used in case of emergencies. There are more than a hundred of them. We had to learn where they were as part of our training.'

'Helped to pass the long hours while we waited for the abatement,' Adam mumbled.

'Abatement?'

'It's the term we use for the Infection dying down, when it was judged safe for the arkies to come out and for the rebuilding to start,' Magda explained. 'Anyway, when I saw the name of that village on a signboard I remembered there was a handset there, so I asked you to stop for me to pee and went behind the war memorial and got this from its hiding place. As soon as I could I told Adam where I was and where I was going. I also told him about you.'

'Why?'

'I didn't know then that you and Kerryl were special, but I knew that our research people were interested in any survivors, and particularly in twins. Of course, as soon as I reported to Adam he knew at once who you were. He knew your home, and he told me what to expect there.'

'Why didn't you tell me? Why didn't you take me directly to him?'

'We were going to do that,' said Adam. 'Magda was on the point of filling you in, but then you found your sister's diaries, you blamed me for her death and you were out for my blood. If we'd met straight away you wouldn't have been in the mood to co-operate. You needed time to cool off. You still do,' he said, rubbing his neck. 'Anyway, when you decided to go to Oxford by canal, that was perfect. We reckoned it would give you a week or more to calm down and come to terms with the changed situation.'

'"Changed situation." Christ! I can't believe you people. Is that all Kerryl's death means to you? A "changed situation"?'

'No, of course not,' Adam said, and Lander was gratified to see that he seemed embarrassed.

'What happened to her, then? What happened to my sister?'

Adam looked at Lander and then very slowly shook his head from side to side. 'I don't know.'

'What do you mean you don't know? Of course you know. You were supposed to be watching her!'

'I was. But I was with you, too. I wasn't with her all the time. I wasn't aware of everything that was going on. It's easy to see what was happening to her when you read her diaries, but I didn't have those. I didn't know she was having hallucinations. I could see she was getting very thin, but I didn't realise she'd been starving herself. I saw her body beside the pool at the Bride Stones. She'd drowned, but exactly why I have no idea. She could have been faint from lack of nourishment and just collapsed into the water. Or she might have done it deliberately, it might have been suicide, that's what her diary seems to say.' He shook his head. 'I don't know.'

'One thing that I know is that you were playing games with her,' said Lander. 'You were pretending to be there, and then not there. She was lonely and she was depressed and she was vulnerable, and you used her to have a bit of fun.'

Adam shook his head, this time more vigorously. 'No, no, no. It wasn't like that. I explained everything to the inquiry. I told them exactly what happened.'

'What enquiry? There was an inquiry?'

'Yes,' said Adam. 'The government put a considerable share of its very limited resources into you and your sister. When things went wrong they wanted to know what had happened. Okay, maybe I misjudged things. Perhaps I didn't see what was coming, but I didn't intend either you or Kerryl to come to any harm. Far from it. From the point of view of our programme it was vital that you both be kept alive and well. Kerryl's death was a complete disaster.'

Adam looked away.

'As soon as Adam knew where you were,' said Magda, 'he came to Walbrough. Straight away. He arrived the night you and Steve went off your heads on the lager, and after I'd put the two of you to bed we met.'

'The extra coffee mug,' said Lander.

'Yes. Smart of you to spot that. Anyway, I showed him the canal route we'd worked out so he could brief the patrols and make sure they left us alone.'

Lander shook his head. So that was why they'd hardly seen any sign of officials, despite sometimes travelling in daylight. That was why, even when they were seen, there'd been no interference. He remembered the bus full of armed soldiers, the way they'd stopped when they'd seen him and Steve on the canal bank. They'd looked as though they were about to step in, but then they just drove off. He'd been manipulated. Operated, like a remote-controlled toy. Adam had moved the joystick, and Magda had made sure he received the commands. He and Steve were puppets.

'And you say you haven't tricked me,' Lander said wearily.

'We neither of us did,' said Adam. 'We fully intended to tell you everything. All we were doing was holding the information back until the time was right. We needed to work out the details and finalise our plans. We hoped that over the couple of weeks it would take you to get to Oxford your grief would die down, you would come to terms with what had happened, and you'd be willing to work with us. We intended that as you got closer, Magda would update you.'

Lander was stupefied. He felt as though he'd been building a structure which he thought was solid, which he believed to be on firm foundations, only to discover when it was almost complete that the whole thing was made of jelly. When he'd read Kerryl's diary he'd become more and more appalled at the cruelty with which she'd been treated. Now these two were trying to explain it, asking him to accept it and move on. He didn't intend to do that.

'You can't read Kerryl's diaries without seeing that being left so alone affected her mind,' said Lander. 'Don't you understand that?'

'Yes, we do,' said Magda. 'But who was it who left her?'

Lander felt something inside him snap. He stood up and faced Magda.

'I left because I thought I was protecting her. That arsehole,' he pointed to Adam, 'knew that. He could see what was going on at the farm. I couldn't because I was being held in prison, or being fed some bullshit in Oxford. So she dies, and then you come along and make the whole thing a thousand times worse.'

Lander's face was inches from Magda's, but she didn't flinch.

'What did your fancy Inquiry say?' said Lander, looking at Adam. 'That you should be locked up for murder?'

'They were concerned, naturally but I had a surprise for them, and I have one for you. What would you say if I told you we could bring your sister back to life?'

LANDER WAS THUNDERSTRUCK. What did Adam mean?

'We intended to get you to Oxford and then brief you properly,' said Magda. 'We hoped that when you had the full picture you'd agree to take part in our programme.

Lander felt lost, out of control. He had no idea what they were talking about. How much of what had happened to him since he first left the farm was random, and how much was part of some elaborate plan? It was a different sort of dream walking, a fantasy in which no one was actually what they at first seemed.

'Was Steve in on this?' he said.

Magda snorted and Adam laughed out loud.

'Steve? What do you think?' said Magda. 'He was useful in helping you to navigate the canals, and of course he came up with the idea of using them in the first place, but apart from that, well, he's hardly the fastest horse in the race, is he?' She turned towards Lander and put her hand on his arm. 'I know you think we've organised all this,' she said, 'but we've not. Coming across you at Mickey's was a complete accident.'

'I don't believe you,' he said, moving away.

'Suit yourself, but it's true. Adam knew about you and how important you might be to a programme he was working on, but after you left the hospital in Oxford no one had any idea where you'd gone. Nobody realised at that time how much we did – do – need you, otherwise we'd have tried harder to find you. Adam and I barely knew each other then. I certainly wasn't aware of what he was working on.

Lander felt used, and he couldn't forgive Adam for what he'd done to Kerryl. But what was he talking about? 'You said you could bring my sister back to life,' he said. 'I'm not stupid. I know you can't do that. I don't believe in magic. So what do you mean, and where do your fancy plans go next?'

'I don't believe in magic either,' said Adam. 'But I do think we can give Kerryl some sort of continued existence. Not the Kerryl we knew, you and I. Sadly she's gone from us. But her heritage.'

'And where do I come in?'

That depends on you,' said Adam. 'Some of what I'm going to share with you now you know already, from *thetruthwillmakeyoufree*, and from what you've discovered since you left home.' He looked to Magda. 'You start. My throat's sore.'

'All right,' said Magda. 'It's like this. When the Infection came we thought it would wipe everyone out, and it's true that most of the people who contracted the virus were killed by it. However, there were a few others. You know about them from *thetruth*. In these cases the system resisted the fever but the virus lodged in the brain. The results were all the same: insanity, usually violent insanity. People infected in this way did crazy things, they fought each other, they took stupid risks. The upshot was that many of them died, just like the others but in different ways. You know them by the term coined by *thetruth*: dream walkers. We prefer to call them "the possessed".

'You and Kerryl were like the possessed,' said Adam. 'You got the virus, avoided the fever, and it migrated to your brains. You might have displayed the classic symptoms but you didn't, because you were different. There were no signs of mental disorder and you both remained calm and rational.

'In Oxford you were in a sheltered situation, so your environment was not a natural one. However, Kerryl was in the real world. And Kerryl was female, whereas everyone else we knew about who'd been infected in this way was male. We needed to observe her and test her responses to what she encountered. We had to see whether she succumbed to hallucinations like the others, so we tried to induce a few. She resisted them, but we noticed something very interesting beginning to happen. Your sister appeared to be constructing a second psyche, another, different Kerryl who existed in the same body, in parallel to the first one but with an independent consciousness. The original Kerryl was there most of the time, but sometimes she was replaced by the other one, the alternative Kerryl. The two operated independently. Neither was aware of the existence of the other.'

Lander remembered the conversation he'd had with Adam and Gwen Matthews, what seemed like a hundred years ago. 'Jekyll and Hyde.'

'Yes,' said Adam. 'Just like the famous Doctor and his alter-ego, one Kerryl could do something and the other Kerryl would know nothing about it.'

'So she was a dream walker.'

'In a way, but she was different from the others. You've seen her diary, you know about the messages she was sending to herself.'

'The ones she thought were coming from you,' said Lander bitterly.

'The tragedy is that she died before we were able to fully understand what was happening to her and could find out the potential of this remarkable quality,' said Magda.

The implications were mind boggling. Lander could remember a movie he'd seen where the hero didn't know who he was and helplessly followed some programme that the state had planted in his brain. What Adam and Magda were describing seemed like that.

'I still think Kerryl's death was your fault,' he said.

'I can understand you blaming me,' said Adam, 'but I hope you can see that Kerryl dying was the exact opposite of what we wanted. In fact it was a tragedy. But listen, I meant it when I said that your sister can live again. Or part of her can, and you and she together can help us move towards an incredible future.'

'What do you mean?' said Lander. He was wary that Adam might again be trying to manipulate him.

'When the Provisional Government was established it set up the arks, using resources and facilities that had been assembled in case of nuclear war. A small number of elite people were singled out to go into the arks to be safe from the Infection.'

'The arkies. I know,' said Lander.

'Yes,' said Adam. 'Well, the idea was that when the Infection had abated the arkies would march out and start all over again. For that reason, when people were chosen for the arks they were selected not only for the skills they could bring to rebuilding society, but also on what was judged to be a vigorous capacity for breeding. What we didn't know was that everyone who went into an ark would come out sterile. The ovaries of the ark women have ceased to function, and the men all fire blanks.'

'Why? I thought the arks were supposed to be safe.'

'They were. All we can think is that somehow a mutation of the virus that had this effect got around before the arks were sealed. It was probably present amongst one or more of the arkies at the pre-lockdown briefings, it was passed around and some of it got into every one of the arks, where it spread.'

'The divine plan,' said Lander.

'What?'

'Oh, nothing. It was just something one of the Nightingale women said. So what happened?'

'The boffins were desperate,' said Magda. 'It looked like the end of everything. They examined the possibility of extracting eggs from women who had died of the infection, but in all the subjects they tried the samples had been tainted by the virus. When Kerryl's body was found up on the moors behind your house, Adam saw an opportunity. He had her taken immediately to a facility in Manchester, where she was put into cold storage. Now, amazingly, our medics have taken cells from her, and from these they've created oocytes.'

It was a word Lander had heard before. No wonder Magda knew so much about this.

'They can be used to develop ova,' said Adam.

Lander could hardly believe his ears. 'You're going to clone her!'

'No, no, no,' said Adam. He was clearly irritated by the suggestion. 'That would be no use at all. Anyway the artificial cloning of humans is impossible.'

'The South Koreans claimed to have done it back in the early two thousands,' said Magda, 'but they were never able to produce any proof, and as far as we know it can't be done.

'In any case, the whole business of cloning is very iffy,' said Adam. 'There's been some success with a range of animals, but it's not reliable. And there's the age problem.'

'What's that?'

'It's quite simple,' said Magda. 'A cloned subject begins its life at the same age as the organism that provided the cells. So a clone of Kerryl would start out at the same age as she was when we took hers.'

'An eighteen-year-old baby,' said Lander.

'Yes,' said Magda.

'Even if we could do it,' said Adam. 'What I'm talking about is different and really has possibilities. However, it's a one-shot chance, and because so much depends on it, the science has to be spot on. What we're after is good old-fashioned IVF.'

'I see,' said Lander, although he was not entirely sure he did. 'The baby farms you'd planned, that Lisa told me about, won't work, so you want to make babies in test tubes instead. You've got some eggs you've made from Kerryl, and you want my permission to get them fertilised.'

'We don't need your permission,' said Adam, coldly.

Lander looked as though he was going to have another go at Adam and Magda held up her hand to calm him. 'It's a bit more than that,' she said. 'We do need your permission, because we want you to fertilise them.'

Lander was speechless. What on earth was this insane woman talking about?

'We need your sperm,' she said. 'The tests in Oxford confirmed that you are fertile.'

'But that's crazy. It's ridiculous. You're mad. Anyway, I can't be the only fertile male in the country. There must be others.'

'We want Kerryl's children to have the dual characteristic she had. There were signs of the same thing coming out in you. When I read Kerryl's diary I saw that the explanation you'd given her for going away was that you were experiencing behaviours like the ones she developed,' said Adam. 'Yours were different, but they were there. This trait is in you, too. If we use sperm from anyone other than you to fertilise Kerryl's eggs, this feature – we call it dual personality syndrome, DPS – most likely won't be replicated. We'll just produce more of the possessed. If we use sperm from you, there's an excellent chance that at least some of your progeny will have this characteristic.' Adam leant forward. He seemed to have forgotten his injuries and there was passion in his eyes and his voice. 'Don't you see what this means?' he said. 'You and Kerryl can be the founders of a new race. Every member of this race will be two people in one, each able to act independently of the other. It will be amazing, a new species of human kind.'

'Homo sapiens will give way to homo duplex,' said Magda.

Lander still couldn't grapple with what was being suggested, but he was starting to see the implications, or some of them. 'But what you're wanting me to do is incest,' he said.

'No, not in the physical sense,' Adam said.

'It's not what Steve was suggesting,' said Magda.

'But it's inbreeding. All it will do is produce idiots.' Lander was remembering the jokes he'd heard about people in isolated communities being mutants and nutters because they were all related to each other.

'Incest has been outlawed and regarded as immoral for societal reasons as much as scientific ones,' said Adam. It's better for the health of society if groups inter-breed. There are biological risks, but we know a lot about gene editing now and we can adjust the DNA of the foetuses to avoid most problems.'

'And if there are any that we can't deal with, sadly we'll have to terminate them,' said Magda.

Lander still couldn't believe what they were saying. It sounded crazy, obscene.

'Imagine it,' said Magda, taking Lander's hand, 'a room full of babies that you and Kerryl have created. I've been talking to the Nightingales. They have agreed to provide host mothers, and they would also care for the infants. We expect some of the other covens will join in too.'

'This is the future,' said Adam.

Is it? thought Lander. It was a sort of future, certainly, but was it a good one? Two people in one? Really? From what he remembered of Jeckyll and Hyde one of the pair was normal, but the other was evil. Would the same happen here? One could commit terrible acts but the other would be totally innocent, their conscience completely clear. One could be made to carry out whatever lunacies its lords and masters decided was necessary, while its parallel would know nothing about them. The implications for deception, for crime, for espionage and warfare were huge. It would also be the last word in social control. And presumably these babies, his and Kerryl's numberless offspring, would be immune to the Infection. The virus could be used as the weapon it was originally intended to be.

'It's time to decide,' said Adam. 'Will you be a new Adam to Kerryl's Eve? Will you help us?'

THIRTY

A DECISION

LANDER HAD FOLLOWED the same path with both Adam and Magda. He had liked them, and trusted them, and they had misled him. Even if what they were proposing was possible, were these the people who should be in control of it? He got to his feet.

'Brave New World, eh?' he said.

'It will be,' said Magda, also standing.

'If you help us,' said Adam. 'Will you join us in making the future?'

Lander paused for a moment. They had power, and so did the people who directed them. There were probably all sorts of ways they could trick or force him into doing what they desired, so it was vital that his answer had impact. When they eventually did to him what they would, he wanted them to remember this moment, and that whatever happened was against his will. He looked from Adam to Magda and back while he chose his words.

'Have you stopped for a moment to think what it was like for Kerryl?' he said. 'What you did to her? You've read her diaries. You know the torment she went through. So how do you imagine the people you propose to create in this obscene way would feel? They would have no free will. They would be lost. They wouldn't know who they were or what was happening to them. They would be more alone than ever Kerryl was. They would be in hell. Help you? Help you to create a race of tortured freaks? No. Not ever.'

Adam looked crestfallen. He was going to say something but Lander had had enough. He turned and walked away across the terrace, the gravel crunching under his feet. He didn't hurry, although he wanted to. He didn't look round, despite feeling their gaze boring into his back.

He reached the grassy slope that skirted the lake, and followed the path that led to a small wood. Once hidden from the house he slowed down and took a deep breath. He sat on a tree stump. It was a perfect afternoon and the land shimmered in an unseasonal heat haze. A few wispy clouds stippled a cornflower sky. The trees were an autumn carnival – layer upon layer of oranges, yellows, russets, ochres. Was it his imagination, or was everything more vibrant, brighter, more intense than it had ever been before the Infection?

He looked at the fields beyond the lake. The one nearest had been planted with wheat, at a time when the farmer had thought it would be needed, but there had been no harvest and the ears had dropped so that only chaff and dead stalks were left. They had been beaten down by wind and rain, flattened swathes meandering into the distance.

There was no sign of human activity; nothing moving, no sounds of life beyond insects droning like distant aircraft and bird calls piercing the silence. It was their land now. Would it ever belong to mankind again? Adam had told him that there had been four thousand people in the arks. Then there were the others, people like Adam himself, and Magda, and Gwen, and Steve, and Lisa, and Mickey, and Edna, and Maisie, and Louise, and even Spencer. People who had not been in the arks, but had managed somehow to survive. For now. Adam had been in no doubt that sooner or later some mutation of the virus would get each of them, too, but for the present they were alive. How many were there? A thousand? Two? Even if it were double that, the total of everyone in the country, arkies and the rest, would be less than the population of Walbrough. Fewer than would fill Leeds Arena. A tenth of a home crowd for Manchester United. Certainly not enough to populate and run a country. Kerryl had thought that despite the misery and death the plague brought, life afterwards would be all right. That there would be enough of everything for everybody. She was wrong. Things would run out, and there would be nobody to replace them. No wonder Adam and his bosses, whoever they were, were desperate to farm babies.

He massaged his hand, painful from the blow he'd struck Adam. What would have happened if Magda hadn't stopped him? Would he have choked Adam to death? He'd felt like it at the time, but he knew he couldn't, just as he couldn't have shot Spencer. Nevertheless, he felt the frustration of unsatisfied revenge, and massive resentment at the way both Adam and Magda had deceived him. If there were to be a brave new world it would need people to make it work. He didn't believe that Adam, Magda and others like them were the ones to do that.

He heard the helicopters long before he saw them, a faint throbbing scarcely perceptible over the noise of the bees. Then he saw two specs in the distance. They grew slowly, coming towards the Manor. One circled and the other landed on the far side of the trees, in front of the house. They couldn't be after him, but what were they doing there?

A dog barked. There were shouts. It was time to leave.

He thought of going through the village and trying to find an abandoned vehicle with the keys still in it, but it was getting harder to do that. They were all either empty of fuel, smashed up, or vandalised for parts. For a moment he thought about trying to get back to Mickey's farm, where Maisie's Mini might be still in the yard. Then he remembered that he already had a means of transport.

Joey was a little slow, but he was reliable, and better still, he was self-fuelling.

Lander broke into a jog, heading for the canal, hoping that Steve and Joey were still there. Not that he intended to take Steve with him. Collect the horse and go, that was his plan.

Go where?

He had no idea, but it hardly mattered. The human race couldn't end like this. There would be a brave new world, he was sure of it, and there would be people who could make it happen. People he could trust. People he could work with to build a new future.

Sooner or later he would find them.

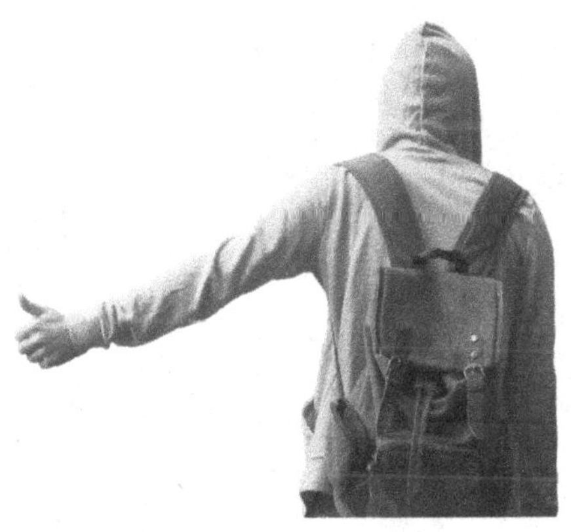

I hope you've enjoyed reading about Lander's journey and I'd love to know what you think. Would you give the book a rating on Amazon? And, if you have time, a short review? Reviews mean a lot to independent authors because they alert other readers to their work. And do please visit my website where you can join my mailing list and download a free collection of my short stories.

www.phillfeatherstone.net

You can also follow me on

Twitter: @PhillFeathers

Facebook: PF-author

Instagram: phillfeathers.

The story continues in REBOOT book 3 –

JERICHO ROSE

The plague is over and it's time to rebuild. Different ideas about how to do this risk destroying the little that's left. Rival groups take sides. Lander and his new friends have something to offer, and there's a final showdown.

"Fast paced, thought-provoking, brilliant! At last it all becomes clear."

Paperback 978-1-9993324-9-5

eBook 978-1-8380035-0-0

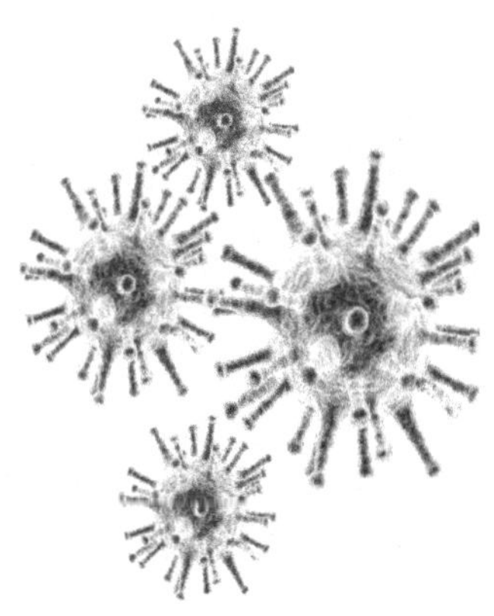

ACKNOWLEDGMENTS

Thank you for reading Aftershocks. I hope you enjoyed it and will go on to the final book in the REBOOT trilogy, Jericho Rose.

Many people have helped, advised and supported me while I've been writing this book. Some of them don't even know they've done it. Several I must thank by name, but there are far too many to list them all.

Firstly, there are my family, who have to get used to me inflicting on them embryonic plot ideas, character speculation and half-finished drafts. They are my son, John, and my daughter, Sarah. This book is dedicated to them.

Just as important, to me and to them, are their partners, Kathy Featherstone and Jeff Durber. Thank you to both of them for their interest in and support for my writing. Their children, Hailey and Ella Featherstone and Bruce and Lenny Durber have also been involved, reading my work, talking to me, or simply by being there. Hailey and Ella live in the USA so are harder to reach. Bruce and Lenny are closer, and it is they who have helped me in my efforts to get inside the mind of a teenager.

As always, my deepest thanks go to my wife, Sally. She is a constant support, and her patience and understanding are boundless. Not only that, her creative ideas and her suggestions for plot, characters and structure have been invaluable throughout the process of writing Aftershocks. Sally not only contributes to the content of the book, she advises me on the production - the covers of Paradise Girl and of this book are largely down to her - and on marketing. Most important, being an author herself she knows what it's like when you have a book in your head and it won't leave you alone.

I feel very fortunate to have a number of friends who are interested in my work and prepared to discuss it with me. Thank you to Rod and Helen Collett, Mark Edwards, Judith Shorrocks, Catherine Corry, Lynn Broadbent, Laurence and Shamshad Cockroft, Chris and Michelle O'Gorman. I am grateful to you all.

When I published the first edition of Paradise Girl it was not in my mind to write a companion or a sequel. However, a number of Facebook friends, bloggers and Amazon and Goodreads reviewers have been kind enough to say they would like to read more by me. Others were curious to know more about Kerryl and Lander. So I opened my laptop and started to tell the story of Lander. My thanks go to all of them for their encouragement and support.

Last, but by no means least, I am enormously grateful to Julie Dexter, who did a magnificent job of proof reading my manuscript and also provided me with some very helpful suggestions for tweaking the plot. Mark Edwards (of MEPPC in Scarborough) gave me enormous help with the IT side of producing this book.

9 781999 332426